American Nights Entertainment

GRANT OVERTON

By GRANT OVERTON

About Books and Authors

AMERICAN NIGHTS ENTERTAINMENT

WHEN WINTER COMES TO MAIN STREET

THE WOMEN WHO MAKE OUR NOVELS

Fiction

ISLAND OF THE INNOCENT

THE ANSWERER

WORLD WITHOUT END

THE THOUSAND-AND-FIRST NIGHT (*In Preparation*)

American Nights Entertainment

BY

GRANT OVERTON

New York, 1923

D. APPLETON & CO. GEORGE H. DORAN COMPANY
DOUBLEDAY, PAGE & CO. CHARLES SCRIBNER'S SONS

PRINTED IN THE UNITED STATES OF AMERICA

First Printing, September, 1923.

Press of
J. J. Little & Ives Company
New York, U. S. A.

Bound in Interlaken-Cloth

This Book

IS DEDICATED TO BOOKSELLERS AND BOOKREADERS EVERYWHERE BY THE AUTHOR AND THE PUBLISHERS WHO HAVE JOINED IN ITS PRODUCTION

Preface

THIS book is written because of the rapid spread of the habit of reading books, developing in its march an interest in the personalities of authors. Indeed, the existence of this book is an evidence of the quick contagion of the book-reading habit, since four publishing houses have joined to make possible the pages that follow.

Few developments of the early part of this century are more encouraging than the new attention to books. The increase in book stores, the very large increase in the number of books sold, the multiplication of libraries and their great patronage, the success of new book review pages and periodicals—all are signs of the change that has come about in recent years, and perhaps especially during and since the war of 1914-18.

And in a narrower department, no development of recent years has borne a more cheerful promise than the resolution of four publishers to associate themselves in an enterprise the disinterestedness of which the reader is invited to assess for himself.

The entire responsibility for the estimates and opinions offered (where they are not directly attributed) is mine. I have tried to tell the truth, use my imagination legitimately, and observe good taste without the sacrifice of valuable insights into character and work.

For example, in addition to biographical facts, in themselves often unenlightening, I have usually tried, as in the account of Mr. Galsworthy, to disclose the personality so carefully (albeit high-mindedly) withheld from the writer's books. Again, as in the chapter on Joseph Conrad, aside from the effort at novelty and freshness of interest by the device of adopting Conrad's own Marlow as the narrator, I have made bold to set down some facts never before printed and not in the least generally known, because they seem to me a side of the picture that it is wrong to obscure.

The wealth of material spread before me has made the task of selection exceedingly difficult, and I cannot pretend to be satisfied with what I have chosen in the light of my knowledge of what has had to be left out. I owe a grateful acknowledgment to the publishers and to individuals in the several publishing houses for their generous assistance.

1 August, 1923.

GRANT OVERTON.

Contents

Portraits

American Nights Entertainment

American Nights ENTERTAINMENT

1. Mr. Galsworthy's Secret Loyalties

i

IN the autumn of 1922 New York began to witness a play by John Galsworthy, called *Loyalties*. Not only the extreme smoothness of the acting by a London company but the almost unblemished perfection of the play as drama excited much praise. Because, of the two principals, one was a Jew and the other was not, with consequent enhancement of the dramatic values in several scenes, it was said (by those who always seek an extrinsic explanation) that *Loyalties* simply could not have avoided being a success in New York. The same type of mind has long been busy with the problem of Mr. Galsworthy as a novelist. It read *The Man of Property* and found the book explained by the fact that the author was a Socialist. Confronted with *The Dark Flower*, it declared this "love life of a man" sheer sentimentalism (in 1913 there was no Freudianism to fall back on). And the powerful play called *Justice* was accounted for by a story that quiet Mr. Galsworthy had "put on old clothes, wrapped a brick in brown paper, stopped in front of a tempting-looking plate-glass window" and let 'er fly. On being "promptly arrested," he "gave an assumed name, and the magistrate, in his turn, gave Galsworthy six months. That's how he found out what the inside of English prisons was like."

A saying has it that it is always the innocent bystander who gets hurt; but the fate of the sympathetic bystander—and such a one John Galsworthy has always been—is more ironic. That peculiar sprite, George Meredith's Comic Spirit, reading all that has been written about Galsworthy would possibly find some adequate comment; but Meredith is dead and the only penetrating characterisation that occurs to me is: "Galsworthy's the kind of man who, if he were in some other station of life, would be a splendid subject for Joseph Conrad."

In the middle of *Loyalties* a character exclaims: "Prejudices—or are they loyalties—I don't know—criss-cross—we all cut each other's throats from the best of motives." Well, in a paper written in 1917 or earlier and included in their book, *Some Modern Novelists*, published in January, 1918, Helen Thomas Follett and Wilson Follett, discussing Galsworthy's early novels put down a now very remarkable sentence, as follows:

"Mr. Galsworthy does not see how two loyalties that conflict can both be right; and he is always interested in the larger loyalty."

So interesting and significant a statement, buried as seed, might easily sprout as novel or play. I have

© *Eugene Hutchinson*

JOHN GALSWORTHY

no atom of evidence that Mr. Galsworthy ever saw the comment; but if he read it and forgot (buried?) the words, then *Loyalties* was written in their effectual disproof. For in this drama, as in all his novels, as in all his other dramas, Mr. Galsworthy is constantly seeing and portraying how conflicting loyalties both are right; he is never interested in the larger loyalty and cannot keep his eye on it through consecutive chapters or through a single act; he is forever presenting the two or more sides and taking none. He once said: "I suppose the hardest lesson we all have to learn in life is that we can't have things both ways." He should have added: "—and I have never learned it!"

ii

"Learned," of course, in the sense of "accepted," of becoming reconciled to the fact. It did not need Mr. St. John Ervine to tell us that "Mr. Galsworthy is the most sensitive figure in the ranks of modern letters"; for of all modern writers the author of *Loyalties* and *The Forsyte Saga* is the most transparent. He is transparent without being in the smallest degree luminous; he refracts, but he does not magnify—a prism through which we may look at society.

Compare him for a moment with Mr. Conrad. Mr. Conrad is by no means always transparent; his opacity is sometimes extraordinary, as in *The Rescue;* and yet from the midst of obscure sentences, like a gleam from those remarkably deep-set eyes, something luminous will shine out, both light and heat are given forth. "In a certain cool paper," explains Galsworthy, "I have tried to come at the effect of the war; but purposely pitched it in a low and sober key; and there is a much more poignant tale of change to tell of each individual human being." But even when telling the more poignant tale, as in *Saint's Progress*, the coolness is noticeable, like the air of an April night; the key is still sober, pitched low; and the trembling passion of a melody proclaimed by violins is quickly muted. Such is his habitual restraint, so strong is his inhibition, that when we hear the orchestral brasses, as we do once or twice in *Justice* and *Loyalties*, it shocks us, like a rowdy outburst in a refined assembly or a terse sentence in Henry James. But it is nothing, nothing. Mr. Galsworthy has momentarily achieved a more perfect than usual transparency; he has suddenly surrendered to the pounce of another of those multitudinous loyalties which give him no peace and the secret of which, except for its continual disclosure in his works, he would most certainly carry with him to the grave.

For he does not talk. No! "You are nearer Galsworthy in reading his books than in a meeting." Another keenly observant person summed up Galsworthy's conversational resources in the one word: "Exhausted!" St. John Ervine: "Whatever of joy and grief he has had in life has been closely retained, and the reticence characteristic of the English people . . . is most clearly to be observed in Mr. Galsworthy. . . . How often have we observed in our relationships that some garrulous person, constantly engaged in egotistical conversation, contrives to conceal knowledge of himself from us, while some silent friend, with lips tightly closed, most amazingly gives himself away. One looks at Mr. Galsworthy's handsome, sensitive face, and is immediately aware of tightened lips! . . . But the lips are not tightened because of things done to him, but because of things done to others." Mr. Galsworthy, in a personal letter: "The fact is I cannot answer your questions. I must leave my philosophy to my work generally, or rather, to what people can make out of that work. The habit of trying to tabloid one's convictions, or lack of convictions, is a pretty fatal one; as I have found to my distaste and discredit." He conducts his own cross-examination, in new books, new plays. He acknowledges, with quiet discontent, the claims upon his sense of loyalty of a dog, a jailbird, two "star-crossed lovers," the wife of a possessive Forsyte, a De Levis unjustly used. His pen moves, with a bold stroke, across the paper; another secret is let out; his lips tighten. He is serene and indignant and completely happy.

Why not? "My experience tells me this: An artist who is by accident of independent means can, if he has talent, give the Public what he, the artist, wants, and sooner or later the public will take whatever he gives it, at his own valuation." And he speaks of such artists as able to "sit on the Public's head and pull the Public's beard, to use the old Sikh saying." Nothing else is worth while—for an artist. "The artist has got to make a stand against being exploited." But if the artist should exploit himself, or anything more human or individual than that impersonal entity, the Public, Mr. Galsworthy's mouth would become grim again; his loyalty would be forfeited, I think. There might be a larger cause, but his concern would be with the other fellow. And however hard you might press him for a verdict, he would bring in only a recommendation for mercy.

iii

The Galsworthys have been in Devonshire as far back as records go—"since the flood—of Saxons, at all events," as John Galsworthy once put it. His mother came of a family named Bartleet, whose county for many centuries was Worcestershire. The boy, John, was born in 1867 at Coombe, in Surrey. "From the first," continues the anonymous but authorised sketch I am quoting, "his salient characteristics were earnestness and tenacity. Not surprisingly brilliant, he was sure and steady; his understanding, not notably quick, was notably sound. At Harrow from 1881-1886 he did well in work and games. At New College, Oxford, 1886-1889, he graduated with an Honour degree in Law. After some further preparation he was called to the bar (Lincoln's Inn) in 1890. It was natural he should have taken up the law, since his father had done so. 'I read,' he says, 'in various chambers, practised almost not at all, and disliked my profession thoroughly.'

"In these circumstances he began to travel. His father, a successful and unusual man in both character and intellect, was 'not in a position to require his son to make money'; his son, therefore, travelled, off and on, for nearly two years, going, amongst other places, to Russia, Canada, British Columbia, Australia, New Zealand, the Fiji Islands, and South Africa. On a sailing-ship voyage between Adelaide and the Cape he met and became a fast friend with the novelist Joseph Conrad, then still a sailor. We do not know whether this friendship influenced Galsworthy in becoming a writer; indeed, we believe that he has somewhere said that it did not. But Galsworthy did take to writing, published his first novel, *Jocelyn*, in 1899, *Villa Rubein* in 1900, *A Man of Devon and Other Stories* in 1901." *Jocelyn* has been dropped from the list of Galsworthy's works, *Villa Rubein* was revised in 1909, *The Island Pharisees*, a satire of English weaknesses which appeared in 1904, was revised four years later; and it was not until the publication of *The Man of Property* in 1906 that our author succeeded in sitting on the Public's head and twining his fingers firmly into the Public's whiskers.

This was the first volume of the then-unplanned *Forsyte Saga* and it led Conrad, who had two years previously dedicated to Galsworthy what remains his greatest novel (*Nostromo*), to write an article in which he said:

"The foundation of Mr. Galsworthy's talent, it seems to me, lies in a remarkable power of ironic insight combined with an extremely keen and faithful eye for all the phenomena on the surface of the life he observes. These are the purveyors of his imagination, whose servant is a style clear, direct, sane, illumined by a perfectly unaffected sincerity. It is the style of a man whose sympathy with mankind is too genuine to allow him the smallest gratification of his vanity at the cost of his fellow-creatures . . . sufficiently pointed to carry deep his remorseless irony and grave enough to be the dignified vehicle of his profound compassion. Its sustained harmony is never interrupted by those bursts of cymbals and fifes which some deaf people acclaim for brilliance. Before all it is a style well under control, and therefore it never betrays this tender and ironic writer into an odious cynicism of laughter and tears.

"From laboriously collected information, I am led to believe that most people read novels for amusement. This is as it should be. But whatever be their motives, I entertain towards all novel-readers the feelings of warm and respectful affection. I would not try to deceive them for worlds. Never! This being understood, I go on to declare, in the peace of my heart and the serenity of my conscience, that if they want amusement they shall find it between the covers of this book. They shall find plenty of it in this episode in the history of the Forsytes, where the reconciliation of a father and son, the dramatic and poignant comedy of Soames Forsyte's marital relations, and the tragedy of Bosinney's failure are exposed to our gaze with the remorseless yet sympathetic irony of Mr. Galsworthy's art, in the light of the unquenchable fire burning on the altar of property. They shall find amusement, and perhaps also something more lasting—if they care for it. I say this with all the reserves and qualifications which strict truth requires around every statement of opinion. Mr. Galsworthy will never be found futile by anyone, and never uninteresting by the most exacting."

Twelve years after the appearance of *The Man of Property*, in the volume *Five Tales* (1918), was included a long short story, *Indian Summer of a Forsyte.* The year 1920 saw publication of the novel, *In Chancery*, and another long short story, *Awakening;* and the following year brought the novel, *To Let.* These five units, separately in the order named or together in the same chronological order in the thick volume called *The Forsyte Saga*, compose a record of three generations of an English family which has very justly been compared to the Esmonds of Thackeray. The Forsytes and their associates and connections are indeed "intensely real as individuals—real in the way that the Esmonds were real; symbolic in their traits, of a section of English society, and reflecting in their lives the changing moods of England in these years." The motif is clearly expressed by certain words of young Jolyon Forsyte in *The Man of Property:*

" 'A Forsyte is not an uncommon animal. There are hundreds among the members of this club. Hundreds out there in the streets; you meet them wherever you go! . . . We are, of course, all of us slaves of property, and I admit that it's a question of degree, but what I call a "Forsyte" is a man who is decidedly more than less a slave of property. He knows a good thing, he knows a safe thing, and his grip on property—it doesn't matter whether it be wives, houses, money, or reputation—is his hallmark. . . . "Property and quality of a Forsyte. This little animal, disturbed by the ridicule of his own sort, is unaffected in his motions by the laughter of strange creatures (you or I). Hereditarily disposed to myopia, he recognises only the persons and habitats of his own species, amongst which he passes an existence of competitive tranquillity." . . . They are half England, and the better half, too, the safe half, the three-per-cent half, the half that counts. It's their wealth and security that makes everything possible; makes your art possible, makes literature, science, even religion, possible. Without Forsytes, who believe in none of these things, but turn them all to use, where should we be?' "

One of Galsworthy's severest critics, St. John Ervine, calls *The Forsyte Saga* "his best work," and breaks the force of many strictures to declare: "The craftsmanship of *To Let* is superb—this novel is, perhaps, the most technically-correct book of our time—but its human value is even greater than its craftsmanship. In a very vivid fashion, Mr. Galsworthy shows the passing of a tradition and an age. He leaves Soames Forsyte in lonely age, but he does not leave him entirely without sympathy; for this muddleheaded man, unable to win or to keep affection on any but commercial terms, contrives in the end to win the pity and almost the love of the reader who has followed his varying fortunes through their stupid career. The frustrate love of Fleur and Jon is certainly one of the tenderest things in modern fiction."

iv

Grove Lodge, The Grove, Hampstead, London, N. W. 3, is the residence of Mr. and Mrs. Galsworthy; if you have occasion to telephone, call Hampstead 3684. The approach to the house is described by Carlton Miles in the Theatre Magazine (December, 1922):

"The Galsworthys live at the bottom of a long, rambling lane called The Grove, in that part of Hampstead that looks calmly down on the crowded chimneypots of northwestern London. To reach the house you must climb a steep hill from the underground station and pass the stone building in which Du Maurier wrote *Peter Ibbetson* and to whose memory it bears a tablet. A few minutes' walk in one direction and you are in Church Row with the historic cemetery in which Du Maurier and Beerbohm Tree rest side by side. Follow the Grove walk and you arrive on Hampstead Heath, black with thousands of workers on Bank Holiday, overlooking the little row of cottages where Leigh Hunt and his followers established their 'Vale of Health.' But, having passed the Du Maurier home, you turn fairly to your left, descend a winding pathway that takes you by the Admiral's House—designated by large signs—erected 159 years ago by an aged commander who built his home in three decks and mounted it with guns. The guns have vanished but the Admiral's House still is one of the sights of Hampstead.

"At the end of the lane a small grilled iron gate shuts off the world from a green yard and a low white house, whose rambling line suggests many passageways and sets of rooms. A sheltered, secluded spot, the place above all others where Galsworthy should live. Peace has been achieved in five minutes' walk from the noisy station. 'The Inn of Tranquillity.'

"A turn down a long hallway, up a short flight of steps—a bright, flower-decked livingroom, a tea table, a dark-eyed, low-voiced hostess, a clasping of hand by host and a bark you interpret as cautious approval from Mark, the sheepdog, lying on the hearth rug. Mark is named for one of Galsworthy's characters"—Mark Lennan in *The Dark Flower?*— " . . . moments flee before you dare steal a look at the middle-aged gentleman sitting quietly in his chair, striving with gentle dignity to place you at the ease he feels not himself.

"Tall, grey-haired he looks astonishingly like his photographs. Reticent to a degree about his own work, he talks freely and with the utmost generosity about that of others. Opinion, formed slowly, is determined. The face, with its faint smile, looks neither disheartened nor sad, yet sometime it has met suffering. Like most Englishmen the eagerness of youth has not been crushed. . . . There is nothing chill about the novelist. He is the embodiment of easy, gracious courtesy. Conversation is far from intimidating, a long flow of material topics with now and then an upward leap of thought. And it is this swift flight that betrays his mental withdrawal. As clearly as if physically present may be seen the robed figure of his thoughts, standing behind him in his own drawingroom. You wonder what may be their burden. About him is the veil of remoteness."

His humility, adorned by his presence and made disarming by what is certainly the most beautiful head and face among the living sons of men, does not always save him from the charge of coldness when manifested impersonally and at a distance. Where nearly all men and women give essential particulars of their lives, not to mention the human touch of their preferred recreations, Mr. Galsworthy, in the English *Who's Who*, besides the long list of his publications, states only the year of his birth, his residence, and his membership in the Athenæum Club. This would hardly support Mr. Ervine's declaration that the Galsworthy sensitiveness "is almost totally impersonal"; and instead of being "startled to discover how destitute of egotism Mr. Galsworthy seems to be" the close student of mankind might be led to speculate upon the variety of egotism he had just encountered. "It may even be argued," pursues Mr. Ervine, cautiously, "that his lack of interest in himself is a sign of inadequate artistry, that it is impossible for a man of supreme quality to be so utterly unconcerned about himself as Mr. Galsworthy is." With due respect to Mr. Ervine, this is nonsense. Whatever Mr. Galsworthy may lack, it is not interest in himself. He has achieved countless satisfactory channels for the extrusion of that interest through other and imaginary men, women and beasts—that is all.

V

It is as if he had long ago said to himself, as perhaps he did: "I am myself, but myself isn't a subject I can decently be concerned about or expose an interest in. Let me forget myself in someone—

in everyone—else!" And since then, if he has ever repented, the spectacle of George Bernard Shaw, and particularly the horridly fascinating spectacle of Herbert George Wells, have been before him, to serve as awful warnings and lasting deterrents. Mr. Wells, in ever-new contortions, like a circus acrobat whose nakedness was gaudily accentuated by spangles, began seeing it through with Ann Veronica and is still exposing the secret places of his heart, while dizzy recollections of marriage, God and tono-bungay yet linger. Mr. Shaw has gone back to . . . evolution.

"I was," Mr. Galsworthy has said in an uninhibited moment, "for many years devoted to the sports of shooting and racing. I gave up shooting because it got on my nerves. I still ride; and I would go to a race-meeting any day if it were not for the din, for I am still under the impression that there is nothing alive quite so beautiful as a thoroughbred horse." His devotion to dogs and other dumb animals is frequently spoken of as it extrudes in *Memories*, Noel's protection of the rabbit in *Saint's Progress* and "For Love of Beasts" in *A Sheaf*. These shifting loyalties were—what were they if not admirable realisations of the Self? But let those who still believe Mr. Galsworthy selfless but read the prefaces to the new and very handsome Manaton Edition of his works. For these volumes he has provided sixteen entirely new prefaces. I quote from the announcement of the edition:

"These"—prefaces—"are peculiarly interesting, for in them he frankly criticises his work; in some cases, too, they reflect the response of readers as he has sensed it. In others he tells of the thought in his mind while writing, and of the changes through which the thought has gone in the process. Again, he speculates on the art of writing in general, on the forms of fiction, on emotional expression and effect in the drama. In short, as he phrases it, 'in writing a preface, one goes into the confessional.'

"Of *The Country House* he says: 'When once Pendyce had taken the bit between his teeth, the book ran away with me, and was more swiftly finished than any of my novels, being written in seven months.'

" 'The germ of *The Patrician*,' he begins the preface to that volume, 'is traceable to a certain dinner party at the House of Commons in 1908 and the face of a young politician on the other side of the table.'

"In the preface to *Fraternity* he says: 'A novelist, however observant of type and sensitive to the shades of character, *does little but describe and dissect himself*. . . . In dissecting Hilary, for instance, in this novel, *his creator feels the knife going sharply into his own flesh, just as he could feel it when dissecting Soames Forsyte or Horace Pendyce*.' "

The italics are my own and I think they are permissible.

Probably not enough attention has hitherto been paid to Mr. Galsworthy as a writer of short tales, but that may be because no collection of his stories has shown his talent so roundly as does the new book *Captures*. This opens with the well-known story "A Feud" and offers also such variety and such virtuosity in the short story form as "The Man Who Kept His Form," "A Hedonist," "Timber," "Santa Lucia," "Blackmail," "Stroke of Lightning," "The Broken Boot," "Virtue," "Conscience," "Salta Pro Nobis," "Heat," "Philanthropy," "A Long Ago Affair," "Acmé," "Late—299." In this book, as in similar collections, there must be put to Mr. Galsworthy's credit his frequent practice of the Continental notion of the short story—the sketch, the impression, the representation of a mood which we find in French and Russian literature and which the American short story too often sacrifices for purely mechanical effects.

Books by John Galsworthy

1900 *Villa Rubein.* Revised Edition, 1909
1904 *The Island Pharisees.* Revised Edition, 1908
1906 *The Man of Property*
1907 *The Country House*
1908 *A Commentary*
1909 *Fraternity*
1909 *Strife.* Drama in Three Acts
1909 *The Silver Box.* Comedy in Three Acts
1909 *Joy.* Play on the Letter "I" in Three Acts
1909 *Plays.* First Series. Containing *The Silver Box*, *Joy*, and *Strife.*
1910 *Justice.* Tragedy in Four Acts
1910 *A Motley*
1911 *The Little Dream.* Allegory in six Scenes
1911 *The Patrician*
1912 *The Inn of Tranquillity.* Studies and Essays

1912 *Moods, Songs, and Doggerels*
1912 *Memories.* Illustrated by Maud Earl
1912 *The Eldest Son.* Domestic Drama in Three Acts
1912 *The Pigeon.* Fantasy in Three Acts
1913 *Plays.* Second Series. Containing *The Eldest Son, The Little Dream, Justice*
1913 *The Dark Flower*
1913 *The Fugitive.* Play in Four Acts
1914 *The Mob.* Play in Four Acts
1914 *Plays.* Third Series. Containing *The Fugitive, The Pigeon, The Mob*
1915 *The Little Man and Other Satires*
1915 *A Bit o' Love.* Play in Three Acts
1915 *The Freelands*
1916 *A Sheaf*
1917 *Beyond*
1918 *Five Tales*
1919 *Another Sheaf*
1919 *Saint's Progress*
1919 *Addresses in America 1919*
1920 *Tatterdemalion*
1920 *In Chancery*
1920 *Awakening*
1920 *The Skin Game.* A Tragi-comedy
1920 *The Foundations.* An Extravagant Play
1920 *Plays.* Fourth Series. Containing *A Bit o' Love, The Foundations, The Skin Game*
1921 *To Let*
1921 *Six Short Plays.* Containing *The First and the Last, The Little Man, Hall-marked, Defeat, The Sun,* and *Punch and Go*
1922 *The Forsyte Saga*

1922 *A Family Man*
1922 *Loyalties*
1923 *Windows.* Comedy in Three Acts
1923 *Plays.* Fifth Series. Containing *Loyalties, Windows, A Family Man*
1923 *The Burning Spear* [first published anonymously in England in 1918]
1923 *Captures*

Sources on John Galsworthy

John Galsworthy: A Sketch of His Life and Works. Booklet published by Mr. Galsworthy's publishers, CHARLES SCRIBNER'S SONS, 1922.

John Galsworthy. Booklet published by Mr. Galsworthy's English publisher, WILLIAM HEINEMANN, 1922. Valuable for its bibliography of the English editions.

J. G. Pamphlet announcing the Manaton Edition of John Galsworthy's works. Procurable from CHARLES SCRIBNER'S SONS. This edition contains some hitherto unpublished material and a rearrangement of the plays.

The Prefaces to the Manaton Edition. Practically the only discussion of his own work by the author.

Some Modern Novelists. Helen Thomas Follett and Wilson Follett. HENRY HOLT & CO. Chapter X. contains a long and careful critical consideration of Galsworthy's work up to and including *The Freelands.*

Some Impressions of My Elders. St. John G. Ervine. THE MACMILLAN COMPANY. For a forceful statement from one of those who strongly criticise Mr. Galsworthy's work, especially for its "indiscriminating pity." Analyses at length the play, *The Fugitive.*

John Galsworthy. Carlton Miles. THE THEATRE MAGAZINE, December, 1922. An interview.

A Middle-Class Family. Joseph Conrad. THE OUTLOOK (London), March 31, 1906. A review of *The Man of Property.*

The interested reader should further consult the READER'S GUIDE TO PERIODICAL LITERATURE for the years since 1906.

A complete Galsworthy bibliography, to be published in England, is now in preparation by Harold A. Marrot.

2. *The Magic Carpet*

i

THE Magic Carpet was one which took you far away, whisked you up and through the air (though not sensibly too fast) and brought you into a foreign but delightful country. There are books like that, taking you out of yourself, so that the preoccupation of a moment before is forgotten, to-morrow's worries are lost, and you exist in a blissful unconsciousness that there can be anything beyond the fine pleasure of this present hour. The "travel book" attempts directly the transfer to some place else; the book of essays, more indirect in its method, is often more successful.

Aldous Huxley has been known to us hitherto as a poet and a writer of fiction. Both his poetry and his fiction have been marked with a graceful artifice and that simplicity which comes only from a completed sophistication. His new book, a collection of essays, is distinguished by those qualities. There is something about Huxley's writing—I don't know what it is and those who know what it is, can't tell —which brings a gleam to the eyes of all who love literature for its own sake. In *On the Margin* Huxley the satirist walks comfortably with Huxley the student. For Aldous Huxley is a very studious young man. Tall, with hair that bushes out from under his broad-brimmed soft hat, he walks with that slight stoop inevitably acquired by those whose heads do not pass readily under all doorways. With his clothes flapping gently around him, his glance peering through thick-lensed spectacles, he advances into a room with the surprising effect of an amiable scarecrow. A first grotesque impression is rapidly dissolved in the gentle acquaintance springing up immediately afterward; for no more likeable person lives. It is not generally known that between the ages of seventeen and nineteen it was thought he would go blind, so that he learned to read Braille type. His interest in America is keen; he would like to come here, and may. Intimates know him as one of the most learned men in England, though devoid of poses and devoted to finding pleasure in the works of Charles Dickens. His scholarliness shows itself in *On the Margin*, where Chaucer, Ben Jonson, and the devilish biographer, Mr. Strachey, divide attention with the question of love as practised in France and England, the justice of Margot Asquith's strictures on modern feminine beauty, and the evolution of ennui.

Recently there died in his ninety-second year Frederic Harrison, who had witnessed the coronation of Victoria in 1838 and every celebration in her reign; who saw her funeral in 1901; who, though past eighty when it began, saw the war of 1914-1918 and the several years of turmoil afterward. An extraordinary life! Before it had ended this man whose span of years was matched by his breadth of knowledge and interests gathered together what he himself regarded as his last book, now published under the title *De Senectute* and blending some of his finest literary criticism with delightful recollections of the great times in which he lived. A personal account of Victoria and Prince Albert, the "Dialogue on Old Age" which affords the title for the volume, a review of the picturesque history of Constantinople through sixteen centuries, fundamental differences between Greek and Elizabethan tragedy, the art of translation with reference to Dante and Molière, some consideration of Fielding and Smollett and Kingsley, and a final chapter upon various schools of philosophy—these are the relics of a glorious life. The book is full of brightness, its effects are sane, and the writing is alike lucid and tinctured with that peculiar zest which, as it was a quality of Frederic Harrison's temperament, goes far to explain the length of his life as well as the grace with which he lived it.

Among essayists there are ladies. But there are not many ladies, nor men, either, who have taken rank in the essay with a single book. I understand that Katharine Fullerton Gerould would rather prefer to be known for her fiction—those short stories, masterly in form, with which she began and such a work as her most recent, the brief novel, *Conquistador*. And such a preference is easily understood. *Conquistador*, a jewel with many facets, would seduce any woman. And yet Mrs. Gerould's collection of essays, *Modes and Morals*, published in 1920, had an extraordinary sale for a book of its character, and still steadily sells. People constantly refer to her discussion of "The Remarkable Rightness of Rudyard Kipling" and the arts of persuasion are constantly brought to bear upon her to assemble another such book. If Mrs. Gerould began with something of the suddenness of a meteor, she persists with a good deal of the steady brilliance of a fixed star. It was, in fact, with the appearance of a story, "Vain Oblations," in Scribner's Magazine for March, 1911, that she first came to general notice. This dark and terrible piece of fictional analysis had for its principal character a New England woman missionary. Other stories followed in Scribner's, the Atlantic and Harper's, and a first collection, under the title *Vain Oblations*, was published in March, 1914. A second book of tales, *The Great Tradition*, was succeeded by a novelette, *A Change of Air;* by the essays comprising *Modes and Morals;* and then by the novel, *Lost Valley. Valiant Dust* offered some more short tales; but with the appearance of *Conquistador* many of us felt Mrs. Gerould for the first time to be perfectly suited in length, form and material alike. Despite her superb technique, she needs more room than the short story gives her; and although she can write of barren New England lives she can write much more effectively of richly-coloured Latin life. Although, as Stuart P. Sherman has observed, she can do dashingly the "picture of a really nice woman meditating a fracture of the seventh commandment in a spacious sun-flooded chamber with a Chinese rug," her deep fictional desires are toward the richly barbaric, and neither Henry-Jamesical nor Edith-Whartonesque. In the atmosphere of Princeton, which is her home (her husband, Gordon Hall Gerould, is a member of the English faculty), she has the leisure and repose necessary to do such essays and short novels as no other living American has given evidence of an equal talent for achieving. Occasionally a bit of travel, perhaps, producing as its direct result a book like her *Hawaii, Scenes and Impressions;* but ultimately much more valuable for its indirect stimulus to her imagination, which belongs to the class of imaginations so dangerous when they are confined.

In fact, the imagination is very little understood, as if it were one of those glands whose mysterious secretions we tinker with nowadays, either not too successfully or with a success so alarming as to threaten the overthrow of all physiology. One of these days we shall have a mental thyroid extract, and then—! It remains to be observed that with most of us the imagination secretes gently, with a fresh annual activation in the direction of old woods and pastures ever-new, rather than new; a circumstance very favourable to David Grayson when, in 1907, he put forth the volume called *Adventures in Contentment.* It is difficult to think of any precise precedent for this mixture of essay, philosophy, homely observation and quiet humour with its essentially American pattern of thought. The febrile character of much American life was already marked, and the remedy of an equally feverish optimism had yet to be widely prescribed. The time was propitious, the sentiment of David Grayson had an ingratiation. When, in 1910, *Adventures in Friendship* was published, a good many thousand people had read the earlier adventures and were alert for these. *The Friendly Road* (1913) was succeeded by *Hempfield* (1915) and a final volume, *Great Possessions* (1917). A half dozen years have passed without relegating these books to the shelves of the Great Unread. As "The Library of the Open Road" they inherit an annual, rather a perennial, popularity.

ii

In the course of reading a great number of travel books, I have come to prefer my Baedekers to all others. The worthy Karl's "handbooks for travellers" are not only the standard guides (and likely to remain so) but they seem to me perfect in their exactitude, their literalness and their discreet prescriptions for the visitor's emotions. If I wish to know the number of yards to walk from the castle gate and the right entrance through which to pass to emerge upon a View, I wish also to know in a general way how to graduate my feelings on beholding the spectacle spread out at my feet. And this, Baedeker tells me. By the unstarred, starred or double-starred nature of his reference to the View, I know with reassurance whether my emotional response should be elementary, intermediate or advanced. Moreover, there is lacking no concrete detail from which the fancy may launch itself. To read Baedeker is to use one's own wings, and not somebody else's. This is a great virtue; for in book travels, as perhaps in other travel, it is much more desirable to make one's own appraisal than to accept another's description of the beauties of a place. And I really have known a novelist to reject every particular travel book dealing with a certain town or region in which his scene was laid, because he felt hampered by their emotionality and their impressionism and a quality of vagueness, and turn with joy and relief to his *Baedeker's Mediterranean* or *Northern Italy* or *Spain and Portugal*. Here the matters essential to accuracy were given—and only a novelist who has heard the protest of literal-minded readers can know the penalties of a topographical mistake—but the perfectly-set stage stood cleared for the actors of his writer's imagination. For the benefit of those attending the assemblies of the League of Nations, one of the most freshly revised volumes is *Baedeker's Switzerland;* another of equal recency is the guide to Canada.

In spite of the twenty-seven books of the Baedeker series, there is a good deal of the world which is not even touched upon in these famous guides, which are, after all and with slight exception, properties for the tourist in Europe and the Mediterranean countries. The tourist, however, more and more declines to stick to Europe, a large number of him having seen Europe pretty thoroughly anyway. As for the tourist in fancy, he goes everywhere. The business man is another traveller who is omni-itinerant. I suppose the widest audience for the series of books called "Carpenter's World Travels" is composed of what one commentator rightly describes as "the incalculable company of stay-at-home travellers." Frank G. Carpenter himself is the best guarantee that the matter and form of the planned twenty-five volumes will remain as excellent as in the seven already brought out. For over thirty years this highly skilled journalist has walked the earth, even to the ends of the earth, and written of what he saw. Some four million copies of his Geographic Readers have sold to the public schools, and an equal number of families now open their newspapers once a week to find his new series of letters from the countries of Europe. In fact, Mr. Carpenter is a publicist of so vast and important an audience that Governments have been glad to give him access to every official source of information, and various rulers and prime ministers have at one and another time especially commissioned him in facilitation of his work. The many and exceptional photographs in his hands have made it possible to plan the use of about one hundred of the best in each volume of the series now under way. *Java and the East Indies* and *France to Scandinavia* (France, Belgium, Holland, Denmark, Norway and Sweden) are his latest additions to the beginning made with *The Holy Land and Syria. From Tangier to Tripoli* (Morocco, Algeria, Tunis and the Sahara), *Alaska, Our Northern Wonderland, The Tail of the Hemisphere* (Chile and Argentina) and *Cairo to Kisumu* (Egypt, the Anglo-Egyptian Sudan, and British East Africa) were the intermediate books.

"Adopted as a motto this year, 'The world is my parish,'" wrote down Stephen Graham, at the end of his travel record for 1921—a record that begins with that first pilgrimage of his to Russia in 1906. Even so, he finds parts of his parish yet unvisited, and the next year saw him off on fresh Latin trails. It had come over him, indeed, to traverse some 15,000 miles that represent one of the most fabulous of mankind's adventures. Graham had a thought to approach our present America in the path of those first explorers and in the spirit of the conquistadores, following Columbus from Spain to the Indies, Balboa to the peak in Darien whence he saw the Pacific, Cortes to the conquest of Montezuma's capital, and Coronado on the fruitless quest into the deserts of New Mexico and Arizona. What happened? Why, in the words of Vachel Lindsay, Graham's tramp companion in the Rockies:

Then I had religion, then I had a vision—

and Graham, whose intimacy with Russian life and thought has deeply enriched a natural mystical endowment, found a significant theme in the Spanish quest for gold succeeded, after four centuries, by the American quest of power—religion the sanctification of one, pan-Americanism the credo of the other. It is this spiritual penetration that makes the fine distinction of Stephen Graham's *In Quest of El Dorado*, joined to the man's unusual literary skill, taste and sense of form. On the point of form there is something more than usually admirable in the start of the book from Madrid and Cadiz and in the conclusion (on a note of wonder) amid the ruins of Mitla, as if the quester for El Dorado would do well to seek its whereabouts in the indecipherable inscriptions placed on their massive memorials by a race that had sunk into silence long before the imperious advent of the Children of the

Sun. These are the refinements of the book for the reader of philosophical or æsthetic tastes; but as such matters should be, they are entirely unobtrusive—present to those who seek them, hidden to those who are indifferent—and in externals Stephen Graham offers a first-hand travel study with cowboys and conquistadores, Indians and Mexicans, the Panama Canal and the jingle of spurs in the changing foreground.

Among those authors whose books of travel win their appreciation from the personality of the adventurer, Mary Roberts Rinehart seems to me quite plainly the foremost. The considerable time that has elapsed since the publication of *Through Glacier Park* and *Tenting Tonight* will sharpen many appetites for the camp fare offered in her new book, *The Out Trail.* With none of the acerbity of her own Tish, Mrs. Rinehart has to the full that lady's derring-do. "I have roughed it," she explains at the beginning of *The Out Trail*, "in one wilderness after another, in camp and on the trail, in the air and on water, in war abroad and in peace at home. I have been scared to death more times than I can remember. Led," she confesses, "by the exigencies of my profession, by feminine curiosity, or by the determination not to be left at home, I have been shaken, thrown, bitten, sunburned, rained on, shot at, stone-bruised, frozen, broiled, and scared, with monotonous regularity." And she adds that on several occasions she has been placed in situations of real danger from which she has clamoured to be extricated with all possible despatch. Two things, if we may judge by her chronicle, seem never to have failed her, in whatever emergency: her sense of drama and her sense of humour. At least, they are keenly in evidence on all the pages of *The Out Trail*, and make it easily among the most entertaining books of its kind—not infrequently exciting, too! If someone thinks that the sense of the humorous must have been missing at the time and have been recaptured later in writing of the adventures, I suspect he is mistaken; for I recall that not so long after I had written a chapter on "The Vitality of Mary Roberts Rinehart" as a novelist, I met Mrs. Rinehart. She was suffering from one of those ferocious colds which make cowards and pessimists of us all, but she only remarked: "I'm afraid you will find the vitality you have just celebrated rather low this morning." This, I submit, is such stuff as humorists are made on.

iii

Among books of essays that successfully spread the Magic Carpet for readers I should like to draw attention to the following (in addition to those described above):

ROBERT CORTES HOLLIDAY'S *In the Neighborhood of Murray Hill.*

J. C. SQUIRE'S *Essays at Large* and his *Books Reviewed.*

HILAIRE BELLOC'S *On.*

Other collections of essays, chiefly on literary and philosophical subjects, are included in or listed after Chapter 15, "For the Literary Investor."

iv

In the matter of books of travel, some classification is necessary, and in addition to the ones just described I am glad to name the following in all their happy variety:

A Group of Books on Ancient Egypt and Present-day Egyptian Explorations.

A History of Egypt From the Earliest Times to the Conquest of the Persians, by JAMES HENRY BREASTED. The ninth printing has just been called for. With 200 illustrations and maps.

History of Assyria, by A. T. OLMSTEAD. A companion volume to Breasted's *History of Egypt*, and equally admirable. With maps and many illustrations.

G. MASPERO'S *Life in Ancient Egypt and Assyria*, his *Egyptian Art: Studies*, and his *History of Art in Egypt*. These remain standard in their field.

TERENCE GRAY'S *And in the Tomb Were Found* and his *The Life of Hatshepsut*. The first is a series of historical studies and sketches including Khufu, builder of the Great Pyramid, and Rameses the Great. Some literal translations of Egyptian love songs are added. The second book is the romance of an Egyptian princess who reigns as a man; the work is cast in the form of a pageant for the sake of greater vividness.

PERCY E. MARTIN'S *Egypt Old and New*, a general account with many illustrations in colour.

PERCY EDWARD NEWBERRY'S *The Valley of the Kings*, which includes the discoveries by the late Lord Carnarvon and Howard Carter in a general account of thirty years' explorations.

ARTHUR WEIGALL'S *Tut-Ankh-Amen and Other Essays* is the work of an Egyptologist and former Inspector-General of Antiquities in Egypt. Mr. Weigall was special correspondent for the London *Daily Mail*, New York *World* and other newspapers at the opening of the tomb of Tut-Ankh-Amen.

A Group of Books About China.

Audacious Angles on China, by ELSIE MCCORMICK, introduces the reader to Chinese life as the Western resident there sees it. The humorous side of such experiences is to the fore, and one part of the book is devoted to "The Unexpurgated Diary of a Shanghai Baby"—an American child's view of the intimacies of Eastern life.

Swinging Lanterns, by ELIZABETH CRUMP ENDERS, is a vivid narrative of what an American woman saw while living and travelling in China. It contains much that is unusual, including such matters as the Yellow Llama Devil Dances, never before described. Fine illustrations.

ROY CHAPMAN ANDREWS'S *Across Mongolian Plains*.

ROY CHAPMAN ANDREWS'S and YVETTE BORUP ANDREWS'S *Camps and Trails in China*.

HERBERT A. GILES'S *A History of Chinese Literature*, a historical account written with much charm and taste and offering translations of the work of various Chinese writers.

The Far East.

C. M. VAN TYNE'S *India in Ferment.* Mahatma Gandhi and the general background by a scholar and skilled observer.

SIR HUGH CLIFFORD'S *A Prince of Malaya* and his earlier book, *The Further Side of Silence.* These are stories, true, fictional and semi-fictional, that take rank as literature. The author, a friend of Joseph Conrad, at the age of twenty-one was "the principal instrument in adding 15,000 square miles to the British dependencies in the East."

SYDNEY A. CLOMAN'S *Myself and a Few Moros.* An American soldier's lively but not unhumorous administrative experiences, with a good picture of what the United States has accomplished in colonial government.

H. O. MORGENTHALER'S *Matahari.* The Frederick O'Brienish adventures of a Swiss engineer prospecting for tin in the Malayan-Siamese jungle.

The Callers of the Wild.

ERNEST THOMPSON SETON'S *Game Animals and the Lives They Live*, Vol. I. There are to be four volumes.

WILLIAM T. HORNADAY'S *The Minds and Manners of Wild Animals*, a book of personal observations by one of the keenest living observers and one who, as director of the New York Zoological Park, has under his eye and care the most complete collection in the world.

SAMUEL A. DERIEUX's *Animal Personalities*, including domesticated animals.

CARL AKELEY's *Men and Animals: An Autobiography* and MARY HASTINGS BRADLEY's *On the Gorilla Trail*. Mr. Akeley went to the Belgian Congo on a gorilla expedition, and Mrs. Bradley, well-known as a novelist, her husband and their five-year-old daughter went, too. Each book enhances the interest of the other.

With Ice.

APSLEY CHERRY-GARRARD's *The Worst Journey in the World*, describing, in its two volumes, Scott's last Antarctic expedition, 1910-13.

Mediterranean.

V. C. SCOTT O'CONNOR's *A Vision of Morocco*, which is both historical and descriptive, and C. E. ANDREWS's *Old Morocco and the Forbidden Atlas*, written in a distinguished prose.

C. R. ASHBEE's *A Palestine Notebook*, the result of administrative experience in 1918-22. The book has interesting personal portraits of Sir Herbert Samuels, General Allenby, Lord Robert Cecil, Lord Morley, the late Lord Northcliffe, Lord Curzon, and others.

G. K. CHESTERTON's *The New Jerusalem*.

ERNEST PEIXOTTO's *Through Spain and Portugal*,

where the author's illustrations are so happily wedded to the text.

ROSITA FORBES'S *The Secret of the Sahara: Kufara.*

South America.

C. REGINALD ENOCK'S *Republics of Central and South America*, his *Spanish America* (two volumes), his *Ecuador*, his *Peru*, and his *Mexico.*

LEO E. MILLER'S *In the Wilds of South America*, an account of six years' explorations.

Unique Books of Travel.

GEORGE EYRE-TODD'S *The Clans of the Scottish Highlands.* By an authority on Scots lore.

VAUGHAN CORNISH'S *A Geography of the Great Capitals*, from the "capital" of the Iroquois Indians, marked by a sacred fire, to the capitals of government, such as Rome and London, or of commerce, such as New York, and including vanished cities as well as existing ones.

THOMAS NELSON PAGE'S *Washington and Its Romance*, really a historical work. Mr. Page had been engaged upon it for several years before his death and left completed his account of the city's early days.

S. R. ROGET'S *Travel in the Two Last Centuries of Three Generations*, a remarkable history, vivid, personal and interesting, derived from the records and letters of a single family and showing what rapid changes transportation underwent in the short period of two hundred years.

B. W. MATZ's *Dickensian Inns and Taverns*, and his *The Inns and Taverns of Pickwick*, and also CECIL ALDIN's magnificent *Old Inns*—for all who hear the post horns blow and the stage coach drive up to the door.

STEPHEN GRAHAM's *Tramping With a Poet in the Rockies*, the description of a vagabondage with Vachel Lindsay, with a report of many conversations which left the ground.

3. *A Breathless Chapter*

i

WHAT actually took my breath away (in the first place) was an inspection of the "general catalogue" of one of our publishing houses, and a discovery therein. Now, a general catalogue, showing all the books published by a particular house and "in print"—that is, procurable new—is in itself a species of adventure. I admit all that Mr. A. Edward Newton puts forward as to the amenities of book collecting—by which, I take it, he means the joys, the sorrows, the moments of irony and the moments of amusement which fall to the lot of the collector of rare books. The quest of the book that is out of print, and must be had at second hand by diligent search and patient waiting, is an exceptional delight. Nevertheless, a special and more accessible pleasure lies in the catalogue, whether of a publisher or a bookshop. All but a handful of us are certain to come upon titles that kindle the imagination or rekindle the memory. Both were lit for me by the entry:

> GABORIAU, Emile
> The Most Complete Library Edition
> Each with new illustrated jackets
> *The Count's Millions.* 12mo. 2.00

And not only *The Count's Millions*, but a roll of eleven others, an even dozen in all, ready to be re-read after these too many years and pleasingly freshened up by the new illustrated jackets! There they were: *Baron Trigault's Vengeance*, *The Clique of Gold*, and a fine array of enticing titles that memory doesn't recall—*The Champdoce Mystery*, *Within an Inch of His Life*, which has the proper ring; *The Widow Lerouge; Other People's Money*, always an engrossing subject; *The Mystery of Orcival* (illustrated by Jules Guerin) and one or two others besides (of course!) *Monsieur Lecoq* and that famous *File No. 113*. It is desolating to reflect that there must be thousands, perhaps millions, to whom the name of Monsieur Lecoq conveys nothing and who are totally unacquainted with *File No. 113*, the most marvellous genealogical mystery story ever written, a tale in which one does not know which more to admire, the genealogy or the plot, until one grasps that the genealogy *is* the plot, and that what is desperately needed is not a detective but an expert in the ascension of family trees. However, that is not the worst. A yet more fearful thought concerns the author himself. It is even possible that there exists a whole generation, and perhaps races of men, to whom the name of Gaboriau is nothing but part of a quatrain (though rather a famous jingle) perpetrated first by Julian Street and James Montgomery Flagg under the auspices (I think) of Franklin P. Adams ("F. P. A."):

> Said Opie Read to E. P. Roe,
> "How do you like Gaboriau?"

A BREATHLESS CHAPTER

"I like him very much indeed!"
Said E. P. Roe to Opie Read.

Too, too flippant! Recalling Monsieur Lecoq, one exclaims: "There were detectives in those days!" And then again, such despondency is excessive. There is, now and occasionally, a detective in these days also. For proof, look at this fellow, Monsieur Jonquelle, in Melville Davisson Post's new book of that title. Ah! M. Davisson Post! It is but to mention him to introduce a new and important subject, *n'est ce pas?*

Mr. Post is worth talking about, certainly; and assuming that you have read him, you have probably discussed what you read afterward. His reputation as a writer of detective-mystery stories was pretty well abroad before the publication of *Uncle Abner, Master of Mysteries*, but that book established the reputation solidly. My recollection is that even before its appearance Mr. Post had written one or two articles in which he explained his theory and practice of story writing. I may simply remark that he went into the matter with as much technical skill and artistic nicety as Poe or de Maupassant; the man is an artist to his finger-tips and his work shows it. One has the feeling of construction and the sense of ornamentation springing from fine tastes; his tales are like beautiful pieces of cabinet work in which, at first sight, the effects of form, of shapeliness and of beauty and power are felt; on a closer examination you fall to admiring the sure hand and the cunning art; and at last your exploring fingers touch a particular joint, disclosing an unsuspected drawer that flies out and reveals the story's secret . . . though not Mr. Post's secret, which, like that of all genuine artists, remains with himself. If this has a ring of exaggeration to your ear, I need only refer you to such a perfect thing as the opening tale, "The Doomdorf Mystery," in *Uncle Abner*. Or you may make the test on *Monsieur Jonquelle*, where likewise all the stories turn on a central character, the Prefect of Police of Paris. *Monsieur Jonquelle* exemplifies very well Mr. Post's method of developing the mystery and its solution side by side. The gain in movement and surprise is the compensation for a technique immensely more difficult than the usual formula, by which a mystery is first built up and then, with inevitable repetition, dispelled. Those who are interested in the mechanism of stories will also find it worth while to consider why Mr. Post varies the narrative standpoint in his new book, so that some of the tales of *Monsieur Jonquelle* are related by the chief character, some by a third person, some by the author. . . . Mr. Post is a native of West Virginia, where he lives (Lost Creek, R. F. D. 2). A lawyer by training, he became particularly interested in the possibilities that lie open for the use of the law to aid the commission of crime; and this led to his first book, *The Strange Schemes of Randolph Mason*, in which this perversion of the law to criminal ends was the tissue of the stories.

A rural free delivery route at Lost Creek, West Virginia, has about it something pleasing in connection with a writer of breathless fiction, but the height of suitability in authors' residences belongs to Beatrice Grimshaw, whose mystery-adventure yarns of the South Pacific begin to be as numerous as a group of Pacific Islands. Indeed, I feel it would be no surprise some day, running before the southeasterly trade wind in a longitude west of 135 degrees and a latitude exceeding 20 degrees south, to sight a succession of dark blue cloud shapes lying on the horizon and be told: "Yonder's the Beatrice Islands of the Grimshaw group—big archipelago." Beatrice Grimshaw lives at Port Moseby, Papua, New Guinea, and is a planter as well as an author. There is practically no place in the South Seas which she has not visited, including the cannibal country of Papua. An old and possibly untrue story recalled by Hector MacQuarrie tells of a time when, on a schooner in mid-Pacific, "the captain, a gentle ancient, thinking that the dark women were having it all their own way, offered to embrace Miss Grimshaw, finding in return a gun pointing at his middle, filling him with quaint surprise that anyone could possibly offer violence in defence of a soul in so delightful a climate." Anyway, the lady knows her corner of the world and the people in it, as anyone may discover by the exciting enterprise of reading such a book as *The Sands of Oro*, with its strange group of five persons bound together by necessity and ugly chance, and committed to each other's fortunes for a term on a lonely Pacific island. Here, as in the author's *Nobody's Island*, the reader is at once let into the general secret with the result of a deepening mystery as to why and how and what next.

In truth, the tale which attempts breathlessness simply by the device of withheld explanations takes our breath away no longer. We have come to demand of the author that he proceed with direct and forward action, producing genuine interest instead of merely artificial suspense. He must hew to the line of his story, must *move*, letting the explanations, chips of his tough puzzle, fall where they may. Thus it has come about that the mystery story which is not also an adventure story fails to capture our interest or stir our curiosity. Of living writers, one of the earliest to grasp this was A. E. W. Mason. With others, I feared a half dozen years ago that he might have forgotten the vital principle; for his story of *The Summons* was quite unlike the Mason who had given us *The Four Feathers*, *The Witness for the Defense*, and other superb novels. But the fear may be dissipated, for in his new book, *The Winding Stair*, Mr. Mason has written a story comparable with his best work. Like *The Four Feathers*, it is a tale of cowardice becoming ultimate bravery; and I do not recall a heroine so pitifully appealing, so desperately lovable, so admirably brave as Marguerite Lambert since Joseph Conrad gave us the girl Lena in *Victory*. Possibly the title of Mr. Mason's newest work may, offhand, convey the wrong flavor to the incipient reader; it is not a yarn of mysterious goings-on in some old mansion but the history of a soldier and the son of a soldier, moving principally in Northern Africa; the very appropriate phrase that christens the book is quoted from no less person than Bacon, "All rising to Great Place is by a winding stair." Seldom does one come upon a novel of adventure which is also so profoundly a novel of character or which has so direct and free an appeal to the emotions, or makes that appeal so successfully. *The Winding Stair* is the work of a masterly storyteller, and such scenes as those of Paul Ravenel's discovery of who he is, his rescue of Marguerite Lambert, and Marguerite's discovery of his self-betrayal sprung from his love for her are something more than exciting drama. There is a breathlessness here that comes from a slowing-down rather than a quickening, from a pause, from a moment of perilous silence in which the only sound or sensation is the painful throbbing of the human heart.

ii

The other way of breathlessness is laughter.

"Laughter, holding both his sides," sang Milton; and, in fact, I once knew a man who sat at a dinner or some place between Don Marquis and Pelham Grenville (P. G.) Wodehouse. It is not necessary to recall what happened to him. Let us draw a veil, and proceed. Don (perhaps you recall it) was under the necessity of conducting a guessing contest in a New York newspaper. The purpose was to guess his real name. People refused to believe that he could be Don Marquis. The Supreme Court, in a case brought as a test, has since decided that such incredulity is not a sign of moral turpitude. Even Donald Robert Perry Marquis, held the Court (seven to two; Holmes, J., and Brandeis, J., dissenting), does not sound sufficiently possible, especially when the evidence shows that he was born in Walnut, Bureau County, Illinois. The Court ruled that Don was conceivably a literary hoax, but that his play, *The Old Soak*, was the real thing and within the Amendment. Popular rather than judicial cognisance has extended to the other and uncollected works of Don Marquis, such as *Prefaces*, his stories in *Carter and Other People*, his truth-telling about a young woman called *Hermione*, his newly rededicated record of *The Cruise of the Jasper B.*, his iliad of *Noah an' Jonah an' Captain John Smith*, his poetry in *Sonnets to a Red-Haired Lady and Famous Love Affairs*, etc., etc. You have read Anatole France's *The Revolt of the Angels*, but are you familiar with Don's *The Revolt of the Oyster*, I ask you? Or *Pandora Lifts the Lid*, by Christopher Morley, writing under the auspices of Don Marquis? Or *The Almost Perfect State*, a vision vouchsafed exclusively to Mr. Marquis?

The truth is, there is a good deal of Mark Twain in Don Marquis. Don is usually as good as ever Mark was and in some cases a good deal superior—and throughout, more genuine. When I make the comparison I am thinking of the best Mark Twain, the satirist and not too easily satisfied thinker; neither the embittered and savage pessimist of those final years nor the facile (too facile) humourist. Marquis, who can sustain the severer comparison with Twain, can also well sustain the comparison on the lighter side; for Don is a humourist, too. The point is in the "too." And the exemplification may be sought in (let us say) *The Almost Perfect State*. "No matter how nearly perfect an Almost

Perfect State may be, it is not nearly perfect enough unless the individuals who compose it can, somewhere between death and birth, have a perfectly corking time for a few years. . . . In the Almost Perfect State every person shall have at least ten years before he dies of easy, carefree, happy living." A place of pay-as-you-enter wars; a heaven where everyone is an aristocrat and there are no professional reformers—in short, a Marquisate. Where Don differs from Mark Twain is in being a poet who sometimes uses poetry as the medium of his expression—see *Dreams and Dust* and his *Poems and Portraits*. Christopher Morley (whose essay on Don Marquis, in *Shandygaff*, deserves to be read) has coaxed Don into a Frank R. Stocktonish enterprise in *Pandora Lifts the Lid*, with its narrative of seven young women snatched from the shades of a young ladies' seminary and—. But as I write, Pandora has lifted the lid on a crack only.

P. G. Wodehouse is another matter, a chap over whose books thousands of people have found themselves unable to keep straight faces. Yet, not long ago, writing in the London Sphere, Clement K. Shorter declared he had never read a single one of the more than twenty Wodehouse yarns. He had never read *Jeeves*, or that new one, *Leave It to Psmith*, or *Mostly Sally*, or *Three Men and a Maid*, or *The Little Warrior*, or *A Damsel in Distress*, or *Piccadilly Jim*—think of it! Or no, don't think of it. It won't bear thinking of, it won't really. The Wodehouse novels, though in most respects like those jolly things he writes to go with music by Jerome Kern, have now and then a page that dips far below the surface of fun into something very deep and true to the inwardness of human nature. Such are some bits in *The Little Warrior*, and such are the more tragic moments for Sally in *Mostly Sally;* and yet Mr. Wodehouse brings his story up again quickly like a diver clutching a pearl and rising up through clear water to sparkling and sunlit air. It is the prettiest talent imaginable, and I can think of no other contemporary writer of light fiction who has the same dexterity.

iii

There is no formula for achieving breathlessness. Those who are most susceptible to what may be loosely called Plot will find an enviable difficulty in breathing while they peruse, besides the stories already mentioned, some of the following tales:

JOHN BUCHAN's *Midwinter* and his *Huntingtower*. Buchan is a master of suspense and a humourist of very exceptional quality. His stories are rightly called "the grandest of grand yarns." Have you ever read *Greenmantle?* The literary merit of these books (quite incidental) is far above the average of their kind.

FRANK L. PACKARD's *The Four Stragglers*, an "unguessable" story with a steady acceleration of excitement, and his new one, *The Locked Book*.

WILLIAM GARRETT's *Friday to Monday*, which will give you the liveliest week-end of your possibly rich experience. Black pearls, a Chinaman, torture, a fight in the dark, a rocky cavern of the sea and an airplane are used.

WILLIAM JOHNSTON'S *The Waddington Cipher.*

H. C. MCNEILE'S *The Dinner Club.* The six members had each to tell two stories worthy of the dinner, and did! Also H. C. McNeile's *The Black Gang*, with its further adventures of Bulldog Drummond.

ALBERT PAYSON TERHUNE'S *The Amateur Inn*, remarkable not only for its mystery puzzle but for the presence of an irresistible maiden lady who says: "A person not ashamed to lock a door with a key, need not be ashamed to lock his mind with a lie."

CAROLYN WELLS'S *Wheels Within Wheels*, another story with Penny Wise as the detective. The village idiot is a protagonist.

C. N. and A. M. WILLIAMSON'S *The Lady From the Air* and their *The Night of the Wedding.*

When Ghost Meets Ghost.

The "borderland" in F. BRITTEN AUSTEN'S *On the Borderland* is the region between the conscious and the subconscious, assuming that such a neutral zone exists. The book offers twelve weird stories striking in their ingenuity.

E. F. BENSON'S *Spook Stories.*

Ordeal by Water.

TRISTRAM TUPPER'S *Adventuring* is entirely off the beaten track of adventure fiction—the story of a middle-aged, ordinary man whose love for the songs of the Grecian Sappho quickens his imagination to a dream of her beauty and leads him into an homeric sea adventure.

A. HYATT VERRILL'S *The Real Story of the Pirate.* A fascinating book about those fellows whose colouring is perhaps a little faded in spite of their being scoundrels of the deepest dye; although (as you may not know) Kidd was by no means so black as he was hanged for being.

A. HYATT VERRILL'S *The Real Story of the Whaler.* More thrills for all of us who had 'em as we watched the film, "Down to the Sea in Ships."

Almost Anything by HAROLD MACGRATH.

His *The World Outside*, or, if you haven't read them:

The Ragged Edge
The Pagan Madonna
The Man With Three Names
The Drums of Jeopardy

iv

Let us approach the subject of humour circumspectly. In addition to the Works of DON MARQUIS, *passim*, as the reference books say, and the Works of P. G. WODEHOUSE, both before-mentioned, and the Works of DONALD OGDEN STEWART (see Chapter 13, "A Parody Outline of Stewart"), and the Works of IRVIN S. COBB in many places, the reader may be well advised to consult at the outset *Tom*

Masson's Annual for 1923, a humorous anthology; KATHARINE DAYTON'S *Loose Leaves*, IRVIN COBB'S collection of the best humorous stories he has ever met, *A Laugh a Day Keeps the Doctor Away*, and —oh, yes!—the Works of OLIVER HERFORD, including *Neither Here Nor There* and *This Giddy Globe*. A word of warning in regard to a couple of others:

FRANCIS B. KEENE'S *Lyrics of the Links*. This is not a humorous book on days when you are off your game. Still, you can't afford to miss Grantland Rice's foreword to the lyrics.

THOMAS L. MASSON'S *That Silver Lining*, although written largely in a humorous vein, is an honest-to-goodness book about new thought, mental healing, psycho-analysis and so forth, by a survivor of twenty-eight years of Life.

4. In the Kingdom of Conrad

i

I ONCE knew such a man," declared Marlow. I don't believe any of us felt moved to reply. To have indicated, by a syllable or two, a polite interest, would have been fatal. Marlow, in the presence of anything but an aloof skepticism or a cynical reserve, becomes tiresome in his pursuit of metaphysical abstraction. He seems to think it can be caught in the butterfly-net of words. . . . Now he sat, sucking his pipe (he always cools it before re-filling) and looking attentively at each of us as the sparks of cigars momentarily threw a faint gleam on our faces. At length:

"You all know him, too," he pronounced. "Chap named Conrad, Joseph Conrad. Teodor Jozef Konrad Korzeniowski. That Polish sailor; writes novels. But he has a master's ticket. Got blackwater fever or something down at the Congo; he was out East before that. Then he settled in Kent, in a little house, where I once went to see him. Of course you've read *Lord Jim;* I don't think a lot of it. Give me *Victory* or *Youth*, or, best of all, *Nostromo*——"

"Personally, Marlow, I always look at the end first, to see how it comes out. Since you are beginning in the middle——"

JOSEPH CONRAD

"I? I'm not, but Conrad was. Did you ever read *Nostromo?* Talk about beginning a story in the middle!"

"Well, if you want to talk about *that,*" sighed a voice. "My impression was, Marlow, that you were undertaking to tell us about a man who knew himself—shall we say?—singularly well."

"Exactly." Marlow uttered the word with something that might have been reluctance. He repeated it, "Exactly." It was time to re-fill his pipe and he made a long job of it. When he had it drawing nicely and began to speak again his voice was veiled, his choice of words was frequently made with a certain hesitation, and we listened without comment or any other interruption than the occasional shifting of a foot on the deck. At least, I can recall nothing; and I know we borrowed our matches by signs—when we thought to borrow them.

ii

"As you have heard something of him, I won't waste my breath on the bare biographical record," Marlow informed us. "I believe you all know he was born in the Ukraine in 1857; sixth of December happened to be the day. His father and mother were Polish patriots and Russian exiles and their death left the boy in the hands of his mother's brother, who used him affectionately and engaged a very capable tutor to fit the young Korzeniowski for the University of Cracow. It is pertinent, I think, that the father had been a man of scholarly tastes and occupation. He had succeeded in translating Shakespeare into Polish. The legendary figure of a great-uncle, whom, however, the boy had seen, made a great impression. Mr. Nicholas B., as Conrad calls him in his book, *A Personal Record*, was in the retreat from Moscow and had the strange misfortune to share in eating a Lithuanian dog. Did you ever read *Falk?* Mr. Nicholas B. transmuted into fiction, I should say. The one had eaten a dog, the other was credited with having eaten human flesh; but the effect is the same. Then there's that other story, *Heart of Darkness*—the one all the authorities acclaim as among the half-dozen greatest stories in English. I have heard Conrad narrate the actual incident as it befell him down at the Congo; I have also read, and heard him read aloud, his tale. Very interesting. Let us admit that truth is frequently stranger than fiction; what then? Why truth is so often unintelligible, void of significance, without meaning. Whereas fiction is the real truth—all we can grasp, anyway. How we abuse words! It is facts, or apparent facts, that are stranger than so-called fiction. Not truth! Let us save that word for finer purposes. The conquest of brute facts? Well, maybe.

"This Polish boy I am telling you about had an incomprehensible wish. I understand that nowadays there is no such animal as an incomprehensible wish. All wishes are fulfilled, or something of the sort. The boy's wish I am speaking of was fulfilled, safe enough, but its comprehensibility is still in doubt. At any rate, he wanted to go to sea. As almost all boys wish urgently to go to sea, this might not appear abnormal. Perhaps, after all the oddity lay chiefly in the attitude of his uncle and tutor, which was strongly adverse; also, to some extent, in the fact that Poland is (or then was) purely an interior country without ships or the enticing sight of sailors to tempt a boy. A country of farmers. And he left it. He has told in *A Personal Record* of the last stand made by the tutor and his uncle. The sight of an Englishman in the Alps had the mysterious effect of making the lad more set in his purpose than ever. Why, as I say, is not comprehensible, unless by those serious scientists who exist in Vienna and play jokes on the rest of the world.

"When he had got clean away, with a sorrowful blessing, he fared to the Mediterranean. He wanted to become not merely a sailor but a British sailor; he knew no English. French, of course, he knew, as befitted a Pole of a good family and some education. It was not so difficult to get berths on Mediterranean vessels. Being in his teens, he was looking for excitement and adventure. This, too, *mare nostrum* provides. It does not really matter, I take it, where one sows his wild oats, provided only he sows thickly; and the waters of the Mediterranean received a bushel or two from Poland (a strictly agricultural land). One harvests such a crop from the sea uncertainly and at a long interval, but the sea's return is often curious and beautiful. Fragments, if you like, but of a loveliness not yielded by the soil of the shore; mother-of-pearl'd, glistening. And out of that uncouth time and those bizarre experiences the man Conrad has got back certain pages in *The Mirror of the Sea*, pages that we all remember. *The Arrow of Gold*, also, is the return of those years when he was irregularly employed in smuggling and gun-running out of Marseilles to the loosely-guarded shores of Spain.

"There is a woman in *The Arrow of Gold*, Rita, you know . . . but it is useless to speculate about women. In a preface provided for the new uniform edition of his works, J. C. explains that the slightly demure Antonia Avellanos, in the pages of *Nostromo*, sprang from the recollection, tenderly cherished, of a young girl, a schoolmate of his back there in Poland. But I would like to know where he got Lena, in *Victory*. If I were Somerset Maugham and came unexpectedly upon Lena in another man's novel there would be no limit to my jealousy. One does not expect a sailor to understand women and I cannot for the life of me comprehend how J. C. got in the way of knowing the sex. Perhaps, for some time, he didn't. Disregarding the mysteries of feminine nature, if he observed any, the youth persisted in his weird determination to become one of the great race of sailors. He shipped on English ships. Richard Curle's book, *Joseph Conrad: A Study*, will even tell you just which English ships. For example, the story called *Youth* with its vessel, the Judæa, harks back to a passage on a hulk called the Palestine. And so on. But what are such things to you and me? I have read Curle's book and I give you my *parole d'honneur* that I found it extraordinarily confusing when not simply rhapsodical. I did! As if J. C. were not, in himself, serious enough to require close attention and profound enough to merit it and pellucid enough to reward our most earnest scrutiny. Along comes Curle and roils up the surface of that clear, deep stream. I have no forgiveness for such a man, upon my word, I have not! May his excellent intentions pave the road to . . . but I suppose they do force one to re-read Conrad if only to get straightened out again.

"Anyway, he stuck to ships, this foreign blighter. You will find all that is pertinent diffused through the pages of *A Personal Record*. Even to the examination in which he passed for his master's ticket. What was he reading in those years? One would give something to have the tally; but certainly he did not neglect the French masters. Those who find in the earlier books, including *The Nigger of the Narcissus*, a style 'too florid,' or 'too consciously sonorous' say it was because J. C. was long in understanding that English prose cannot display the crystal resonance of French. Mind you, I don't in the least accept their premise; to me, *The Nigger of the Narcissus* is so perfect that when I came upon it I was seized with a most violent nostalgia. I wanted, in a foolish, incredible way, to be back in the fo'c's'le or on the deck of a certain squarerigger called the Wayfarer which carried me around Cape Stiff in—how long ago?—in 1909. It seems a century. Youth! The splendid, the immortal time!

"The ships bore him eastward. Only the thoughtless, griped by the vain longing for empire or inflated with a nauseating self-importance, will go west. One goes east when one is in search of wisdom, and this man was. The greatest piece of wisdom is the knowledge of oneself; seek that in

India or China or the ocean islands, whichever you please; the road lies eastward. You see, he had already acquired some self-knowledge; not a great deal, perhaps, but beyond the average. Or was he born with it? At a surprisingly early age he had known that he must, as the saying is, 'follow the sea.' This senseless conviction must be put down to the score of self-knowledge. When a man is not misled by that logical apparatus, his brain, it is astonishing to what clearness of perception he may attain. Do you recall that gentle, highly ironic sentence Conrad uses in *The Rescue* about d'Alcacer? 'Mr. d'Alcacer, being a Latin, was not afraid of introspection.' Exactly. J. C. isn't a Latin but neither is he afflicted like us, who shrink from a look inward in a way to arouse the recording angel's darkest suspicion. The best advice, I believe, is that which counsels a man to look into his heart and write. The best advice extant, but it can be bettered. J. C. looked into his heart a long time before he began writing.

"All that he saw there we have had steadily reflected in the succession of novels and tales of a surprisingly varied character and a deep, a very deep, inner relevance to the discovered self within him. Externals do not matter. And yet they have taken aback visitors to J. C., persons already acquainted with the true person and who should therefore have known better. They found, in a cottage in Kent, a man quitting middle age, the victim of an atrocious rheumatism (or what seemed to be rheumatism) who dosed himself with all sorts of concoctions that he had heard of, until the house looked like a laboratory of disused patent medicine bottles. Well, perhaps that is an exaggeration. Tall and broadly ample Jessie Conrad beamed on the very infrequent visitors and would sometimes confide to them, with a giggle: 'You know, they say in London that Conrad lives in the country with his cook!' But she, Jessie, Mrs. Conrad, was a great deal more than just an excellent cook, a capable mother, all that. She was, in J. C.'s words, 'the fortune of the house,' a pair of eyes that guarded watchfully over this unhappy man when, for eighteen months, hardly knowing whether he ate or slept, and sitting all day long at a table, he struggled desperately for 'the breath of life' which had to be blown into the shapes of men and women, 'Latin and Saxon, Jew and Gentile' who people the pages of that miraculous novel, *Nostromo*. That book is unique. You may get some idea of its cost in toil and sheer creative effort from J. C.'s own words in *A Personal Record*. Just so; but then an American editor comes along, some years later, and finds Conrad as nervous as a cat. Actually! The editor particularly noticed that Conrad would never turn his back upon him while they were together in that room and always sat so as to face, or partly face, the door. He appeared like a man who wanted to feel the wall at his back; and with his deep-set eyes and the overhang of his forehead, the Slav contour of the cheekbones, the greying beard, the silences and the restlessness, the jumpiness—everything—J. C. made on the American editor a memorable and fantastic impression. That editor came away convinced that

J. C. had seen some wild goings-on and been in some devilish tight places in his seafaring days; and altogether was spending his later years like Stevenson's chap at the Admiral Benbow, waiting for some old, blind, tap-tap-tapping Pew to come along and tip him the black spot. Fact! But the editor carried no black spot, only large sums of American money which he was prepared to part with in exchange for the very best English fiction, both spot and future delivery. J. C. was then busy writing the novel called *Victory*, and gave it to the American to read. The next morning the American ripped it to pieces, on certain plot details. His, the American's, account of that interview is instructive. He says Conrad sat, fingers clawing the arms of his chair, speechless and infuriated, for nearly an hour, while our editor stressed the importance of the return of the shawl that belonged to Mrs. Schomberg in the story and other matters that the meticulous would find fault with. And finally, I suppose when he was able to speak at all, the editor tells that J. C. came around, ending up by quite handsomely admitting the editor to be right, and promising to make the necessary changes. What I cannot get over is the fact that after, as the story goes, Conrad had re-written 70,000 words and added 60,000 more, in order to run *Victory* complete in a single number, the American cut out of it everything but the conversation and the shooting. The resulting skeleton was, to some readers at least, very imperfectly articulated. That manuscript had a curious history and certainly deserves a place in a Museum. I heard lately that Gabriel Wells, the American collector, has got hold of it. J. C. had made alterations in black ink, the magazine editor had gashed it horribly in red; and when the book publisher came to restore the mangled corpus he could do so, intelligibly for the printer, only by an extravagant use of green ink. You see, there was no duplicate copy of the original. Always make duplicates. If you don't, and if you are a writer of J. C.'s size, your manuscripts may some day be priceless. Even though they are typewritten; for the fact that they are not in handwriting is offset by the touching fact that perhaps your wife got up in the middle of the night to type them off, so you could see how they would look in the neat similitude of printed words.

iii

"But there! Let us not talk about the value of manuscripts. That is adventitious, a sort of excrescence on the process of moneygetting, which, in turn, perhaps, is an excrescence on all the forms of art. Do I sound like one of those absurd persons who wail because an artist must make money? If so, I beg your pardon, I do, humbly. Perhaps you would like me to do it kneeling here on the deck. My knees are bent. I would no more absolve the artist from the urgence of making a living than I would absolve him from the necessity of drawing breath to live. After all, isn't it the same thing? So surely as you breathe, you must suffer; and what is the wage problem but a visitation, like sickness, or misfortune, or mental anguish inseparable from the act of living? If art cannot triumph over these things, if a novelist could not continue to write novels in spite of the awful pangs of rheumatism, the element of struggle would be lost and all our values would exist in a vacuum. It is their merit, and sometimes their sole merit, that they exist in the air under atmospheric pressures averaging fifteen pounds to the square inch and of only the very slightest variation. The need to make money is the atmosphere in which we all live. By a sublime law of nature, of human nature, I should say, the more we make, the more we need. Human nature abhors a vacuum. But, as I was saying—

"What a pill it would be to a man engaged in writing his first few great novels if he had seriously to consider the fact that, some years later but yet within his lifetime, these blackened pages would be worth a modest fortune. Such a consideration might well drive him quite off his head. What actually steadies him is the indisputable fact that *this* book has simply got to earn him enough to live on for a whole year, including the younger boy's annual six pairs of shoes. Then, when the book doesn't, a way is provided. Don't snort, please. I admit that, on the face of it, such a solution is improbable. The answer to that objection is: The solution arrives. Take J. C. He came ashore with the remnants of this tropical fever infesting him and a definite medical mandate enjoining him from all future notion of following the sea. When a chap is nearing forty and has spent all his life from boyhood working up to a master's ticket and a ship to command, a decree of that sort is calculated to knock him out completely. He is in splendid shape to be counted out in a prostrate condition, lying prone and never recovering consciousness. J. C. had no more idea what to do——. He dug up the manuscript of that tentative story or novel he had been working on at intervals for about five years. The one which, to the extent of about the first nine chapters, he had shown to a young Englishman on a passage between Adelaide and the Cape. This was a young Cambridge student, named Jacques, who was aboard as a passenger. You remember that Jacques handed the manuscript back and J. C. ventured to ask if the story seemed worth finishing. Jacques answered. 'Distinctly.' So the beginnings of *Almayer's Folly* escaped being thrown overboard to puzzle the fishes.

"Ashore, J. C. finished the thing and it got published. No appreciable sum of money rewarded him, of course, and he has told how he wondered whatever he should do afterward, and he submitted his dilemma to Edward Garnett one evening after the publication of *Almayer's Folly*. Finally Garnett brought forth a suggestion which, in its unoriginality, was a piece of the most authentic inspiration. 'Why don't you write another?' he asked. But, of course, that is the only safe suggestion to make to a person who has written one novel. J. C. admits that from the moment those words crossed Garnett's lips, *An Outcast of the Islands* was merely a matter of time. All the same, he had to live. Shortly, he was marrying, and at suitable intervals Boris and John were added to the family unit. Capel House was a Kentish cottage but there were rates to pay. For some years the pension provided by the Civil List was an affair of serious importance. There is a man or two now living and a man or two now dead who could throw light on this phase of J. C.'s special problem. Conrad's present American publisher dropped in one day on the late William Heinemann in London, with his usual question of what, or more accurately whom, Heinemann had got. The reply was: A comparatively new writer who would some day be as important as Kipling. However, it appeared that in order to attain this importance he would have to live. 'Suppose,' suggested Heinemann, with every aspect of intense earnestness, 'you and I back him. He has a novel he wants to do. I think if we both put in ten pounds—fifty dollars—a month——.' For a moment it seemed as if this blithe proposal might terminate the interview. And, after all, a publisher, who has to foot the cost of a book anyway on what is often the slenderest chance, might well draw back before the prospect of investing $50 a month for a year or two as a preliminary to risking as much more. But it was done. In the end, J. C. told them frankly that he could not give them the book. He had got seven-eighths of the way through and he was unable to bring the story out. Stuck for an ending would be the other way of stating the case. The two, Heinemann and Frank N. Doubleday, accepted this disappointment with a most commendable calmness. J. C. went on to write other things, *The Nigger of the Narcissus*, *Lord Jim*, since so widely hailed and at the time so little heeded and so immensely unlucrative; *Nostromo.*

James B. Pinker (you knew Pinker, the author's agent) handled the stuff. In the American phrase, Pinker 'grubstaked' Conrad; and among long-term investments of the very highest grade J. C. has been one of the very best in the world. Ah, yes! He has! No one who ever invested in Conrad and held on, held 'for the rise,' has ever lost a penny—or failed to make an enormous per cent. Why, take Heinemann and F. N. D. They, in effect, bought at away below par twenty-year bonds that matured and were paid off at par. For after twenty years J. C. picked up the all-but-finished novel, put it through in triumphant fashion and gave it to them under the title of *The Rescue*. By that time, he was made. He was selling in America practically seventeen times as many copies as when they put their money in—maybe more. And any publisher in America or England would, by then, have given his upper and lower teeth to possess Conrad. The Civil List was at liberty to take care of someone else and lucky if it found another half so rewarding.

"Do I give the impression that this result was brought about in the least meteorically? That would be inexcusable on my part. Let me see: There were *Almayer's Folly* and *An Outcast of the Islands* and *The Nigger* and *Lord Jim* and *Nostromo* and *The Secret Agent* and *Under Western Eyes*. Seven novels, not counting the two he wrote with Ford Madox Hueffer and four or five books of short stories. I am speaking now of the nineteen years that lay between Conrad's first book and his novel, *Chance;* and I am avoiding all exaggeration when I tell you flatly that in all those nineteen years not one single book—not the succession of all those books—made enough money for the reasonable needs of himself and his family. Oh, I don't say that he was entirely dependent on these books and the far-sightedness of men like those investors I have mentioned. W. E. Henley serialised *The Nigger;* in America, the North American Review serialised *Under Western Eyes;* there was a bit of money, now and again from the magazine sale of one of the short-stories, no doubt. I stick to my point: The income from the books was not enough. By the way, he also wrote in those years the two autobiographical books, *The Mirror of the Sea* and *A Personal Record.* H'm. The American publishers of *A Personal Record* printed it from type. You know; print a few and throw the type away.

"*Chance* was published in 1914 and sold 20,000 copies in England and the long ordeal was over.

iv

"One ordeal, that is. Ordeals, as such, are never over. After the trial by water, the trial by fire; and you are not to suppose that because one has survived the trial of the spirit he will therefore triumph easily over the trials of the flesh. Not at all. What is the malady of rheumatism beside the torture of shyness? And Conrad has always been distinctly shy. His American publisher, for a long time, did not meet him; J. C. backed out of it, until, finally, a perfectly reasonable impatience seized upon Mr. Doubleday, who said to himself, in a mild tone: 'Confound it all. This sort of thing has got to stop.' And that sort of thing did stop. J. C. at length was induced to come to a London hotel and shake hands—about all he did do, in fact, for at once a severe attack of shyness set in. For quite a while that interview went—very badly? Goodness knows it did not even go badly; it simply did not go at all. But then, as he knew Conrad was planning a new book, Mr. Doubleday asked a few questions natural to a person who has something at stake in a prospective venture. J. C. answered with entire willingness, began explaining what he had in mind and—pouf! Where was that shyness any longer? They parted as very good friends and have remained such ever since. So it came about that at last J. C. visited America as the guest of Mr. Doubleday. As you can imagine, lecture bureaus, societies and every sort of outfit had been after J. C. for years to speak in public. He had always turned down such offers, but before coming to America he explained to Mr. Doubleday that he should like to tell a few people, not more than a dozen, over the luncheon table of his Congo experience, and then read to them from his story, *Heart of Darkness*, the same affair as it came out in fiction. 'If I am able to interest those few,' J. C. went on, 'perhaps I might try the same thing with a larger number, say fifty or even a hundred; I don't think I could ever address more than a hundred.' You see, he knew himself. He is the kind of man who is at his best in an intimate surrounding. Perhaps you have noticed the very special quality of intimacy achieved in his stories under practically all conditions. He inhabits other people's breasts.

A self-conscious tendency as great as his own or greater excites his friendly compassion. I know an American novelist, at one time editor of an American magazine and then in England meeting people and questing material. Several people were present but Conrad noticed the extreme ill-ease of the American editor. J. C. got up and came over and sat beside the stranger, who then lost some of his discomfort and eventually plucked up enough to say to J. C. that he would like to get some short stories from him. 'Ah! Short stories,' J. C. commented with that markedly foreign accent or intonation. He paused. 'I do not pick short stories out of my sleeve.' It was said with an inflection pleasantly humorous that did not conceal the seriousness of the fact. He simply wasn't that kind of a conjuror. This was not the editor who handled *Victory*. American editors, according to my impression, are a varied lot. The mixture they make is a literary cocktail which appears to go to the heads of so many American authors. I know an American editor who bought a Conrad novel as a serial when all his—confrères?—had rejected the story because of the impossible length. This man printed the 147,000 words without the sacrifice of one. This was after *Victory* and as the editor in question knew nothing of that case, his was an unconscious as well as a vicarious atonement. But let that pass. We are not concerned with American editors, and neither, except momentarily, has Conrad been. His preoccupation has been unbrokenly with the problem of a sufficient self-knowledge. Must he not know himself better than any other possibly could?

Of course, and for two imperative purposes: In the first place to write, in the second place, to keep his courage. It is no use being able to write unless you can keep your courage. Too, the world is full of brave souls who have bravery and . . . nothing else. No gift, I mean. Nothing in the world is so cheap as courage, so common. But look you!—if a man undertakes self-examination, his courage goes. The scale of values is hopelessly deranged and either the self rises to sublime heights of despair or sinks into a hopeless, sticky complacency. J. C. is not an unblemished exception to this general law, or deplorable result—whichever term you prefer. He had gone to revisit Poland and was there when the Great War unleashed itself. The story of how he got out of Europe has never been told and, in fact, I don't see how it can be. Or, well, why not? What do a few bribes matter, in a good cause? Some fairly influential persons, including an American Ambassador, were called upon to extricate Conrad from the extremely troublesome complications caused by the fact that he, a Pole by race and a Russian subject by birth, was a naturalised Englishman. The American Ambassador, appointed in the first place because of his large personal means, enabling him to support an Ambassadorship in the style to which it had been accustomed, may have used his private pocketbook; but in my judgment the matter was one to which he could quite conscientiously have devoted the public funds. Let that pass, too. They say that J. C. hates Russians and is frequently irascible. He also understands Russians, as any disbeliever may discover by reading *Under Western Eyes.* As for his irascibility, the results of self-examination justify any reasonable amount of irritation. If it had been one of you who had written seven-eighths of *The Rescue* and found himself stuck for an ending I daresay the detonations would have been terrific. A volcano can blow its head off but an artist must not be permitted to let a little steam escape! What sort of a doctrine is that? J. C., of late years, has lost a good deal of his nervousness. He has written his *Lord Jim* long ago. He has accomplished the most satisfactory definition we possess of the novel —where he calls it 'a conviction of our fellowmen's existence strong enough to take upon itself a form of imagined life clearer than reality.' I call your attention to the last three words. If the 'form of imagined life' is not clearer to us than life as we observe it, there is no novel. Now, life is never clear unless we hold a little fragment of it in front of the mirror of each one of us, his own heart. Always, then, something different from what we expected is then clear, recognisable. J. C. has never done anything else. The story of *The Secret Sharer*, that chap who haunted the captain's cabin and persisted in the captain's thoughts, is the symbol of all Conrad's work. I believe he has called it his favourite story; does anyone need to ask why? Giorgio Viola in *Nostromo*, Mrs. Gould in the same novel, the nigger in the story of the Narcissus, Haldin in *Under Western Eyes*, our friend, the anarchist, in *The Secret Agent;* Captain MacWhirr in *Typhoon* and Jim in *Lord Jim;* Axel Heyst in *Victory;* Flora de Barral and others in *Chance*—

you know as well as I do that these are simply persons we encounter and depreciate or else dismiss as incomprehensible. But Conrad holds them up to the mirror of his own heart and behold! they are reflected in new shapes, pathetic shapes, heroic shapes, twisted and tortured shapes, but shapes that are unfailingly intelligible. It is not quite the same thing as saying: 'There, but for the grace of God, goes Joseph Conrad.' It is equivalent, perhaps, to saying: 'Here, by the grace of God, is the affinity with Joseph Conrad.' The meaning of the universe is, as the Spaniards say, with God; but what we feel about it is of perpetual fascination and very real importance. J. C. has found that out, in the course of a fairly long and extremely surprising lifetime. The world is a ship that will never make port, it is fair to assume, in our lifetimes; its exact position, then, as witnessed to by the sun and the stars, is of little moment. But those who are aboard—let us have a clear understanding about them, if we can.

"To do that, one must feel the deck beneath his feet, like that old fellow Peyrol, in Conrad's newest novel which you will so soon be reading. Coming after *The Rescue*—how long it has been! Three years after!—*The Rover* has surprised me with an unexpected simplicity of strain, like a clear little thread of blue in a riot of scarlet, the bright background of Revolutionary France and Napoleon's day. Peyrol, I ought to tell you, was a French waif whose sea exile led him to the coast of India and to membership in the strange fraternity of pirates who called themselves Brothers of the Coast. But this was all before; we open upon the return of

Peyrol to France and an inconspicuous repose in a little farmhouse where dwell an old woman, a bloodthirsty scarecrow, and a young girl whose eyes, having looked upon the spurting blood of the Terror, can remain fixed on nothing for consecutive instants since. And there's a young French officer sent to the farm on duty connected with the blockade. Far down below the rim of the horizon, you understand, sails the fleet commanded by Lord Nelson. The complete affair is one of those episodes in which a handful of people are wholly at the mercy of destiny if a single one of them fails to sustain his illusion, whether of love, of wrath, of mercy, of hope, or, perhaps, of a sublime despair. Despair? Why, certainly; from what other sentiment could old Peyrol have acted as he did, in the grand emergency, cutting the knot that bound up together those few lives, whose only importance was the supreme importance of the insignificant and humble? Peyrol, the ex-pirate, flashing out over the water to his final earthly adventure is the latest and most beautiful incarnation of that old sailor whom Conrad knew in the flesh and has translated so often —the 'Ulysses' we meet in *The Mirror of the Sea*, who is also Nostromo, who appears under his actual name and in his true rôle in *The Arrow of Gold*. In the closing pages of *The Rover* we get a brief glimpse of the great Nelson, but he does not dwarf Peyrol.

"A Mediterranean story, a tale of that sea which is 'the charmer and deceiver of audacious men,' like Life itself, which also keeps 'the secret of its fascination.' "

V

Marlow ceased to speak. It was beautifully dark. The river, in our stretch of it, was composed to the beauty of that darkness and won to the felicity of a nearly perfect silence. I can't speak for the others, of course. Personally I was absorbed in trying to remember the man Conrad's exact words—in the so long suppressed preface to *The Nigger*. You must have read them:

"The artist appeals to that part of our being that is not dependent on wisdom; to that in us which is a gift and not a mere acquisition—and, therefore, more permanently enduring. He speaks to our capacity for delight and wonder, to the sense of mystery surrounding our lives; to our sense of pity, and beauty, and pain: to the latent feeling of fellowship with all creation—and to the subtle but invincible conviction of solidarity that knits together the loneliness of innumerable hearts, to the solidarity in dreams, in joy, in sorrow, in aspirations, in illusions, in hope, in fear, which binds men to each other, which binds together all humanity—the dead to the living and the living to the unborn."

Books by Joseph Conrad

NOVELS:

1895 *Almayer's Folly*
1896 *An Outcast of the Islands*
1898 *The Nigger of the Narcissus* [first published in America as *The Children of the Sea*]

1900 *Lord Jim*
1903 *Nostromo*
1907 *The Secret Agent*
1911 *Under Western Eyes*
1914 *Chance*
1915 *Victory*
1917 *The Shadow Line: A Confession*
1919 *The Arrow of Gold*
1920 *The Rescue*
1923 *The Rover*

NOVELS IN COLLABORATION WITH FORD MADOX HUEFFER:

1901 *The Inheritors: An Extravagant Story*
1903 *Romance*

TALES AND SHORT STORIES:

1898 *Tales of Unrest*
1902 *Youth: A Narrative; Heart of Darkness; The End of the Tether*
1903 *Typhoon and Other Stories* [in America *Typhoon* is published separately and the volume is *Falk and Other Stories*]
1908 *A Set of Six*
1912 *'Twixt Land and Sea*
1916 *Within the Tides*

AUTOBIOGRAPHICAL:

1906 *The Mirror of the Sea: Memories and Impressions*
1912 *A Personal Record* [published in England as *Some Reminiscences*]

CRITICAL:

1921 *Notes on Life and Letters*

Sources on Joseph Conrad

Joseph Conrad: His Romantic-Realism, by RUTH M. STAUFFER (Boston: Four Seas Company, 1922). This study of Conrad is of first importance because of its thirty pages of appendices, consisting of:

I. Conrad Bibliographies
II. Conrad's Works
  (A) Chronological List of Novels and Tales (with Original Editions)
  (B) Alphabetical List of Short Stories
  (C) Miscellaneous Writings by Conrad
III. Criticisms of Conrad
  (A) Books on Conrad. With a paragraph of characterisation of each.
  (B) Articles About Conrad. With notes as to the character of each article. There is given a "first," a "second" and a "third" list, according to the estimate of an article's value.
IV. Book Reviews. Described as a "partial list only," but recording fully 200 reviews in principal English and American magazines and newspapers.
V. Miscellaneous
  (A) Brief Articles on the Personality of Conrad

(B) Poems to Conrad
(C) A list of Portraits of Conrad

All of Conrad's short stories are credited to their respective volumes, serial publication is invariably noted, etc.

Joseph Conrad—The Man, by Elbridge L. Adams, in THE OUTLOOK for 18 April, 1923. One of the most complete accounts of a visit and report of the everyday Conrad.

The chapter on Joseph Conrad, by Leland Hall, in *English Literature During the Last Half Century*, by JOHN W. CUNLIFFE. The Macmillan Company, revised edition, 1923.

Some Modern Novelists, by HELEN THOMAS FOLLETT and WILSON FOLLETT. Henry Holt & Company, 1918.

Joseph Conrad, A Study, by RICHARD CURLE. Doubleday, Page & Company, 1914.

Private Information.

The reader may consult the references available in the New York Public Library or the Library of Congress, Washington, D. C., and should also consult the annual READER'S GUIDE TO PERIODICAL LITERATURE especially since 1914. He should also consult the map showing the locations of Conrad's stories, printed as an end-paper in some editions of his books, particularly *Victory*.

5. *The Documents in the Case of Arthur Train*

i

THE first and most important is a volume of over two hundred pages—very large pages, somewhat larger, in fact, than those of Cosmopolitan magazine, a trifle smaller than those of Vanity Fair. The volume is bound in heavy yellow paper which says, in neat letters at the upper left, "Indictment No. 1." Inside the cover is a long table of contents; the printed pages that follow are made either more enlightening or more alarming, according to your variety of intelligence, by the presence of charts and diagrams. One such, when unfolded, shows green, red and black inks. The purpose is to make it easier for the eye to trace the intricate handlings of certain considerable sums of money. . . .

This mysterious book, possessed of no title-page and honouring no one as its author, represents the capacity of Arthur Train for hard work. In 1914 Henry Siegel, a New York merchant and banker, was to be prosecuted, and Arthur Train was entrusted with the prosecution. Counsel for Siegel secured a change of venue and the trial was transferred to Geneseo, New York. The case for the prosecution, in its mathematical and extremely complicated demonstration, seemed only too likely to be lost before a jury of farmers completely unfamiliar with Mr. Siegel's affairs. Mr. Siegel was in banking companies, merchandising corporations, realty corporations, a securities company, an express company and other enterprises. It was quite necessary to explore the labyrinth; something like $50,000 was expended by Arthur Train, the explorer, and the printed and bound book, *Indictment No. 1*, was a mere preliminary to the battle in court.

In 1914 Arthur Train was already the author of quite a number of books of fiction. In a general way, they represented pleasant recreation.

ii

Other documents are these books and stories of his, the work of leisure intervals and an active imagination. Some of them were done by dictation, dictation interrupted by telephone calls, by days in court, by this or that or the other. He acquired the faculty of dropping and picking up again in the middle of a chapter, a paragraph, a sentence. He didn't worry over the stuff; he didn't fuss about it, as some men do about their golf, when they're off their game. The business of life was transacted in the gloomy chambers of the Criminal Courts Building, New York, where the air is bad, the light poor, but the saturation with human nature, perfect. To prepare a case was rather frequently interesting, to try a case was scarcely ever without its thrill. And the cases, despite the common misconception of them, were not assorted East Side vendettas or Chinatown murders. A large percentage of them

ARTHUR TRAIN

and, if not at the end of it, nearer to the end than to the beginning. When did our materialistic age begin? At the end of Mrs. Wharton's *Age of Innocence*, of course.

Mr. Train's motif is the dominant characteristic of an age we all lived in, and what that characteristic led to. He writes, of course, about old Peter B. Kayne, "The Pirate," and his children and grandchildren; these are the little group of people in the immediate foreground. They are the larger world in little, people who set the fashion and make the pace, watched and aped by thousands. Their ambitions, their discontents, their achievements in every direction, including sensation, scandal and disgrace are the best commentary on—themselves as individuals? Not at all; on certain forces and tendencies more powerful than they.

So considered, *His Children's Children* is a perfectly documented study of the third generation since the beginning of the era of "big business" in America. To the Forsytes the termination came with a sign, "To Let." With us it has more frequently come with some such scene as that closing Mr. Train's able novel; I mean old Peter B. Kayne, ill and helpless upstairs, and the auctioneer at his stand below. To the once redoubtable Pirate comes the sound of a rising murmur from down there; he manages to get up and struggle feebly to a place where he can look upon the alien affair going on in the house—in his, Peter B. Kayne's, house. The auctioneer's voice is lifted above the rest, in a louder smoothness, in an accent of barter; ambitions and ideals, so far as realised, are here knocked down to the highest bidder. What price are we offered on certain tangible results of a desire to get on? To the highest bidder. . . . Perhaps, after all, Peter B. Kayne's was the high bid.

iv

A "documented" study; I chose my word there, also. For an immense amount of work went into *His Children's Children.* You may take my word for it, as much as went into the authorship of *Indictment No. 1.* Or, no, you need not take my word. Take a fact, instead. Mr. Train is now at work upon a very remarkable novel of which it is not my privilege to speak here except to say that its first chapter exemplifies his infinitely painstaking method to-day. In common with a very few other novelists, he likes to derive clearly through several antecedent generations his principal characters. His writing undergoes many corrections but in his first draft he gives himself full rein. In the novel that is to follow *His Children's Children*, he spent much time on the first chapter. By a "cut-back" he traced his hero's family from about the year 1790 to the opening of the story, in the present. This, mind you, was with the deliberate intention that the first chapter should ultimately be of not much, if any, more than ordinary chapter length—perhaps thirty typewritten pages.

Well, he knew he had written a good deal, but the first chapter, first draft, was written and he sent it to be typed. The manuscript had been returned to him on a day when I called; it made exactly 184 typewritten pages—about half the length of an ordinary full-length novel, maybe somewhat more.

V

Arthur (Cheney) Train was born in Boston, 6 September 1875, the son of Charles Russell Train and Sarah M. (Cheney) Train. His father was Attorney-General of Massachusetts, 1873-1880. Arthur Train was graduated from Harvard (A.B.) in 1896 and received the law degree three years later. In 1897 he married Ethel Kissam, daughter of Benjamin P. Kissam, of New York. Mrs. Train, also a writer, died in the spring of 1923. Her book, *"Son" and Other Stories of Childhood and Age* is being published posthumously.

Arthur Train went almost immediately into the District Attorney's office in New York. He never entirely sacrificed his connection with it until 1916, when he became a member of the firm of Perkins & Train. As a special deputy Attorney-General of the State of New York, in 1910, he brought about the indictment of over one hundred persons, political offenders in Queens County, in the city of New York. He is a member of the Century, University and Harvard Clubs of New York, and of the Downtown Association. In his attractive home, at 113 East Seventy-third street, New York, there is a room, up one flight, occupying the whole width of the front of the house, with southerly windows, book-lined walls, an ample desk, and a roomy davenport confronting a fireplace. The fireplace is fenced about and the top of the fence is leather-cushioned, making a comfortable seat. Nothing could be more pleasant than to sink into the davenport and face Mr. Train, who has seated himself on the fireplace fence and lighted a cigarette.

"But don't you mind the interruptions?" you ask him. "Suppose you are in the middle of a novel and a big case comes along——"

"That's very refreshing," he answers. "I come back to the novel as from a vacation."

And you recall the early writing, done, so to speak, between telephone calls.

There *has* been a change; Mr. Train freely acknowledges it. "I can't say exactly when it occurred. It was during the war. I felt differently about my writing. I felt much more intent about it. It took hold of me very strongly when I was writing about Ephraim Tutt—*Tutt and Mr. Tutt*, you know. I think those were possibly the first stories I had written which made me feel emotion."

It is easy to see why, easier, perhaps, in Mr. Train's new collection of these tales, *Tut, Tut! Mr. Tutt*, than in the first book. For the emphasis upon Ephraim Tutt's attitude is more pronounced as we see him deliberately employing the tricks of the law in the interests of justice. Himself moved by that most permanent of human emotions, the desire for the just, and by that most continual of human delights, the extraction of good from evil or even good wreaked by means of evil, and moved also by that human protest against the application of general rules to individual dilemmas, Mr. Tutt would be strange if he did not arouse in his creator the emotion inseparable from any act of art.

Once felt, never without. The practise of law seems less important than once it did to Arthur Train. The number of cases that really are interesting—are they growing fewer? There is something about private practise . . . duller than the old court work, less stimulating. . . .

He has "an infinite capacity for taking pains." It has been proven. There, I think, our case rests.

Books by Arthur Train

1905 *McAllister and His Double*
1906 *The Prisoner at the Bar*
1908 *True Stories of Crime*
1909 *The Butler's Story*
1909 *Mortmain*
1909 *Confessions of Artemas Quibble*
1910 *C. Q., or In the Wireless House*
1911 *Courts, Criminals and the Camorra*
1914 *The "Goldfish."* This book, published anonymously, caused a sensation by its satirisation of American social life
1915 *The Man Who Rocked the Earth* (with ROBERT WILLIAMS WOOD)
1917 *The World and Thomas Kelly*
1918 *The Earthquake*
1920 *Tutt and Mr. Tutt*
1921 *By Advice of Counsel*
1921 *The Hermit of Turkey Hollow*
1923 *His Children's Children*
1923 *Tut, Tut! Mr. Tutt*

6. The Lady of a Tradition, Miss Sackville-West

i

THERE are two sides from which you may first profitably look at the house. One is from the park, the north side. From here the pile shows best the vastness of its size; it looks like a mediæval village. It is heaped with no attempt at symmetry; it is sombre and frowning; the grey towers rise; the battlements cut out their square regularity against the sky; the buttresses of the old twelfth-century tithe-barn give a rough impression of fortifications. There is a line of trees in one of the inner court-yards, and their green heads show above the roofs of the old breweries; but although they are actually trees of a considerable size they are dwarfed and unnoticeable against the mass of the buildings blocked behind them. The whole pile soars to a peak which is the clock-tower with its pointed roof; it might be the spire of the church on the summit of the hill crowning the mediæval village. At sun-set I have seen the silhouette of the great building stand dead black on a red sky; on moonlight nights it stands black and silent, with glinting windows, like an enchanted castle. On misty autumn nights I have seen it emerging partially from the trails of

V. SACKVILLE-WEST

vapour, and heard the lonely roar of the red deer roaming under the walls."

Such is the opening page of V. Sackville-West's volume, *Knole and the Sackvilles*, a handsomely printed and illustrated account of the seat of the Earls and Dukes of Dorset. Authentic record of the family goes not beyond that Herbrand de Sackville who came to England with William the Conqueror. Knole, bought by Archbishop Bourchier in 1456, and held by Cardinal Morton, Cranmer, Henry VIII., Edward VI., Queen Mary and Elizabeth, was granted, in 1586 by Elizabeth, to Thomas Sackville, Lord Buckhurst, first Earl of Dorset. The name "West" enters with the marriage of Lady Elizabeth Sackville, sister of the fourth Duke, to John West, Earl de la Warr.

The house, of seven courts to correspond with the days of the week, fifty-two staircases matching the weeks of the year and 365 rooms answering to the days of the year * "is gentle and venerable. It has the deep inward gaiety of some very old woman who has always been beautiful, who has had many lovers and seen many generations come and go, smiled wisely over their sorrows and their joys, and learnt an imperishable secret of tolerance and humour. It is, above all, an English house." The garden side is the gay, the princely side. When, in

* "I cannot truthfully say," writes Miss Sackville-West in *Knole and the Sackvilles,* "that I have ever verified these counts, and it may be that their accuracy is accepted solely on the strength of the legend; but, if this is so, then it has been a very persistent legend, and I prefer to sympathise with the amusement of the ultimate architect on making the discovery that by a judicious juggling with his additions he could bring courts, stairs and rooms up to that satisfactory total."

summer, the great oak doors of the second gate-house were left open, "it has sometimes happened that I have found a stag in the banqueting hall, puzzled but still dignified, strayed in from the park since no barrier checked him."

ii

In 1825 the duchess Arabella Diana died and her estate devolved upon her two daughters, Mary and Elizabeth. Elizabeth, as has been told, became the wife of Lord de la Warr. Dying in 1870 she left Buckhurst to her elder sons and Knole to her younger sons, one of whom was Miss Sackville-West's grandfather. He was eighty and she perhaps eight, and as he shared "the family failing of unsociability" it fell to the child's lot to show the house to visitors. In this, as in more natural ways, she became highly familiar with Knole and from her earliest years must have loved the place. On receipt of a telegram that people were coming, Grandpapa would take the next train for London, "returning in the evening when the coast was clear." The Cartoon Gallery, the Leicester Gallery, the Brown Gallery; Lady Betty Germaine's bedchamber; the three principal bedrooms, the Spangled Room, the Venetian Ambassador's and the King's chamber, "the only vulgar room in the house" with furniture made entirely in silver and articles of silver, "even to a little eye-bath"—the procession of the days and years was not more certain than the procession of the curious, the inquisitive and the wonder-struck through these. You will fashion your own picture of the daughter of the Sackvilles standing before the portrait of Lady Margaret Sackville (over the fireplace in Lady Betty Germaine's sitting room) and endeavouring, quite vainly, to do her own hair in the elaborate manner of young Lady Margaret's. Or, it may be, she had been naughty that day, and had hid herself inside the pulpit of the Chapel of the Archbishops, where, in spite of private steps leading out of her bedroom straight into the Family Pew, "they never found me." Grandpapa was "a queer and silent old man," as Miss Sackville-West remembers him. "He knew nothing whatever about the works of art in the house; he spent hours gazing at the flowers, followed about the garden by two grave demoiselle cranes. . . . He and I, who so often shared the house alone between us, were companions in a shy and undemonstrative way. Although he had nothing to say to his unfortunate guests, he could understand a child. . . . When we were at Knole alone together I used to go down to his sitting-room in the evening to play draughts with him—and never knew whether I played to please him, or he played to please me—and sometimes, very rarely, he told me stories of when he was a small boy, and played with the rocking-horse, and of the journeys by coach with his father and mother from Buckhurst to Knole or from Knole to London; of their taking the silver with them under the seat; of their having outriders with pistols; and of his father and mother never addressing each other, in their children's presence, as anything but 'my Lord' and 'my Lady.' I clasped my knees and stared at him when he told me these stories of an age which already seemed so remote, and his pale blue eyes gazed away into the past, and suddenly his shyness would return to him and the clock in the corner would begin to wheeze in preparation to striking the hour, and he would say that it was time for me to go to bed. . . ."

iii

At the age of thirteen Miss Sackville-West wrote "an enormous novel" about the figure of Edward Sackville, fourth Earl of Dorset, who seemed to her the embodiment of Cavalier romance. And perhaps he was. "He had the advantage of starting with the Vandyck portrait in the hall, the flame-coloured doublet, the blue Garter, the characteristic swaggering attitude, the sword, the love-locks, the key of office painted dangling from his hip and the actual key dangling on a ribbon from the frame of the picture." The dashing career of this follower of King Charles, who fought a duel with Lord Bruce and whose younger son was murdered by the Roundheads, became "a source of rich romance to a youthful imagination nourished on *Cyrano* and *The Three Musketeers*." The half-grown girl re-examined certain old nail-studded trunks in the attics, mute witnesses to Cromwellian violence, some of them curved to fit the roof of a barouche. "The battered trunks were stacked near the entrance to the hiding-place, which, without the smallest justification save an old candlestick and a rope-ladder found therein, I peopled with the fugitive figures of priests and Royalists. I peeped into the trunks: they contained only a dusty jumble of broken ironwork, some old books, some bits of hairy plaster fallen from the ceiling, some numbers of Punch for 1850. Nevertheless, there were the gaping holes where the locks had been prised off the trunks, and the lid forced back upon the hinges by an impatient hand. Down in the Poets' Parlour, where I lunched with my grandfather, taciturn unless he happened to crack one of his little stock-in-trade of jokes, Cromwell's soldiers had held their Court of Sequestration. The Guard Room was empty of arms or armour, save for a few pikes and halberds, because Cromwell's soldiers had taken all the armour away. The past mingled with the present in constant reminder; and out in the summer-house, after luncheon, with the bees blundering among the flowers of the Sunk Garden and the dragon-flies flashing over the pond, I returned to the immense ledger in which I was writing my novel, while Grandpapa retired to his little sitting-room and whittled paper-knives from the lids of cigar-boxes, and thought about—Heaven knows what *he* thought about."

iv

Miss Sackville-West is writing of Knole, of course, in her long story called *The Heir*. The manor of Blackboys with its peacocks is not Knole; I suppose no one makes the mistake of literal identification of people and places in fiction; at least, none should do so. What is truly identifiable is never anything tangible at all; it is merely an emotion. When we read *The Heir*, subtitled "A

Love Story," and acquaint ourselves in a leisurely sufficience with the fellow Chase we should be stupid indeed if we grasped at the substance and neglected the shadow. It is shadow and its correspondent sunlight for which, after all, mankind lives a life wherein the things of substance are the final unreality. . . .

But her first book, which was brought to the attention of the American publisher by Hugh Walpole, was a novel called *Heritage*, an unusual story of young lovers. The breath of distinction upon the tale more than redeemed its faults of construction, of which, perhaps, after all, the most serious was merely the device of a letter immensely longer than any epistle probable to be written. Then, in point of publication, at least, came *The Dragon in Shallow Waters*, also a novel. Some two years elapsed before the appearance of her third novel, *Challenge*, a piece of work of such a character as to demand our earnest scrutiny. *Challenge* is being followed by *Grey Wethers* and *The Heir*.

I have been speaking of American publication; in England Miss Sackville-West first came to notice as a poet. Her *Poems of West and East* was followed by another collection called *Orchard and Vineyard*. Her work in verse exhibited austerity of expression joined to an emotional and descriptive power difficult to appraise. Although it may be, as has been said, that the chief use of poetry, written when one is young, is to produce a finer prose when one is older.

Of *The Heir* it is best to say little since a few betraying words can so easily spoil its secret for the reader. In the same volume appear *The Christmas Party*, *Patience*, *Her Son* and *The Parrot*, a vignette dedicated to "H. G. N." All the qualities present in *The Heir* may be found in the other tales, so varyingly shorter—delicacy, precision, dramatic power and a perception of beauty translated almost without the use of a single emotional word. In *The Christmas Party* we have the deferred revenge of a woman, a theatrical costumer, upon her strait-minded family; *Patience* is an elderly man's recollection, in perfectly domesticated surroundings, of his youthful affair; *Her Son* is the inevitable cruelty inflicted upon a mother by the passage of the years; the story of *The Parrot* points to the only escape from the . . . cage.

The "H. G. N." of its dedication is the Honourable Harold G. Nicolson. Except as an author, the lady of Knole is no longer Victoria Sackville-West but the Honourable Mrs. Harold G. Nicolson.

V

Challenge, a novel that may instructively be compared with Joseph Conrad's *Nostromo*, had the curious fortune to be published first in America and—what is more remarkable—only in America. It might seem altogether extraordinary that one of the most noteworthy novels by an Englishwoman in years should not only not be published first in England but should not be published there at all. It might seem very extraordinary; and it is. The circumstances were perhaps without a precedent and, it may be hoped, will be without a duplication.

In 1920 an English publisher had accepted *Challenge* and prepared it for issuance. That is to say, type had been set, plates had been cast, the sheets of the novel had been printed, folded and sewed. Nothing remained but to encase them in cloth—a matter of a week, usually—when the book would be ready to go on sale. It was the eleventh hour; 11.59 to be precise. Then fate intervened.

It transpired (or was allowed to transpire) that Miss Sackville-West had written her novel about an actual family, portraying that family in general and possibly in particular. The family was part of her own, or shall we say, connected with her own; and it was not without influence. This influence was immediately exerted to secure the suppression of *Challenge*. How far the influence succeeded, by virtue of its own force and considerations, and how far it was aided by the peculiarity of the English libel law, which recognises technical libel, I am unable to say; but succeed it did. *Challenge* remained unbound and the English house either put it down as a loss or, with a sanguineness born of much publishing experience, carried it in its inventory. There were all those folded and sewed sheets constituting a very fair-sized edition, as English editions go, packed away in some sufficiently dry place. At Knole and in Cornwall and it may be in other places Miss Sackville-West continued writing.

Probably the only challenge to the suppressors of the novel in England lay in the single figurative word of the title. Miss Sackville-West could be said to be writing of the actual family only in the same sense that we can say, in alluding to the manor of Blackboys in *The Heir*, that she writes of Knole. Some South American republic, indeed, any South American republic, would be equally justified in beginning suit for libel against Conrad for the picture of Costaguana in *Nostromo*—could a court be discovered in which such a suit would be justiciable? It is charitable to suppose that the suppressors beheld themselves mirrored in the pages of *Challenge* because they were victims of a narcism complex. However, the interesting disabilities of these people were of no serious importance on this side of the Atlantic; Miss Sackville-West had done no work of such importance as the unborn *Challenge*; and after all those unbound sheets had lain untouched for two years or longer the day came when an American publisher took the whole lot, together with the plates to enable him to print more, and *Challenge* saw the light in the United States early in 1923.

It is still unpublishable in England and seems destined indefinitely to remain so. Not indignation nor ridicule is likely to alter this state of affairs, since the prototypes of Miss Sackville-West's Davenants must be conceived of as resembling Galsworthy's Forsytes in one respect: They are almost certainly impervious to the wrath or derision of any except their own kind, and this will hardly be forthcoming.

Challenge, admirable in its technique, begins with an epilogue, giving us through the eyes of disinterested bystanders a glimpse of Julian Davenant many years afterward. We see him with his wife at a great affair in London. He has power, wealth, distinction; and his wife is perfectly equipped for her rôle. Many people expect that Davenant will be the next Viceroy; he has already been in the Cabinet. A cynical man, who believes in nothing —and a philanthropist, really. His face, or his eyes, give one the impression that he has "learnt all the sorrow of the world"; they are inexpressibly weary. And the two onlookers, a man and a woman, recall that there was some "crazy adventure" in Julian Davenant's youth. "Very romantic, but we all start by being romantic until we have outgrown it."

The three parts which follow narrate in a strictly chronological order the details of that "crazy adventure." Julian Davenant was the young son of a house of English Levantines, that is to say, an English family established for several generations in the Levant and possessing, at the time of the story, besides much land, the site of valuable vineyards, prestige and influence and political power. It will be recalled that the Goulds of Costaguana in *Nostromo* constituted a similar clan. Such English exoterics (not to say exotics) are only moderately rare. It is not proper to speak of them as hybrids, since in their marriages they are careful to avoid a non-English admixture and their sons are invariably sent to England for their education. Without in any essential degree sacrificing a single one of those peculiarly tenacious English traits of character and without any alteration of the English habit of thought, they are in most other matters assimilated to the country of their holdings. They come to understand it, its ways, its habit of thought and policy of conduct and instinct of behaviour with a completeness that amounts to perfection and reposes, as a rule and deep down, on a sincere distaste. They are really marvellous, whether Goulds in South America or Davenants in Greece. And their young men . . .

In any comparison of *Nostromo* and *Challenge* it will be found that the most obvious likenesses are purely superficial. In *Nostromo* we have the son, Charles Gould, determined to avenge, by a patient commercialism and a silent political sagacity, the fate of his Uncle Harry and the killing worry of his father; the instrumentality to his hand is the silver of the mine. In *Challenge* young Julian Davenant is the victim of the romantic impulse which causes him to respond, at any cost, to the patriotic appeal of the Islands lying off the coast and unwillingly a part of the tiny republic of Herakleion. The girl, Eve, and the woman, Kato, a native of the Islands and a famous singer, are the personal contending forces in the struggle over Julian Davenant. Eve is Julian's cousin. In the developing story of her love for Julian, in its culminating struggle and final disaster a precise comparison with *Nostromo*—even in respect of the tragedy that befell Linda Viola—is a waste of our attention.

vi

What may profitably be compared in Mr. Conrad's acknowledged masterpiece and Miss Sackville-West's dramatic novel is the identity of method and art. I say "identity" without any hesitation, for in both cases I think the artist has achieved a proportionately impressive and living and beautiful result. As to method, the reader will observe for himself that either novel might have been written by either author. In each case the actual knowledge of a totally foreign country is perhaps the same; and in neither case is it very great or very important. Again, in each case, the imaginative creation is on a plane so much above the level attained in other (and very excellent) novels that the book must definitely be set in a class apart. One accounts for the intense imaginative insight of *The Old Wives' Tale* and *My Antonia* (to choose two especially fine examples) by saying that, after all, both Arnold Bennett and Willa Cather had the immeasurable aid of childhood's unblunted perceptiveness; and in so partially accounting for the sheer fact, one does quite rightly. But neither memory nor the deepest well of sympathy serves to explain *Nostromo* and *Challenge;* in these two novels the imagination had to create something *de novo* and actively body it forth; memories, hearsay, would be an actual interference and the existence of an outer world a positive interruption. They are both novels of a perfectly valid idea recreated in terms of the subconscious personality. If that is too cloudy an explanation I will ask you to think of the subconscious mind as a happily benevolent oyster, of the germ-idea as an infinitesimal particle of irritant sand, and of the accomplished story as the resulting pearl. It is as near as I can come to conveying what I mean . . . and know to be at least subjectively true.

Abandoning this difficult region and ascending to the surface on which most art and literary method lies, the comparison becomes so easy that one feels superfluous in making it. Have we not the same complexity of persons presented in an intimate relation to each other and composing a little world, complete socially, politically and in their attitudes; so that we can perfectly conceive them in any set of circumstances? Have we not also an atmosphere resulting from a multitude of impalpable small touches? Is not the effect in each case more exact than any impression to be derived from personal familiarity with either South America or Greece? Is not the same impersonal viewpoint present? the same astringent humour in evidence in its application to the incongruities of the life presented? In both cases the avoidance of any expression of emotion, the final austerity of the highest art, exercises an effect out of all predictable proportion on the emotions of the reader. He is led to feel amusement, ridicule, sympathy, indignation, dismay, horror and grief; because never is it intimated to him that it is his duty to feel any of these things.

vii

The new novel, *Grey Wethers*, taking its name from those ancient sacrificial stones of the Druids which are the symbols of the story, traces back in substance to Miss Sackville-West's *Heritage*, but is free from the faults of construction which made her first novel so unsatisfactory. The fineness of her hand upon this more familiar material is the delicate reward for her incessant painstaking. She is not a person to rest satisfied, but an artist. An artist . . .

"What was the promise of that mediocre ease beside the certainty of these exquisite privations?" So Chase questioned himself, in Miss Sackville-West's story of *The Heir*. "What was that drudgery beside this beauty, this pride, this Quixotism?" There is only one answer. If you would be an artist you do not even bother with the answer. But your heart leaps.

Books by V. Sackville-West

Poems of West and East [in England]
1921 *Orchard and Vineyard* [in England]
1918 *Heritage*
1920 *The Dragon in Shallow Waters*
1923 *Knole and the Sackvilles*
1923 *Challenge* [withdrawn in England prior to publication, 1920]
1923 *Grey Wethers*
1924 *The Heir and Other Stories*

Sources on V. Sackville-West

Knole and the Sackvilles, generally, and also pages 11, 17, 68, 82, 83, 219 and 220
Who's Who [in England]
Private Information

7. *Harold Bell Wright*

i

FROM *Who's Who in America*, 1922-1923 (Volume 12):

"WRIGHT, HAROLD BELL, author: born, Rome, Oneida County, New York, May 4, 1872; son, William A. Wright and Alma T. (Watson) Wright; student two years, preparatory department, Hiram College, Ohio; married, Frances E. Long, of Buffalo, New York, July 18, 1899; married, second, Mrs. Winifred Mary Potter Duncan, of Los Angeles, California, August 5, 1920. Painter and decorator, 1887-92; landscape painter, 1892-7; pastor, Christian (Disciples) Church, Pierce City, Missouri, 1897-8, Pittsburg, Kansas, 1898-1903, Forest Avenue Church, Kansas City, Missouri, 1903-5, Lebanon, Missouri, 1905-7, Redlands, California, 1907-8; retired from ministry, 1908. Author: *That Printer of Udell's*, 1903; *The Shepherd of the Hills*, 1907; *The Calling of Dan Matthews*, 1909; *The Uncrowned King*, 1910; *The Winning of Barbara Worth*, 1911; *Their Yesterdays*, 1912; *The Eyes of the World*, 1914; *When A Man's a Man*, 1916; *The Re-Creation of Brian Kent*, 1919; *Helen of the Old House*, 1921. Home: Tucson, Arizona."

Such is the outline derived by the compilers of an invaluable work of reference whose method is to ask of the individual certain standard questions which he may answer in his discretion and which he may supplement—in the editor's discretion—by further information about himself. The latitude allowed in such a work as *Who's Who in America*, is necessarily rather small; it would, however, have permitted Mr. Wright to say that the sales of his fiction exceed those of any other living American writer—perhaps those of any other living writer anywhere. He did not say it. The impression given by the words "landscape painter" may be misleading, for Mr. Wright at that time made his living by sign painting and house painting; but also he made sketches and water colors which he sold as he went along. Let this tiny matter be as a warning that, on his own terms and in his own fashion of speech, Harold Bell Wright is to be taken literally.

Always! Is there metaphor in his writing? Was there metaphor in *Pilgrim's Progress?* Are there parables in the Bible? Do sermons contain allegories? We know that allegories embody sermons. Mr. Wright has never concealed the purpose behind his novels, stories. It is to say plainly some word that he believes will be of help, if uttered, to men and women. In his strange personal history lies the seed of a novel more absorbing, if less credible, than any he has written. The poor boy, the boy left motherless at ten, the man out of work, the man with an empty stomach and no means of filling it, the man who has been told that "the rock

HAROLD BELL WRIGHT

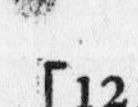

pile was intended for fellows like you!"—and through it all the sleazy thread of ill-health, downright sickness, and the bright scarlet stain of disease. . . . Two years at a little college, cut short by illness; two years financed by hard work and ground down in disappointment. Then the haphazard wandering, the tramping afoot outdoors, the small painting jobs, the inability to find work at times, the hardships of climate—and at last he finds himself in the Ozark Mountains looking for . . . what? For the chance to live, first of all. It was there that he preached his first sermon, and there he found a background and a setting for some of the stories he was eventually to write. They were very far off, then, those stories, below the horizon, out of sight as were so many other things that were to dawn on his life when he should be thirty.

ii

In any consideration of Harold Bell Wright as an author, the usual approaches are of no value, and not only of no value but so without meaning as to be absurd. Almost he raises the fundamental question: What is an author, anyway? Of course the word does apply to all whose writing achieves publication, especially as a book or books; and perhaps it may be used of a person who remains unpublished. But, as always, there is here a meaning within a meaning; the word generally carries with it some suggestion of literary skill or a pretension thereto—as "doctor" implies a medical training, or "lawyer" admission to practise at the bar. However, Mr. Wright neither possesses any literary skill nor ever pretended to have any, comparatively speaking. He has more than once uttered an emphatic disclaimer, but like other very popular writers his sensitiveness to adverse criticism is keen.

He is a moralist, a fabulist, a preacher of sermons, a Sayer, and an Utterer. There is in the impoverished English language no word for his rôle. The English language, so full of words for things that do not exist, has none for this type of man who has always existed among the English-speaking peoples though rather sparsely among other peoples. When forced to recognise his existence as a power for evil in politics, we borrow the word demagogue; if his activity is rather indefinitely "religious," we affix the word evangelist. There is a common factor in John Bunyan, Theodore Roosevelt, James Whitcomb Riley, Harold Bell Wright easily recognised in whatever field it operates. In the case of Mr. Wright, it has been said that he appeals "to the thousands upon thousands who crave to see their humble doings, their paper fantasies exalted and made memorable in the bright guise of a seeming romance." Unfortunately for the success of this diagnosis, it is not the great masses of mankind who are sentimental, but the minority who have accustomed themselves to the contemplation of mankind in great masses. If Mr. Roosevelt had addressed himself to the "thousands upon thousands" he would have been almost without influence; and Mr. Riley's verses are most noteworthy for their intimate personal appeal. Such a Sayer as Walt Whitman, speaking to men *en masse*, receives from men small attention. One can neither speak, write, paint, carve or build for the thousands; one must do it for the individual every time. In a short study of Roosevelt some years ago the editor of the Atlantic Monthly, Ellery Sedgwick, admirably indicated Roosevelt's real achievement, which was—not that he moulded national policies but that he made the homegoing day labourer, sitting in a trolley car, his empty lunch pail beside him, trace with a stubby forefinger in the evening newspaper the simple precept for that day, whether a command against race suicide or a "Don't flinch! Don't foul! Hit the line hard!" He who would speak to many men and women must always address each one; he must not make the mistake of appealing to a lowest common intelligence and he must perfectly understand that what is called "sentimentality" is not a weakness but a sign of health—pink thoughts like pink cheeks.

iii

"She stood before him in all the beautiful strength of her young womanhood."

"He was really a fine looking young man with the appearance of being exceptionally well-bred and well-kept. Indeed the most casual of observers would not have hesitated to pronounce him a thoroughbred and a good individual of the best type that the race has produced. . . ."

These sentences, from Wright's novel, *The Winning of Barbara Worth*, have been quoted with the comment that Wright himself is that casual observer and that, to the more thoughtful, Abraham Lincoln, who "was anything but a thoroughbred, anything but well-kept" is the best type of individual that the race has produced. Mr. Wright could crushingly reply that Lincoln was not a type; but the failure in perception goes much deeper. The critic of the passage quoted must know very well that the respect of mankind for appearances is well-founded. Appearances can be arrived at and kept up, being thus one of the few things definitely within our powers of accomplishment and control; for what lies under the appearance may be beyond our power to make or change. It is not instinct, or even reason, but a solid regard for fact that prizes appearance. Further, in the affair in question, two subjects for a possible mating, the usual man or woman is as unromantic and unsentimental as possible in his or her satisfaction at the good looks of hero and heroine. Those good looks and good manners are something to go upon. Each has an asset with the other and there is some chance for the children, if any. Only a dangerous sentimentalist would wish the man to be a mongrel. Mr. Wright knows all this; so do we all of us; why, then, is he called a sentimentalist?

Because, I suppose, an inveterate tradition of the minority brands the majority as sentimental. Were they so, they could not live. The majority, not being victims of self-delusion, go through life, eating, sleeping, working and feeling. The capacity to feel has not in them been weakened. They may be robbed of their cheeks' pinkness, but it is more difficult to take away the pinkness of their thoughts (the mere mental accompaniments of their feelings). Indeed, it has so far proved impossible to enslave them by any intellectual system, as they have been enslaved by this or that economic system. If it were possible to persuade these men and women that physical mongrelism should take the place of Mr. Wright's hero's thoroughbreeding, the world would have become sentimental with a vengeance likely to recoil on the heads of those who wrought the persuasion. The French Revolution would be as nothing to the new era then dawning.

In other words, the young man used to advertise linen collars (and Mr. Wright, at the young man's age, might easily have served as the model) is the people's proper hero. He represents, to a considerable extent, something within the average power to become. No more suggestive antithesis can be imagined than between a novel like *The Shepherd of the Hills* and such a work of fiction as Mr. Sinclair Lewis's *Main Street*, crammed with the things beyond the average power to alter. It is the interesting inevitability of the visitor to humble homes in out of the way American places to encounter, on the parlour table or its equivalent, a Bible, a "gift" edition of Longfellow's Poems, *The Wreck of the "Titanic"* (with complete horrors, last words of all on board, and full text of "Nearer, My God, to Thee," as played by the ship's band) and a copy of *The Shepherd of the Hills*, or, perhaps, *When a Man's a Man*. But *Main Street?* That, if it was ever in the house, has gone the way of all wood pulp very quickly. For these people have none of that difficulty experienced by the literary critic in distinguishing books, and their applied canons are not matters of taste or sentiment or intellectual theory, but principles of living as they are compelled to practise them daily, personal and intimate, directed toward the best appearance, unsentimental, unintellectual, individual, healthful, sensibly ambitious, emotionally direct and . . . free.

iv

Suppose, instead of audibly deploring Mr. Wright, and uttering in their assaults upon him an unconscionable amount of twaddle, the literary critics were to transform themselves into students of the popular psychology. In such case they would see at once how the usual person unsentimentally proceeds through life with the assistance of attainable ideals. Of course, definitions of sentimentality may and do differ. My idea here is simply that to espouse the shadowy ideal is to come much more under the charge of being sentimental than to aspire to wear the newest style of linen collar, or acquire good manners. I think at once, too, of a writer whose best work meets the severe tests applied by the critic of literature, Mr. Arnold Bennett. What is *The Old Wives' Tale*, what is *Clayhanger*, each a work of accepted art, but a faithful transcription of the average person's utter unsentimentality and complete devotion to the attainable ideal? Mr. Bennett made the same veracious observation as Mr. Wright makes; it is only the presentation that is different—objective in the case of Bennett, immersed in the case of Wright. For Bennett's purpose literary art is essential, for Wright's, literary art is a handicap. Moreover, the identification is unlike. The people Bennett writes about, with the exception of Clayhanger, would not recognise themselves in his two novels; the people of Mr. Wright, would. Why? Because Wright expresses them in their own fractions—known to themselves. Bennett carries them out to a decimal repetend—.142857142857142857 and so on, instead of 1/7, subscribed by Mr. Wright. Virtue, vice, greed, ambition, youth and the like are the simple fractions in which Mr. Wright's characters are stated. Whatever realities these names represent, it had better be realised that they are in themselves the simplest, most necessary conventions. And as such, and as such only, has Wright used them.

His method of work was, I think, the innocent source of the general misunderstanding surrounding him in the discussions of the minority. It is well-known that before writing a novel he prepares a short argument, as other writers prepare an outline or plot. "The system I use," he has explained, "may have been used for centuries, or it may be no one else has ever used it. I have wondered whether it is old or new. Whichever it may be, here it is: When I start to write a novel, the first thing I do is to figure out why I am going to write it. Not what is the story, but why? I mull this over a while, and when it is pretty straight in my mind, I write out an argument. No suggestion of plot, you see. No incidents, scenes, location, nothing done at first except the argument, but it is the heart and soul of the novel. The novel is merely this argument presented through the medium of characters, plot, incidents, and the other properties of the story. Next come the characters, each standing for some element or factor in the argument. Up to the last copying of *The Eyes of the World*, not a character had been named. They were called in the copy, Greed, Ambition, Youth, or whatever they represented to me in the writing of the story." This simple explanation has been derided by asserting that "Mr. Wright seeks to prove some abstract notion of his own concerning good and evil by means of a picked assembly of human beings." But how so? They are not picked human beings at all, but like Bunyan's characters, expressions of the One. They prove nothing and are intended to prove nothing, being merely expository, fabulous, moralistic, and the natural presentation of no easy notion but some familiar fact—far from abstract! Take *The Re-Creation of Brian Kent*, one of Wright's least satisfactory books to its author and to many readers and released by Wright with great reluctance. An abstract notion is the last thing in the world it touches upon; all is simple, vivid, commonplace, centred around the actuality that, with another chance, many a man can set his life straight.

If there is any shortcoming it arises from Wright's personal strength. The man who can do what he has done, persistently fighting tuberculosis, risking public opinion in several matters and adhering to his method in spite of a great change of personal attitude and a personal revolution in ideas—

that man is no weakling. It would be interesting to survey the personal change in Mr. Wright but as it nowhere extrudes in his work, there is no justification for an inquest. But the very circumstance has its positive value in establishing him for what he is not, namely, an artist. But there is another aspect of Mr. Wright as phenomenon (not as person) and his success cannot be understood without examining that aspect.

V

Wright's boyhood, to the age of ten when he lost her, was focussed about the personality of his mother. When she died he lost, if not perhaps his only friend, his strongest. Before he could read she had told him the Hiawatha legends, had read aloud to him the stories of the Bible (the King James version), had retold Shakespeare for him. Her death made him clutch to his heart these books, as well as the *Pilgrim's Progress* and the portions of Ruskin they had read and re-read together in the home—which, by the way, was really at Wrightstown, just outside Rome, New York, though Wright's birthplace is spoken of as "Rome." A feeling that these books of his mother's were as sacred books was fixed in the boy's mind. Wright has never ceased to read them, nor to try to pour himself into those molds; and in conversation he sometimes lets slip a phrase from one of them. Without literary aptitude and with a very ragged species of formal education, he speaks in his extraordinary fashion and the millions hearken. So much so that his success from the outset may be said to have entirely reconstructed—for the purpose of merchandising his books—the retail machinery of book-selling.

The author of *That Printer of Udell's* had the means of reaching the folks in little villages and on isolated farms, people who could scarcely be reached by any of the books ordinarily being published. The very inadequate machinery of retail distribution serving the book trade was insufficient for his purpose. It is insufficient for most purposes, but its insufficiency in the case of Harold Bell Wright was painful and intolerable. With the most remarkable courage, effort and persistence the publishers constructed a new and complete retail mechanism to serve the special need. Those who have no knowledge of the problems of merchandising will be unable to appreciate what they did. A few details are in order. First, the larger book publishers in the United States seldom sell directly to retailers in cities of less than 50,000; smaller publishers seldom enter cities of less than 100,000. The needs of bookstores in little cities and towns, mixed and important only in the aggregate, are taken care of by jobbers. There are possibly 1,000 first-rate bookstores to serve a nation of well over 100,000,000 people—of whom, however, some 20,000,000 are incapable of ever reading a book of any importance in an understanding way. There are cities of 50,000 in which no first-rate bookstore exists. On the other hand a magazine like Pictorial Review, solidly established on the demand for dress patterns, or a magazine like Saturday Evening Post.

promulgating fiction patterns, penetrates into places where no new book is ever seen. So, too, do certain denominational religious papers. And in vast areas of the Middle and Far West, there is a seepage from those reservoirs of modern merchandising, the mail order houses, the Roosevelt Dams of commerce, constantly seeking, more and more achieving the reclamation of the deserts of trade.

The "producers," in stage parlance, of Harold Bell Wright determined to utilise all these channels. It was a great risk of judgment and money at the outset but it succeeded. This is no place to go into the history of a unique performance in merchandising but the results have a distinct place in any record of the author exploited. For one thing, it may be asked if the success with Wright is of value in selling other authors, and while there can be no dogmatic answer to the question it is probable that in most cases it is not. And another phase of the results throws a significant light on the nature of Wright's work, confirming what we have said about the terms of his appeal to his readers. When a Wright novel is published the orders pile in from stores and places with which a publisher has ordinarily no contact; and the order from a hamlet in North Carolina is likely to exceed the order from Brentano's in New York.

This means two things. It means, naturally, that with the heavy campaigns of advertising in all sorts of periodicals from Saturday Evening Post to Zion's Herald, the publishers reach the people who buy a book a year or less often. But also it means that Wright is the moralist, the fabulist and the Sayer we have termed him. On the technical side, perhaps the most instructive detail of this selling performance is the way in which it is initiated. Six months before a new Wright story is to be published, thousands of tradespeople all over the United States know that the story is to be published, and when, and with what enormous advertising placed in forty specified periodicals and several dozen newspapers it will be "pushed"; and then begins the steady succession of personal letters and even telegrams, circulars and placards and posters, honest-minded persons in remote settlements discuss with enthusiasm and awe the prodigious sum of money to be expended on "just this one book, a *book*," librarians grow anxious and advertising men eager, preachers prepare sermons, in thousands upon thousands of homes the Christmas gift to Mother is pre-determined,—until at last, in a wide-rolling wave of excitement, a vast surge of the people of simple faith and worthy ideals, the day comes when the book is born. . . .

vi

It has been said that Wright is of magnetic personality, with fine, clean, inspiring ideals, a man of tireless endeavour, a person who "stirs in one emotions of which one is not ashamed." Also that "he radiates a Lincolnian type of rugged honesty" . . . and much more of the same sort. All such lingo is meaningless outside the atmosphere of Wright's books. The language of those novels is not one of literary conventions but of certain inalterable thought-conventions; and so, necessarily, is language addressed to those who read Wright. "She stood before him in all the beautiful strength of her young womanhood." . . . "It is his almost clairvoyant power of reading the human soul that has made Mr. Wright's books among the most remarkable of the present age." These two statements are demonstrably true to the many whose minds, struck by such sentences, give back the ring of silver. They are not true in themselves; but then, we know no things that are. To be "true" is simply to signify enough, at a given time, in particular circumstances, to some individual or individuals.

That truth Mr. Wright has had enormously, and still has. His newest novel, *The Mine With the Iron Door*, although in no way an elaboration of the traditional tale of that mine—it was supposed to be a wonder mine, where the old Spanish Fathers got the gold that enriched their splendid altars—weaves the old legend through its texture of incident. This gives to the novel a colour beyond the colour it has from its Arizona setting; but the point with Mr. Wright is something like this: Every life has its "mine with the iron door," its dreams that can never come true, its hopes that belong to a past that is forever dead. Nevertheless, he will have you believe, though the lost mine may never be found nor the iron door opened, some riches of happiness is still possible. Were it not for this element, this presentation of something that at a given time and in particular circumstances can signify truth to many, many people, Mr. Wright's new novel would be no more than a picturesque and exciting adventure narrative of the Arizona desert.

vii

Mr. Wright went to Tucson, Arizona, some ten years ago on a business errand. Three days after reaching the city he had bought a cottage. Now he owns eighty acres outside Tucson and has built a new home, a comfortable but by no means pretentious house with a garden transplanted from the neighbouring desert. The scale of living is modest. Wright and his wife take care of the grounds and house, to a large extent; and there is usually not more than one servant. Mr. Wright has a motor car that he has driven for six years and will continue to drive for some years yet. He is fond of horseback riding and spends as much time camping as at home. Two or three tents, the car, some tinned stuff and staples and plenty of ammunition are all Mr. and Mrs. Wright need, for both are good marksmen. They shoot for food, but Wright will not kill a deer.

The stories are frequently written, or largely written, on these expeditions into the desert. Because he is not an artist, Wright has a sadly difficult time. He will submit a story like *The Winning of Barbara Worth* to five engineers in order that they may check up his account of the irrigation of the desert. A long time was spent in worrisome "looking over the ground," visiting factory towns, interviewing employers and workmen, before *Helen of the Old House* took even preliminary shape. As a rule, the incidents Wright uses are transcribed from life, producing the effect of extreme incredibility of which his readers sometimes complain. Being his readers, they are silenced when he tells them of the actual occurrence.

Hildegarde Hawthorne has pointed out the very great and incontestable service of Wright: He creates book readers. It requires very little examination of the facts to discover that thousands whose reading has been nothing but newspapers and magazines have been led by Wright's stories into the habit of reading a book occasionally. That is an accomplishment of an importance hard to overrate.

As for the man, there is one story I like better than any he has written. Some years ago, riding horseback on a narrow trail, Wright was struck by an automobile that came suddenly around a corner of rock. Horse and rider were pitched into a gully; the horse was killed and Wright's particularly bad lung so suffered by the fall that everyone assured him there was nothing left but to die. He said: "I won't die." Because he couldn't be moved, a tent had to be erected over him there in the gully, so that he might die in the shade. Lying there under the tent, he fulfilled his purpose by getting well. He also, under the same tent and in the same place, wrote *When a Man's a Man*. . . . And now he is again in good physical shape, riding his horses after the day's work is over through the desert or up into the foothills of the Catalina Mountains.

The preacher he began, the preacher he must probably remain. There may, perhaps, be something pitiful in the spectacle of a man struggling with the palette of words, as there is something bizarre in the voice proceeding from the wilderness with a perfectly mundane message: That every valley had better be filled, every mountain and hill nicely graded; the crooked carefully straightened, the rough ways . . . paved with asphalt.

Books by Harold Bell Wright

1903 *That Printer of Udell's*
1907 *The Shepherd of the Hills*
1909 *The Calling of Dan Matthews*
1910 *The Uncrowned King*
1911 *The Winning of Barbara Worth*
1912 *Their Yesterdays*
1914 *The Eyes of the World*
1916 *When a Man's a Man*
1919 *The Re-Creation of Brian Kent*
1921 *Helen of the Old House*
1923 *The Mine With the Iron Door*

Sources on Harold Bell Wright

Harold Bell Wright. Booklet published by D. Appleton & Company
Harold Bell Wright, the Man Behind the Novels, by HILDEGARDE HAWTHORNE. Booklet published by D. Appleton & Company
Private Information

8. *"Ah, Did You Once See Shelley Plain?"*

i

Ah, did you once see Shelley plain,
  And did he stop and speak to you?
And did you speak to him again?
  How strange it seems, and new!

BROWNING: *Memorabilia*

THE four lines, and, indeed, the twelve remaining lines of this one of Robert Browning's shorter poems illustrate very well the man's superlative faculty of drama. With a little of our Edwin Arlington Robinson, he mixed a little of our Eugene O'Neill; and, on occasion, expressed himself with point and passion. Such was his simplicity that he appeared (it is now laughable to remember) rather especially unintelligible. Not far distant yet are the days when we banded together to understand him. But the number of Browning Clubs now surviving must be very few. How curious that we never thought to try to understand the man himself! How queer that we didn't concentrate, as he would have concentrated in a similar instance, upon the thirteen years that unlock his life; but we didn't. We generalised about him concerning whom, of all men of his day, it was least safe to generalise. It has remained for Frances M. Sim in her *Robert Browning, The Poet and the Man: 1833-1846* to do the thing that has so needed doing. She has very wisely avoided the form of the full biography and equally the form, which would be sterile in this instance, of a full-length critique. Her book is at once a freely-handled and intensive study of the years that lay between the publication of Browning's first poem, "Pauline," and his marriage with Elizabeth Barrett. She starts with "Pauline," accompanies him to Russia and with him brings back "Paracelsus," goes with him to Italy and re-creates "Sordello." Then, with almost no preliminaries, we are into the love affair. When that has been lived again to its fruition, we are in possession of "the poet and the man" in the only possible fashion apart from the body of his work. Frances M. Sim has given us a valuable and interesting study, and simply by obeying the wisdom in Arthur Waugh's words: "Browning's marriage, in short, was the last stage in his artistic education"—words that open a fascinating path of speculative insights into the lives of how many of the world's artists!

Contrast, if you will, the temperamental difference between such a man as Robert Browning, who had his early and well-nigh fatal intoxication from reading the poetry of Shelley, and a fellow like Joseph Farington, the painter, whose death occurred when Browning was a lad of nine. No literary discovery in years has made half the sensation of the finding of *The Farington Diary*, and quite rightly, for what could be compared to the disclosure of a contemporary account in which Boswell, Burke, Goldsmith, Horace Walpole, the Thrales, Garrick, Mrs. Siddons, Nelson, Howe, Mirabeau, Marat, Napoleon, Hoppner, Turner, Pitt, Warren Hastings, Lady Hamilton and Robert Burns were intimately noted? And yet Farington, ruler of the Royal Academy though a most indifferent artist, came into touch with all these personages and was apparently never for one moment carried off his feet. I think it is quite true, as Robert Cortes Holliday suggests in a review of *The Farington Diary* (The Bookman, June, 1923) that Farington saw only the surface of that great age, that he was devoid of humour and lacked the malice which a diarist should feel. He was sane, not to say stupid; but as a conscientious accumulator of facts I can think of no one who is his equal. Amid riches and grandeur, intriguery and wars and revolutions, surrounded by a glittering society in which one knew not which to worship, genius or scintillance, Joseph Farington scrupulously set down all the diseases of people he knew, all the dishes served at a dinner, how much everything cost and the money that everyone made, inherited, bequeathed or borrowed. It was only accidentally that matters touched with human interest flowed from the point of his pen; but in a fairly long lifetime the number of such leakages runs high, and the result, despite every exasperation and handicap, is to make a book of very great and most indubitable value. The first volume of *The Farington Diary*, covering the years 1793-1802, is the most complete portrait album we have of its time; the remaining volumes, which, it is understood, go on to Farington's death in 1821, should not be less valuable.

ii

Great times, in producing great men, produce great books as well. In the lifetime of Walter H. Page, publisher, business man and American Ambassador to the Court of St. James's, the number of persons who had any comprehension of his greatness was singularly small. Those who had the fine fortune to be associated with him in the day's work knew, of course, the stature of the man; but it was scarcely possible to impress their knowledge on others. When Mr. Page at last became conspicuous in the public service it was at a post where his work and the character enforcing it were necessarily almost completely obscured. An American Ambassador at the Court of St. James's at the present time may conceivably bring himself into a good deal of notice; it is not impossible to be done and the opportunities for doing it legitimately are not infrequent; but Mr. Page was never one for that sort of thing, and I doubt whether, even if the war had not hidden him in its drifting mists as he steered the ship, he would have come in all his lifetime to our not always intelligently directed attention. There are some men, and among them our greatest, whom death alone fully discloses. Such was Walter H. Page, and in the magnificent biography wrought by Burton J. Hendrick, *The Life and Letters of Walter H. Page*, the subject is handled with a justness and a careful proportioning for which praise should not be stinted, and has not been. Unquestionably this is one of the great American books in the biographical field; this life and these letters have something so vital that one hunts a ready comparison in vain. At times they seem to paint the man with rich colour and a splendid handling of light; at other times they carve and sculpture him in some detail of a rare personality; but the figure fails before the ruddiness, the mobile vigour and the unresting intellect which the book sets forth. In a day when the state of America is rather often canvassed and most often with pessimistic conclusions, it is significant that *The Life and Letters of Walter H. Page*, a fairly expensive work in two volumes, has sold half a hundred thousand copies and now, a year after its publication, continues to lead in sales of non-fiction.

It is but one, of course, of a number of great books yielded by the times we have lived in. *The Irish Guards in the Great War*, by Rudyard Kipling, is surely another. Mr. Kipling has not always been regarded as a sympathetic and understanding friend of Irishmen. His son, John Kipling, was an officer of the Irish Guards and, as such, gave his life. The choice of Mr. Kipling as the historian of the regiment was one which only the resultant chronicle would justify; but to my mind there is no possible question that the work justifies and more than justifies. The reviewer for the London Times puts the matter pithily when he says: "The true gold of Mr. Kipling is to be found unalloyed in this memorial." The temptation to embitteredness, the impulse to "handle" and fashion his material or to give it stylistic treatment and the natural inclination to fix the point of view have all been quietly laid aside; and we have a book of continuous vividness that results from the inner perspective to which Mr. Kipling rigidly holds his account. He constantly uses the sentences on the lips of his Irishmen and we are seldom conscious of a narrator—then only when some Kiplingesque epithet or phrase carries us above the trench and, as it were, above the battle. The London Times reviewer speaks of the "wealth of detail, varied, terrible, and sometimes grotesque, as in the best Gothic" in the presentation of which Kipling manages to preserve a clean simplicity of outline and a unity or totality of effect; but this is merely a way of saying that the book is epically written. Mere largeness of subject has nowadays a way of being taken for "epic" treatment, although the word should properly be confined to a treatment in which a great mass of detail is not allowed to obscure the simplicity of the whole. But I do not think anyone can fail in appreciation of *The Irish Guards*, and to any who may be tempted to forgo the reading of the history let me quote these closing words: "Of all these things nothing but the memory would remain. And, as they moved—little more than a company strong—in the wake of their seniors, one saw, here and there among the wounded in civil kit, young men with eyes that did not match their age, shaken beyond speech or tears by the splendour and the grief of that memory."

The final distinction of Mr. Kipling's book is, to be sure, that it is the work of a man who knows how to write. This distinction it shares with the fewest possible number of contemporary histories, but *The World Crisis*, by Winston Churchill, must be admitted within the slender group. Perhaps we had rather forgotten Winston Churchill, the young journalist in Africa during the Boer War (and the hero, incidentally, of one of the greatest prisoner escapes to be found in all history). There may also be some heredity in Winston Churchill's literary gift, as in his other brilliant personal endowments. But that's no matter. As a former British Home Secretary, First Lord of the Admiralty, 1911-15, and Minister of Munitions in 1917—above all, perhaps, as the man chiefly held responsible for the Gallipoli venture—Mr. Churchill's account would be of the very first interest and importance were he never so unskilful among words. But *The World Crisis* makes apparent what some of us had suspected before, that among leading statesmen there has rarely been one whose ability to defend his course and make other courses appear small has equalled Winston Churchill's. The sense of scale amid vastness in sums of money, tonnage of ships and lives of men that Mr. Churchill possesses is laid by some commentators to his American blood. "He savours hugeness like a dainty; and when he writes of carnage or battle he dips his pen in blood," says Filson Young, adding, "But he never for a moment loses his grip of the subject, or his sense of ever-marching destiny; and he never fails to thrill the reader with the sense of the human tragedy lurking in its every step." Mr. Young thinks *The World Crisis* places its author "in the very first rank of British historians; and I think it places him in very nearly the first rank of British statesmen." The two most famous living British statesmen, Mr. Lloyd George and Mr. Asquith, flank Mr. Churchill's book with what went before and what may come after. The Right Honourable Herbert Henry Asquith's *The Genesis of the War* contains, of course, many noteworthy pen portraits; no doubt these will make the most immediate appeal to readers; yet his disclosures regarding the British War Book, begun in 1910 and his exposition of "the purposes and methods of British policy" in the pre-war years are the book's greatest justification and its strongest historical importance. Mr. Lloyd George, characteristically, is far less concerned about the past than about the future. In *Where Are We Going?* he moves alertly over troubled ground of European affairs, discussing the League of Nations, Russian republicanism, Socialism, national armaments, the Irish Treaty, the position of France, England's war debt, prohibition, the disclosure of war secrets, "the next war" and many other topics. His preface is particularly interesting.

iii

Naturally, the climax of interest is reached when we can say: "This man has written of himself." G. Stanley Hall's *Life and Confessions of a Psychologist* is an autobiography of which one feels a keen anxiety lest the many whom it can reward may somehow miss reading it. "I am far older than my years"—he is seventy-seven—"for I have laid aside more of the illusions and transcended more of the limitations with which I started than most." These simple and striking words define his attitude. The truly popular result of a work that has been undertaken and carried through in such a spirit ought to be emphasised. Dr. Hall is the author of important treatises on *Adolescence* and *Senescence*, exhaustive in character and highly technical in their bearing; but I have yet to read anything of his which was not to a very large extent "popularly written" as well as scientifically valuable. Certainly his *Life and Confessions of a Psychologist* deserves the wider audience. It begins on a New England farm with some chapters that reflect with ampleness and feeling and charm the life of New England in the 1850s; it continues through the various stages of an unusually rounded education; in its record of teaching and college executiveship the book constitutes a sort of history of the American college in the last half-century, and this is enlarged and given the value of ripened conclusions by a longer chapter near the close of the book. There is also a tremendous chapter covering "Process in Psychology" and practically constituting a history of the science in Dr. Hall's long lifetime—one might almost say since psychology was recognised as a science at all. But these points, while they demonstrate easily enough that the book is one no teacher or psychologist can afford to omit attending, do not make the case for the book as a sample of autobiography or as a work of popular interest. Then let some of the contents make it! Here is the report of an American who has known Mark Hopkins, Charles Eliot Norton, Henry Ward

Beecher, George Bancroft, Treitschke, Wundt, Helmholtz, William James, Lord Kelvin, Jowett, Pasteur and many others; an American who can write of his boyhood with something of the charm of W. H. Hudson and much the same feeling for nature; who can write with frankness of the *vita sexualis* in the New England of Emerson; who can —we fall back upon it—write!

A fellow-scientist of Dr. Hall's though in quite another field has also written his autobiography, and the extraordinary circumstances of Michael Idvorsky Pupin's life will be enough to attract popular attention to his *From Immigrant to Inventor*. Forty-eight years ago a Serbian boy who hadn't a cent and who couldn't speak a word of English landed in New York. Since 1901 this immigrant has been professor of electro-mechanics at Columbia University; he is the inventor of the Pupin coil, which, by reducing the necessary diameter of copper wire, has saved millions of dollars, and he also invented the device for tuning which many people use daily on radio sets. Michael Pupin was born at Idvor, Banat, Hungary, in a little community of Serbs rewarded for their services against the Turks by the gift of some land and political rights. In assessing his performance it must be borne in mind that he had the handicap of an utterly alien race and culture and speech to overcome in a far greater degree than Jacob A. Riis, who was Danish, or Edward Bok, who came from Holland. Pupin's autobiography is of manifold interest; for one thing, he seems completely in sympathy with an American tradition which so many immigrants have never been able whole-heartedly to accept; for another, he traces the developments of electrical science by the bright thread of his interest and participation in them, and he does actually succeed in making some very difficult scientific achievements quite simple and beautifully plain.

iv

Very different, if possible more magical, has been the career of the Russian glovemaker whose adopted surname is now known everywhere that motion pictures are exhibited—Samuel Goldwyn. It is only about nine years since he paid ten cents to see a two-reel picture in depressing surroundings on Broadway, and came home to tell his brother-in-law, Jesse Lasky, that a fortune could be made in five-reel pictures! Samuel Goldwyn's book, *Behind the Screen*, showing on every page the fine journalistic skill of his collaborator, Corinne Lowe, is less an autobiography than a personal record of the people of the screen. Charlie Chaplin, Mary Pickford, Douglas Fairbanks, Mary Garden, Pauline Frederick, Geraldine Farrar and plenty of others are here described with an intimacy and a frankness and a general wit and good humour that it isn't easy to imagine will be soon surpassed. The popular appeal of such a series of "closeups" should be as limitless as the movie audience, but the book will serve a less immediate and more important purpose to the reader whose interest, not fervidly personal, goes into the general subject of the films—how they came about, what and why they are, what may come of them. I do not mean that Mr. Goldwyn concerns himself directly with any of these questions, for he scarcely touches them; and yet I think that the indirect light he throws may be more finally enlightening than anything else that has come out of Hollywood—certainly more so than would be likely to be got by any outsider who might go there in a direct search. But let that pass. The book, as a book, is irresistible reading.

V

The boundaries between history, biography, autobiography, memoirs and the best journalism are often uncertain and are better so. It does not matter except to formal minds whether an interest begins with a person or an event, or in what direction it proceeds; for the mind, like the body, has its own system of nutrition, and within pretty broad limits should be allowed its own dietary. The suggestions below are additional to those books already discussed and the classifications need not be taken as anything more than a general convenience:

Historical.

ADMIRAL SIMS'S *The Victory at Sea* (World War).

BRAND WHITLOCK'S *Belgium* (World War).

RAY STANNARD BAKER'S *Woodrow Wilson and World Settlement.*

Ambassador Morgenthau's Story (World War).

Memories of a Turkish Statesman, 1913-1919,

by DJEMAL PASHA. A very spirited account, well-written; almost unique as a book from the Turkish side. Interesting in its contradictions of Morgenthau.

An Ambassador's Memoirs, by MAURICE PALEOLOGUE. By the last French Ambassador to Russia. Volume I. covers July 3, 1914–June 2, 1915; Volume II. continues to August 18, 1916.

LAURANCE LYON's *The Pomp of Power* and his *When There Is No Peace*, both published anonymously. The author is in close touch with French policy.

Old Diplomacy and New: 1876-1922: From Salisbury to Lloyd George, by A. L. KENNEDY.

The Drama of Sinn Fein, by SHAW DESMOND. A new and pretty complete history.

The Life of Sir William Harcourt, by A. G. GARDINER. Harcourt was born before Victoria ascended the throne and he outlived her; Mr. Gardiner brings unusual talents to what becomes less a biography of one man than a portrayal of an era.

Memoirs of the Empress Eugenie, by COMTE FLEURY. Here likewise the historical interest is as strong as the biographical.

Lady Palmerston and Her Times, by MABELL, COUNTESS OF AIRLIE. Of value for its picture of the period from George III. to the middle of the Nineteenth Century.

PAUL VAN DYKE's *Catherine de Medici*, in two volumes, now in its third printing, is distinguished by lucidity, an avoidance of easy ornament and floridity, and by great literary charm.

More Purely Personal.

The Letters of Lord and Lady Wolseley, edited by SIR GEORGE ARTHUR. The intimacies of a great soldier and his brilliant wife, with many glimpses of British society from 1870 to 1911.

Margot Asquith: An Autobiography. Volumes III. and IV., although dealing with British war politics, are chiefly personal in interest.

Memories of Later Years, by OSCAR BROWNING. By a much-travelled Englishman, a friend of Queen Mary, Lord Curzon and Lloyd George, now past eighty. He deals principally with persons and events since 1897. Arthur Bartlett Maurice, reviewing the book in the New York Herald, speaks of the book as "a narrative which gives the flavor of Europe of yesterday, of a world that is gone." The volume is a mine of anecdotes of the great.

Post Mortem, by C. MACLAURIN, M.D., somewhat resembles Dr. Joseph Collins's *The Doctor Looks at Literature*—only in this case historical figures are the persons dissected. Henry VIII., the historian Gibbon, Joan of Arc, and Samuel Pepys are some of the subjects.

A Nineteenth Century Romance, by MAJOR C. H. DUDLEY WARD. A love story in two generations based on authentic letters and beginning in the days of Napoleon the Great with the love letters of Dora Best to George Brett and continuing with the love affair of their son who, in 1897, became Viscount Esher.

Lady Rose Weigall, by RACHEL WEIGALL. Lady

Rose was the favourite niece of the great Duke of Wellington. Her long life (1834-1921) brought her in contact with Meyerbeer, Mendelssohn, Rubenstein, Jenny Lind, Bismarck, Browning, Disraeli, Lord Palmerston, Dickens, the Empress Eugenie and many royalties. Not the least interesting things are her letters exchanged with Germany during the World War.

"Indiscretions" of Lady Susan, by LADY SUSAN TOWNLEY. Entertaining and well-edged gossip by the wife of a diplomat who was stationed in many countries.

The Literary Spotlight, with an introduction by JOHN FARRAR. Personal portraits of contemporary American writers, first published in The Bookman, and anonymous to permit greater candour. Louis Untermeyer, Mary Johnston, F. Scott Fitzgerald, Floyd Dell, Sinclair Lewis, Owen Johnson, Edna Ferber, Amy Lowell and others are included.

Unusual Biographies and Autobiographies.

Thomas Nelson Page: A Memoir of a Virginia Gentleman, by ROSWELL PAGE.

All in a Lifetime, by HENRY MORGENTHAU.

My Life and Work, by HENRY FORD in collaboration with SAMUEL CROWTHER.

My Boyhood, by JOHN BURROUGHS.

Lord Northcliffe: a Memoir, by MAX PEMBERTON.

Fourteen Years a Sailor, by JOHN KENLON. The Chief of the New York Fire Department in a naïve and pleasing account of his Irish boyhood.

The Life of an American Sailor: Admiral William Hemsley Emory, from his letters and memoirs edited by ADMIRAL ALBERT GLEAVES.

Mr. Lloyd George, by E. T. RAYMOND.

The Americanization of Edward Bok, by EDWARD W. BOK. One of the most widely read of American autobiographies and still in strong demand.

A Man From Maine, by EDWARD W. BOK. A biography of Cyrus H. K. Curtis, head of the Curtis Publishing Company of Philadelphia.

From McKinley to Harding: Personal Recollections of Our Presidents, by H. H. KOHLSAAT. The political interest is strong.

The Print of My Remembrance, by AUGUSTUS THOMAS. For all who are interested in the theatre and its people.

WALTER DAMROSCH'S *My Musical Life* begins with a childhood in Germany and aside from its autobiographical interest constitutes to some extent a history of orchestral music in America.

My Memories of Eighty Years, by CHAUNCEY M. DEPEW. About evenly personal and political in interest.

Letters of James Gibbons Huneker, edited by JOSEPHINE HUNEKER, and MR. HUNEKER'S *Steeplejack* (autobiographical). The record of one of our most brilliant critics, versatile in all the arts.

John H. Patterson: The Pioneer in Industrial Welfare, by SAMUEL CROWTHER. Of a similar interest with HENRY FORD'S *My Life and Work*.

The Editorials of Henry Watterson, edited by ARTHUR KROCK. They complete his own account of himself in "*Marse Henry.*" The political interest is naturally the main thing and is exceedingly vivid (1868-1921).

The Life of Lord Rosebery, by E. T. RAYMOND. Analytical biography.

C. K. S., An Autobiography, by CLEMENT K. SHORTER. The author is a veteran English critic and writer.

The Life of William Schwenk Gilbert, by SIDNEY DARK. Gilbert of Gilbert and Sullivan, "The Mikado," "H. M. S. Pinafore," etc.

FRANK SWINNERTON'S *George Gissing: A Critical Study*, and his *Robert Louis Stevenson: A Critical Study*. The interest is literary rather than biographical.

Tennyson: A Modern Portrait, by HUGH I'ANSON FAUSSET. Both literary and biographical in its interest. Richard Le Gallienne, in the New York Times, says: "The manner of this portrait is very attractive. Biography and criticism are artfully and suggestively blended, and the influence of Tennyson's environment throughout his life on the development of his character and his poetry is vividly and for the most part convincingly illuminated."

The Life of William Hazlitt, by P. P. HOWE. The only biography we have of a remarkable literary figure.

Victor Hugo: His Work and Love, by ANDREW C. P. HAGGARD. A new account. The romantic element in Hugo's life is emphasised. although not unduly.

Embassies I Have Known, by WALBURGA, LADY

PAGET. The English, German and Austrian Courts in the last half-century.

Two Books About English Seats.

Knole and the Sackvilles, by V. SACKVILLE-WEST. See Chapter 6.

Earlham, by PERCY LUBBOCK.

9. Alice in Authorland and Penrod's Five-Foot Shelf

Alice in Authorland.

STUFF and nonsense!" said Alice, to the White Queen, flinging the book on the floor.

"Exactly," the White Queen replied.

"Haven't you anything a self-respecting person can read?" Alice inquired.

"A self-respecting person," answered the White Queen, "would not ask such a silly question. She would accompany me into Authorland and make the acquaintance of the people there and learn to find her way about. Instead," added the White Queen, cuttingly, "instead of bothering me. I am very busy."

"Well, if you're very busy, you won't want to take me with you and introduce me to all those people," Alice observed, a trifle sulkily.

"Of course I will!" The White Queen spoke with annoyance but also with cheerfulness, for she prided herself on seldom being one-sided. "I am never too busy to loiter. And let me tell you that when *you* become too busy to loiter you will find everyone else too lazy to live with—and then what will you do?"

Alice admitted she didn't know. The White Queen was in a great hurry because, as she said, once in Authorland it would only be possible to make haste slowly. They looked up the timetable and found any number of editions just leaving. As they were entering a compartment the guard came along, crying: "Here! You can't go in there! That's reserved for fairies"—but a very pleasant-looking woman who was already seated inside stuck out her head and said: "Oh, do let the little girl come in. Besides, she's with the White Queen, who may ride anywhere." So the guard let them in, with a good deal of grumbling, slammed the door and blew his whistle and they were off. The pleasant-faced woman smiled at Alice, and Alice took courage to ask:

"Are you a fairy, then?"

"No, my dear, but I write about them. It's more fun than being one, really. My name is Rose Fyleman and I live part of the time in London and part of it in Fairy Hills—that's the nice residence section of Authorland, you know."

"What are your books, please?" Alice asked, primly.

"Oh, there's *Rose Fyleman's Fairy Book*, and *The Fairy Flute*, and *The Fairy Green* and *Fairies and Chimneys*—all poems—and *The Rainbow Cat*, whom I knew very well and admired no end. He used to walk about the Child's Garden of Verse—that's the little village green with flower-beds in Fairy Hills."

Rose Fyleman lent Alice some of her books to read on the train. The White Queen slept in a corner, but finally sprang up, crying: "We're here, we're here!"

"But the train isn't stopping," protested Alice. Rose Fyleman and the White Queen laughed. "Silly," said the White Queen, "it isn't a train, it's an edition, and editions never stop in Authorland. You just jump off anywhere." And with that she jumped. So did Rose Fyleman, pausing to say: "You won't mind it. Landing in a heap of books is such fun." Alice finally summoned her courage and jumped, too. A man six feet tall and over caught her nicely and set her down right side up. Then he very politely introduced himself. He was Frederick Arnold Kummer, he said, and it was his business to catch girls and boys and set them down right side up. "With care," he added.

Alice thanked him and took the two books he handed her, *The First Days of Man* and another called *The First Days of Knowledge*. "You won't need these here," he explained, "but you'll find them very useful and probably interesting and maybe exciting when you go back."

There was no trace of the White Queen, so Alice went down the road, picking her way among the books planted everywhere, until a white-haired and smiling old lady sent out her boy, Nils, to show her the way about. Nils said the white-haired woman was Selma Lagerlöf, and she had written for him two sets of wonderful adventures. He had been a rather bad boy and Selma Lagerlöf had turned him into an elf and later had sent him through animal land. "I'll give you the books," said Nils, picking out a couple that stood between two book ends at corners of the road. "Here they are—*The Wonderful Adventures of Nils* and *The Further Adventures of Nils*."

Alice thought she should like to go back and talk with Selma Lagerlöf, whose smile had seemed mysterious and wonderful, but Nils was bent on showing her the animals. Of these there were quantities, and Nils knew them all, it appeared, and their owners.

"That there's Brer Rabbit," he was beginning, when Alice interrupted to say, "You can't say 'that there.' " "Yes, I can," he retorted, "I've just said it." Alice saw he was hopeless, like all boys, and paid no further attention to his grammar, while Nils discussed the creatures, both wild and tame, all about. Some grazed peacefully, some were frisking and playing, and a few gyred and gimbled in the wabe like the silthy toves Alice had heard her friend, Mr. Lewis Carroll, tell about. Brer Rabbit didn't in the least resemble the White Rabbit, being brown in colour and having no vest pocket with a watch and chain. Uncle Remus and Uncle Remus's friend, Joel Chandler Harris, kept tabs on Brer Rabbit. Forrestine C. Hooker was feeding lumps of sugar to the Comanche pony named Star that she has written about in *Star: The Story of an Indian Pony*, and Prince Jan, the St. Bernard of her other book, stood gravely by her. Ernest Thompson Seton, looking more wild than his wildest animals, was racing about, trying to keep track of his grey squirrel, Bannertail, of Krag and Randy and Johnny Bear and Chink, of Lobo, Rag and Vixen, and especially of the Sandhill Stag. "It's the hardest work," he assured Alice, stopping for a moment to subdue his hair and wipe his forehead, "to observe all their habits. I simply couldn't ever do it if I didn't have wide margins in my books and make a little drawing whenever I noted a new habit. Bad habits in the lefthand margins, good habits in the righthand margins." "But," said Alice, wonderingly, "the drawings all look alike to me." "You might as well say all animals look alike to you," said Mr. Seton, impatiently. "But they don't know good and bad, though; all they know is habits. Now, if children only had habits they would be as interesting as animals." "I'm sure I don't know," answered Alice, doubtfully.

Nils had disappeared and the White Queen was nowhere in sight, either. "It's a strange place," thought Alice. "It is, indeed," said a man who was busy painting magnificent pictures in most glowing colours. "It's strange because no one ever stays long enough to bore you." "Oh, is that it?" Alice answered. But she was really much impressed. She looked at the gorgeous paintings, each signed "N. C. Wyeth" and each outdoing the one before. She thought with secret ecstasy: "I'm only going to have books with his pictures in them." Mr. Wyeth, who seemed to understand her thought, said out loud: "You'll find others—Kay Nielsen and Arthur Rackham and Edmund Dulac and Noel Pocock." Alice said, "Yes, no doubt," but in her own mind she decided it must be because he was as modest as he was wonderful.

"Do you like boys' stories?" asked a boy much older than Nils, who had come up suddenly. "Of course!" Alice responded. She looked at him more closely. "Why you must be the boy in *High Benton*, aren't you?" He grinned. "I guess I am. I was only going to say, if you like boys' stories—and all the girls I know do—my friend, William Heyliger, has written a new one, *The Spirit of the Leader*. It's stuff like *High Benton*, a high school story. Great!" Alice was about to ask him for the book when all the editions began running past so rapidly that she became dizzy and screamed and shut her eyes. When she opened them a moment later, Authorland had vanished and she was back at her starting place and the White Queen was asking with sharpness:

"Have you been all this time deciding on something to read? You have to read, you know, in order to grow up; and at this rate you'll never grow up at all!"

Penrod's Five-Foot Shelf.

Feeling the need of solitude, Penrod Schofield moved slowly toward the barn. As he walked he kicked desultorily at such objects, animate and inanimate, as obtruded themselves in his path—the round top of the water cutoff in the lawn, on which he had broken the blades of the lawn mower last Saturday; a bag of clothes pins reposing harmlessly on its side, and the white cat, Sherlock Holmes. "Ole cat!" Sherlock, untarnished by the hostile toe, trotted off complacently. Creatures like Penrod were little in the life of one who had been victor over the hound of the neighbouring Baskervilles.

Choosing Entrance Two, the youth ascended to Apartment B-3 of the barn, a second-story location offering an outside window with no bath but with proper seclusion. Here on a conscientiously measured shelf of his own manufacture was the beginning of the Penrod Schofield Library. The shelf, constructed in his leisure hours, was exactly five feet in length, a noted educator having assured Penrod and others, through the medium of many full-page advertisements, that the books on a five-foot shelf could furnish the equivalent of a college education. With a passion for exactitude, and in pursuance of a further condition, Penrod was devoting to the books on his five-foot shelf a requisite fifteen minutes a day.

"Five feet divided by fifteen minutes a day makes —makes——." The youth struggled for a while with this intricate problem in arithmetic, at length muttering: "I know. Y' count the pages, and then divide by fifteen; no, by the number of pages y' c'n read in fifteen minutes;—no, that ain't right either, is it?" There was no answer; there would be none if he looked in the back of one of the books, either; and for a while Penrod had a doubt whether, on looking in the back of the noted educator's head, any answer would be found there. He did not understand how the educator could possibly be right, nohow, for of course the first and indispensable item for any book shelf was the complete works of G. A. Henty. He ran his eye along these:

Bravest of the Brave; or, With Peterborough in Spain

By Sheer Pluck: A Tale of the Ashanti War

With Clive in India; or, The Beginnings of an Empire

Few, but still a beginning. A catalogue recently procured assured him that there were at least thirty-five more that he should possess. Allowing an inch per volume, which he had found necessary, fully three feet of the five must be reserved for the author of *By Pike and Dyke: A Tale of the Rise of the Dutch Republic* and other classical studies in the historical field. Still, the two feet remaining gave probable space for a coupla dozen lesser masterpieces. He examined the volumes already in place:

Treasure Island, by ROBERT LOUIS STEVENSON

It had sixteen full-page pictures in colour, lining papers and a coloured title page by Wyeth, and was quite satisfactory.

The Boy Scouts' Year Book: 1923

Penrod had belonged to a troop which had busted up and there was no use joining another as he expected to begin smoking shortly, anyway. However, this book was useful, containing stories and talks on sports and tales of true adventure and Dan Beard's camping stuff and "Boys Who Have Made Good" and a bunch of funny stories and—best of all—all about radio

For the Good of the Team, by RALPH HENRY BARBOUR

This was a brand-new, regular hot story about Stuart Harven captaining the football team at Manning School and his roommate, Neal Orr, and other fellows. Penrod regarded it as a slick story and nobody was going to borrow it from him for a darn good long while because it was brand-new and a hot story.

Lochinvar Luck, by ALBERT PAYSON TERHUNE

One of those he-men, you said it, this Albert Payson Terhune and two-fisted and all, and writes the grandest dog stories a fellow ever gets hold of, no Black Beauty here-nice-doggie story but a corkin' story about how Jamie Mackellar, a plucky little truck driver, mortgages his truck to own a fine th'rough-bred collie and the kennel owner who is a crook stings him bad; but the measly pup runs away and lives wild and grows a wonderful bone and coat; and then Jamie captures him back and takes him to the show and what Jamie and the dog do to that crook kennel owner is some cautionary warning to all crooks.

Fourteen Years a Sailor, by JOHN KENLON

This here's a good sea story, especially when they get shipwrecked on the desolate Crozet Islands and make a wonderful escape, hard to believe but it musta been so, because Kenlon he comes to New York later and sees a fire panic in a theatre and that turns him to be a fireman. Now he's Chief of the New York City Fire Department, can you beat it?

What wouldn't I give to ride to a four-alarm fire with him, going like mad!

Kim, by RUDYARD KIPLING

Things in this story of *Kim* I don't just get hold of, but it's a great story all right and I've read it twice and I bet I read it some more. Got to get the *Jungle Books* and *Captains Courageous* to put alongside it. Certainly Kipling's the real thing, most especially on India.

The Boy's Book of Inventions, by RAY STANNARD BAKER

Well, of course. A fellow 'd have to have that, and the on'y thing was to get hold of the other, *The Boy's Second Book of Inventions* it was called, to go with it. Couldn't have too many books like that which besides being useful, and the kind you c'n always get your folks to give you for presents, was interesting, like most of the books they give hardly ever are.

Penrod reflected. No use to worry. He had room for 'most twenty more books, anyway, allowing for Henty; and when he had read some of these enough he could give one away now and then. Or maybe start a circulating library, a cent a week, which would leave room on the shelves and bring in money for new books. . . . From the distance came a voice: "Penrod!" His mother was calling, and as it unquestionably was a call to supper, perhaps he had better respond. He moved away. "Gosh, my fifteen minutes was gone an' I never read anything. Takes fifteen darn minutes a day deciding what to read. Maybe she's got strawberry shortcake I c'd eat five feet of that no trouble at all!"

Books for Alices and Penrods.

It has become the fashion to try to classify books for boys and girls by ages, but as children's mental ages, tastes, interests and other details vary not less widely than adults', it is much more discreet to arrange the "juveniles," so-called, by general characters. Books not explicitly named above are included in the following very limited and rather carefully chosen groups:

All About Animals.

MARGERY WILLIAMS'S *The Velveteen Rabbit*, with colour pictures by William Nicholson. Unusual pictures drawn on stone by the artist

MARSHALL SAUNDERS'S *Bonnie Prince Fetlar* and her *The Wandering Dog*

ALBERT PAYSON TERHUNE'S *Buff: A Collie* and his *Further Adventures of Lad*

WILLIAM T. HORNADAY'S *The Minds and Manners of Wild Animals*

ERNEST THOMPSON SETON'S *Bannertail: The Story of a Grey Squirrel*, his *Wild Animals I Have Known*, his *Lives of the Hunted*—all illustrated by the author.

JOEL CHANDLER HARRIS'S *Uncle Remus: His Songs and Sayings*, with 112 illustrations by A. B.

Frost. Mostly about animals. It is important to have Mr. Frost's pictures

RUDYARD KIPLING'S *The Jungle Book* and *The Second Jungle Book* have been mentioned; likewise FORRESTINE HOOKER'S *Star* and her *Prince Jan: St. Bernard*. *The Elephant's Child, the Sing-Song of Old Man Kangaroo*, and *How the Alphabet Was Made* are Kipling selections now published as separate small books

For quite little boys and girls there are the MAY BYRON books: *The Little Black Bear, The Little Brown Rooster, The Little Yellow Duckling*, and *The Little Tan Terrier;* and also books by JOHN BRECK, as follows:

Mostly About Nibble the Bunny
Nibble Rabbit Makes More Friends
The Sins of Silvertip the Fox
Tad Coon's Tricks
The Wavy Tailed Warrior
Tad Coon's Great Adventure
The Bad Little Owls
The Jay Bird Who Went Tame

Introducing Fairies.

All the books named above by ROSE FYLEMAN, including *The Rainbow Cat*

Fairy Tales by the BROTHERS GRIMM, illustrated by Noel Pocock

The Twelve Dancing Princesses and Other Tales for Children, retold by SIR ARTHUR QUILLER-COUCH and illustrated by Kay Nielsen

The Fairy Ring Series: Andersen's Fairy Tales

illustrated by Dugald Stewart Walker—*Thumbelisa and Other Stories*, *The Mermaid and Other Stories*, and *The Garden of Paradise and Other Stories*

KATE DOUGLAS WIGGIN'S and NORA A. SMITH'S *The Fairy Ring, with Children's Bookplate*, and their *Magic Casements: A Second Fairy Book*

The Most Wonderful Pictures.

The series of classics illustrated in colour by N. C. Wyeth includes:

The Scottish Chiefs, by JANE PORTER, edited by KATE DOUGLAS WIGGIN and NORA A. SMITH

Westward Ho! by CHARLES KINGSLEY

The Last of the Mohicans, by J. FENIMORE COOPER

The Boy's King Arthur, by SIDNEY LANIER

The Black Arrow, by ROBERT LOUIS STEVENSON

Kidnapped, by ROBERT LOUIS STEVENSON

Treasure Island, by ROBERT LOUIS STEVENSON

The Mysterious Island, by JULES VERNE

Poems of American Patriotism, chosen by BRANDER MATTHEWS

Among the books illustrated by Howard Pyle are:

The Merry Adventures of Robin Hood, of Great Renown in Nottinghamshire

The Story of King Arthur and His Knights

The Story of the Champions of the Round Table

The Story of Sir Launcelot and His Companions

The Story of the Grail and the Passing of Arthur

The two books illustrated by Kay Nielsen are:

The Twelve Dancing Princesses and Other Tales for Children retold by SIR ARTHUR QUILLER-COUCH

East of the Sun and West of the Moon: Old Tales from the North

Here are two books illustrated by Maxfield Parrish:

The Arabian Nights, edited by KATE DOUGLAS WIGGIN and NORA A. SMITH

Poems of Childhood, by EUGENE FIELD

Some other books with especially fine illustrations in colour are:

A Child's Garden of Verses, by ROBERT LOUIS STEVENSON, illustrated by Jessie Willcox Smith

The Wind in the Willows, by KENNETH GRAHAME, illustrated by Nancy Barnhart

LOUIS DODGE's *The Sandman's Forest* and his *The Sandman's Mountain*, both illustrated by Paul Bransom

MARY MAPES DODGE's *Hans Brinker, or, The Silver Skates*, illustrated by George Wharton Edwards

FRANCES HODGSON BURNETT's *Little Lord Fauntleroy*, with illustrations by Reginald B. Birch

MAUDE RADFORD WARREN's and EVE DAVENPORT's *Tales Told by the Gander* and their *Adventures in the Old Woman's Shoe*, both illustrated by C. A. Federer

The History of Don Quixote de la Mancha, edited by J. B. TREND and illustrated by Jean de Bosschere

Robinson Crusoe, by DANIEL DEFOE, illustrated by Noel Pocock

Stories from Hans Andersen, illustrated by Edmund Dulac

Stories from the Arabian Nights, retold by LAURENCE HOUSMAN, with pictures by Edmund Dulac

The Sleeping Beauty and Other Fairy Tales from the Old French, retold by SIR ARTHUR QUILLER-COUCH, illustrated by Edmund Dulac

HAWTHORNE'S *A Wonder Book*, illustrated by Arthur Rackham

ÆSOP'S *Fables*, illustrated by Arthur Rackham

A Fairy Book, illustrated by Arthur Rackham

The Outdoor Life.

WARREN H. MILLER'S *Camping Out*, his *The Boy's Book of Hunting and Fishing*, and his *Canoeing, Sailing and Motorboating*

The Boy Scouts' Year Book for 1923 or earlier years, as each annual contains outdoor information of permanent interest

The Boy Scouts' Book of Campfire Stories, and the *Boy Scouts' Book of Stories*, both edited by FRANKLIN K. MATHIEWS

EDWARD CAVE'S *Boy Scout's Hike Book* and his *The Boy's Camp Book*

ERNEST THOMPSON SETON'S *The Book of Woodcraft*, his *Sign Talk*, his *Woodcraft Manual for Boys*, and his *Woodcraft Manual for Girls*

JEANNETTE MARKS'S *Vacation Camping for Girls*

DAN BEARD'S *Shelters, Shacks and Shanties*, his *Boat-Building and Boating: A Handy Book for Beginners*, his *The Field and Forest Handy Book*, his *The Jack of All Trades*, his *The Outdoor Handy Book*, and his *The American Boy's Handy Book*

LINA and ADELIA B. BEARD's *Recreations for Girls* and their *The American Girl's Handy Book*

Fiction.

JOSEPH A. ALTSHELER's stories. Altsheler wrote seven romances (*The Last Rebel*, etc.), eight books in The Young Trailers Series, beginning with *The Young Trailers;* three books in The Texan Series (*The Texas Star*, etc.) and three miscellaneous Indian stories (*The Last of the Chiefs*, *The Quest of the Four* and *Apache Gold*) as well as two of The Great West Series, *The Great Sioux Trail* and *The Lost Hunters.* He wrote three stories dealing with the World War, but his French and Indian War Series (six books beginning with *The Hunters of the Hills*) and his Civil War Series (eight books, beginning with *The Guns of Bull Run*) are old favourites

RALPH HENRY BARBOUR. School stories. Besides fifteen not in any series and the Yardley Hall stories (eight, beginning with *Forward Pass*) five series of three books each—Hilton, Erskine, the "Big Four," Purple Pennant and Grafton

WILLIAM HEYLIGER. The author of *High Benton* and *High Benton, Worker.* There are three books in the Fairview Series, five in the St. Mary's Series, six in the Lansing Series, besides the extremely popular books about Don Strong in the Boy Scout Series—*Don Strong of the Wolf Patrol*, *Don Strong, Patrol Leader*, and *Don Strong, American*

FRANK T. BULLEN's *The Cruise of the Cachalot*, a classic for boys

RALPH D. PAINE'S *A Cadet of the Black Star Line*, his *The Fugitive Freshman*, his *The Head Coach*, his *College Years*, his *Campus Days*, his *Sandy Sawyer, Sophomore*, his *The Stroke Oar*, and his *Sons of Eli*

LAWRENCE PERRY'S *For the Game's Sake*, his *The Big Game*, and his *The Fullback* (Fair Play Series)

DAN BEARD'S *The Black Wolf Pack*

FRANK B. LINDERMAN'S *Lige Mounts: Free Trapper*

FRANCIS LYNDE'S *The Golden Spider*

LEO E. MILLER'S *Adrift on the Amazon*, his *In the Tiger's Lair*, his *The Hidden People* and his *The Black Phantom*

ARTHUR STANWOOD PIER'S *The Boys of Saint Timothy's*

JULES VERNE'S *Around the World in Eighty Days*, his *A Journey to the Centre of the Earth*, his *From the Earth to the Moon*, and his *Twenty Thousand Leagues Under the Sea*

RICHARD HARDING DAVIS'S *The Boy Scout and Other Stories for Boys*

JESSE LYNCH WILLIAMS'S *The Adventures of a Freshman*, his *Princeton Stories*, and his *The Day Dreamer* ("The Stolen Story," a newspaper classic)

FRANCIS ROLT-WHEELER'S Young Journalists Round the World Series—*Plotting in Pirate Seas*, *Hunting Hidden Treasure in the Andes*, *Heroes of the Ruins*, *A Toreador of Spain*, *The Magic-Makers of Morocco*

STEWART EDWARD WHITE'S *The Adventures of Bobby Orde*

RUSSELL DOUBLEDAY'S *Cattle Ranch to College*, and his *A Gunner Aboard the "Yankee"*

O. HENRY'S *The Ransom of Red Chief and Other O. Henry Stories for Boys*

RALPH STOCK'S *The Cruise of the Dream Ship*. The hobo seafaring adventures of a boy. A fine book, not nearly well enough known

LEWIS E. THEISS'S *A Champion of the Foothills*

CAROLINE DALE SNEDEKER'S *The Perilous Seat*. The story of a young Greek girl who saved her country

JOSLYN GRAY'S *Elsie Marley*, her *Rosemary Greenaway*, and her newest tale, *The Old Mary Metcalf Place*. Other Joslyn Gray stories are *Bouncing Bet*, *The January Girl*, *Rusty Miller*, and *Kathleen's Probation*

MARGARET W. EGGLESTON'S *Fireside Stories for Girls in Their Teens*

E. F. BENSON'S *David Blaize* and his *David Blaize and the Blue Door*

ISLA MAY MULLINS'S *Captain Pluck* (founded on fact)

MARION AMES TAGGART'S *The Annes*, her *Captain Sylvia*, her *The Daughters of the Little Grey House* (*The Little Grey House* should be read first) and her "*Who Is Sylvia?*" (a sequel to *Captain Sylvia*)

Mainly Historical.

FRANCIS ROLT-WHEELER'S Romance-History of America Series—*In the Days Before Columbus*, *The Quest of the Western World*, and *The Coming of the Peoples*, each illustrated by C. A. Federer

NOAH BROOKS's *First Across the Continent.* The story of the Lewis and Clark expedition

CYRUS TOWNSEND BRADY's *In the Wasp's Nest* (War of 1812) and *On the Old Kearsage* (Civil War)

SIDNEY DARK's *The Child's Book of England* and his *The Child's Book of France*

BASIL MATHEWS's *The Quest of Liberty: The Adventures of the "Mayflower" Pilgrims*

H. E. MARSHALL's *This Country of Ours: The Story of the United States*

EVERETT T. TOMLINSON's *Young People's History of the American Revolution*, his *Places Young Americans Want to Know*, his *Fighters Young Americans Want to Know*, his *The Story of General Pershing*, his *Scouting on the Border*, his *Mysterious Rifleman*

Young Heroes of Our Navy, a series comprising ROSSITER JOHNSON's *The Hero of Manila*, J. BARNES's *Commodore Bainbridge*, his *With the Flag in the Channel*, his *Midshipman Farragut*, and his *The Hero of Erie* (Commodore Perry); and MOLLY ELLIOTT SEAWELL's *Decatur and Somers*, her *Paul Jones*, and her *Little Jarvis, the Heroic Midshipman*

Theodore Roosevelt's Letters to His Children, edited by JOSEPH BUCKLIN BISHOP

RICHARD HARDING DAVIS's *Real Soldiers of Fortune* and his *With Both Armies in South Africa*

A. HYATT VERRILL's *The Real Story of the Pirate*, and his *The Real Story of the Whaler*

STEWART EDWARD WHITE's *Daniel Boone: Wilderness Scout*

BERNARD MARSHALL's *The Torch Bearers*, a new novel of the time of Oliver Cromwell

RUSSELL DOUBLEDAY's *Stories of Inventors*

Inventions, Games, Plays, and the Fascinations of Science.

A. FREDERICK COLLINS's *The Book of the Microscope*, his *The Book of Wireless Telegraph and Telephone*, his *The Book of Stars*, *The Book of Magic*, *The Book of Electricity*, *The Home Handy Book*, *How to Fly*, *The Amateur Mechanic*

FRANK M. RICH's *The Jolly Tinker.* How to make all sorts of things out of the simplest materials, how to mend shoes, repair books, make a cardboard loom, etc.

RAY STANNARD BAKER's *The Boy's Book of Inventions* and his *The Boy's Second Book of Inventions* have already been mentioned

GILBERT T. PEARSON's *The Bird Study Book*

FRANK M. CHAPMAN's *Bird Life*, his *Our Winter Birds*, his *What Bird Is That?* and his *Handbook of Birds of Eastern North America*

Birds Worth Knowing, by NELTJE BLANCHAN; *Butterflies Worth Knowing*, by CLARENCE M. WEED; *Flowers Worth Knowing* (NELTJE BLANCHAN adapted by ASA DON DICKINSON); and *Trees Worth Knowing*, by JULIA ELLEN ROGERS

Game books by EDNA GEISTER—*It Is To Laugh*, her *Let's Play*, and her *Fun Book*

The Magic Sea Shell and Other Plays for Children, by JOHN FARRAR

THREE BOOKS FOR PARENTS

Three to Make Ready, by LOUISE AYRES GARNETT. Plays

Ten Minutes by the Clock, by ALICE C. D. RILEY. Plays

S. LYLE CUMMINS's *Plays for Children*

Three Books for Parents.

FLORENCE V. BARRY'S *A Century of Children's Books*

ANNIE CARROLL MOORE'S *New Roads to Childhood*, and her *Roads to Childhood: Views and Reviews of Children's Books*. By the supervisor of work with children in the New York Public Library

10. The Man Called Ralph Connor

i

ONCE upon a time there was a Scotsman of Clan Gordon, those Highlanders ye ken of Blair Athol in the North Country, properly named with a God-fearing name, Daniel, and a fine, stirring preacher, too. Fire was on his lips but the flame burning in his heart was tender and you should have lived to hear him piping "Lochaber No More." The pibrochs sounded something beautiful as he played; and when he stopped piping it was to begin relating wonderful old stories; he kenned them all. Away back in the 1840s it was he came out to Canada with other folk from the North of Scotland and fetched up in a Highland settlement in Ontario, Glengarry, in the Indian Lands. Full twenty years this man of God spent in Glengarry, taking a wife from among the Robertsons. Her father had come to New England first, moving on to Sherbrooke in the Province of Quebec. I could tell you a deal about her family; there was a cousin, Andrew Murray, of Clairvaux, led the Dutch Reformed South African Church; ye'll have heard of Robertson Smith and he was another cousin; the writer M. M. Robertson was a sister. Mary Robertson taught philosophy as a lass of twenty in Mount Holyoke College in New England. They offered to make her principal on the death of Mary Lyons and she was duly considering for a while. She was of the Robertsons of Aberdeen, ye ken, and twenty-two years aged. But there was this young Highlander, Daniel Gordon of Glengarry in the Indian Lands, who was swaying congregations. Well, then, she turned her small, straight back on the principalship and married him, and went away from that pleasant place and company and fine position that stood waiting for her to live in the backwoods of Canada, a rare wild parish with the railway twenty-five miles off and a long journey to everywhere. She was a remarkable woman. Daniel Gordon took her to his home in the woods. In the year 1860 she bore him a son; they named the boy Charles. The laddie played about the square brick house with wide verandas that stood in a natural park of pines and maples, with a glebe of some twenty-four acres and forest all about. Two miles by a path through the woods took him to school in a clearing, and two miles back. They played games in the shadows of the pines. There was a rich green darkness and a curious coolness and a curious warmth there for them; the tops of the pines murmured like distant bagpipes and everything smelt sharp and sweet.

On a day when the boy was eleven Daniel Gordon went to sway another congregation in Western Ontario, taking his wife and the boy along, for that there were better schools for Charley to go to. What with this, and high school in a neighbouring town, the lad makes ready for Toronto and the University.

He didna do badly at the University, though he was no sober-sided student. He sang in the glee club and played quarterback at Rugby football in the champion team for Western Ontario. Some honours in classics he got and went on to the study of theology at Knox College. He was not too strong in those years and capturing scholarships and prizes in the three years' courses at Knox College did him no good bodily. So then it was settled he should take a year abroad, spent mostly in Edinburgh, where he could walk along gay Princes Street and see the grand sight of Castle Rock, or climb to Arthur's Seat and look over the Firth of Forth with its speckle of green islands and white sails and the bare country of the Kingdom of Fife, or pace slowly down the Royal Mile to Holyrood, with every step a threefold memory and an historic lesson. I'll not say this did him any harm, maybe, and what it lacked in one way he made up on his return to Canada, taking his brother and travelling deep into the forest on Lake Nipissing, they seeing no other white man for three months. To crown these journeyings and to confirm the habit of health Charles Gordon spent two more years at Banff. There, in the heart of the Rockies, he climbed mountains and rejoiced in wildness. "Yes, I ought to have been an Indian!" he used to exclaim.

ii

He was ripe to receive his call at last, and it came. It took him to a life of rough hardship as a missioner in the North-West, all among lumbermen and miners with a congregation to be gathered first, and sore deeficult to sway in assembly. He came well-shod to the work of treading out the harvest in the Lord's vineyard. He could go into the woods and come out again, or face a man mad with drink, or comfort a sick mother. A tall, slender, well set up young missioner with no very much ruddiness of complexion and a thoughtful, serious face that could yet smile, for a' that, with crinkles in the eye corners. You would know him for Scots by his look, but the rest is puir American. And he loved those men among whom his work lay. When, along in 1894 and him just well into his thirties, he was asked to a city church, he didna want to respond favourably until he saw where his duty lay. Well, then, he came to Winnipeg and to the ministry of St. Stephen's because it offered him the grand chance to help those roughened men whose needs he knew. Ye ken, perhaps, Mr. J. A. MacDonald of the Toronto Globe newspaper. MacDonald had been a classmate of Charley Gordon's and a year or two after Charley Gordon came as preacher to St. Stephen's, MacDonald was owner of a new little paper called The Westminster and concerned with Canadian Presbyterianism—a frank experiment. Into the office of The Westminster dropped Charley Gordon one fine day. He was in a great heat for money to put into the foothills and the mountain camps. They needed missions out there; I'm burning up with the wish to write an article telling about those men in the pines and along the upland lakes, Charley Gordon tells MacDonald. I've facts and figures. MacDonald was quick to say, if Charley wanted to bring home his message to people and loosen the purse-strings, he had a duty to write the thing as a tale, paint a picture with lifelike figures and a warm feeling running through it all. Gordon minded himself of what he had seen and heard in such good plenty; and he went home and sat down to write a story of Christmas Eve among the lumbermen in the Selkirk mountains. When he was fair into it, he found himself carried back and away, so much so that in reading it through after he didna see what brother clergymen might make out of the ringing speech of some of his characters. MacDonald agreed, but sent to find out what name to put on the story. Gordon invented a name, Cannor, out of the first letters of "Canada" and "North-West." MacDonald picked up the reply telegram and snorted disdain. Cannor, he commented, what sort of a name is that! I'll make it Connor. And where's a first name? Frank? Fred? Chris? No. Ralph? Aye, we'll make it that. This was the birth and christening together, ye'll ken. The tale of the lumbermen's Christmas Eve in the mountains was later to become the first chapter of the novel, *Black Rock*, the first novel by Ralph Connor, that was read everywhere.

iii

I'll not have to be telling you what it was in *Black Rock* won so many readers for Ralph Connor. Humour and pathos are bound up in the lives the young minister of St. Stephen's was writing about; ye could lay hold quickly of his sympathy for those men who were in some ways as helpless as bairns and were half-brutalised by their work and surroundings. It's the effect they have on each other, too. Them picking up *Black Rock* to read were struck with something fresh and wild and clean, withal. They sensed a tenderness about the feeling of the story, like heather softening the bare hillside, and more than a morsel of the everlasting hope in which men endure hard and lonely toils. The same held true of the books that followed *Black Rock;* for there had to be other books. Ye mind *The Sky Pilot* and *The Man From Glengarry* and *The Foreigner* and *Corporal Cameron* and *The Patrol of the Sun Dance Trail*. Take *The Foreigner*. On the edge of Winnipeg, Charles Gordon found a Settlement of Slavs—Ruthenians, Russians, Galicians and who not. They lived in a grim little collection of huts, a dozen in a room, all huddled up, drinking and dirty and violent; and on them was still the shadow of tyrannies in the Old Country. Drinking and dirty and violent with a violence dark and beautiful, Charles Gordon found them. Aye, he found the huts and the men, and Ralph Connor that was in him found a story. Ralph Connor took the splendid young heart in Kalmar, the son of a nihilist, and brought it to fight its way out of the ruck of aliens and make for the new country beyond the Saskatchewan, where there is prairie and where the lakes lie on the surface of the prairie like jewels on a woman's breasts. Then, in *Corporal Cameron*, was Connoring the first grand tale of the North-West Mounted Police, by a man who kenned them, as followers in his tracks scarce can be said to. A richt fine love story is this of the lad who was born in a Scottish glen and came to ride out in the Canadian blizzards; it's furthered in *The Patrol of the Sun Dance Trail*, which makes use of the half-breed and Indian rebellion of Louis Riel. But there's a muckle I love in the book besides the adventure—Cameron and his gold-haired, plucky wife and the hesitant wonder of the first fine feeling of the lover. It fashes me how a man says what's down in the hearts of such a many other men and women. Give me to understand how it's done! Here's the Reverend Charles Gordon dwelling this quarter century and longer in Winnipeg, building up St. Stephen's and seeing it transformed from a plain chapel of wood into a handsome church of stone, with a church house where the young men without homes can live, and where there's sewing and amateur acting and films and bowling every night of the week. In the daytime the Reverend Gordon will maybe attend court to help get some boy straightened out and become a guardian to him; or he'll be at meetings in his church where revolutionary agitators are spouting the downfall of all institutions and then voting thanks to the preacher because, as they put it, he has given us an absolutely square deal. And after supper you would find him in his home at evening prayers with the three youngsters who appeared to enjoy their devotions. There's no stiltedness in the man at all. He reads from Scripture concerning Paul taking Timothy with him to learn what were the problems of that day. And he closes the book on his finger to remark what a sensible, canny thing for

Paul to do. Some of our theological seminaries, adds the father, shut a man out from contact with life, shut him up with professors, and when he comes out of his cloister he canna recognise a social problem if it walks up to him on the street. The trouble with me, he finishes, when I had gotten out of the seminary.

But he's generous to a fault sore in a son of Scots folk. If his right hand is earning moneys with a pen, his left hand is spending lavish and free. There's his salary as minister to the kirk goes flowing out several times over in gifts and helpings to people. I mind the year quite long back when the Presbyterian General Assembly of Canada was meeting in Toronto and Doctor the Reverend Gordon put down $10,000 so every missionary minister and his wife in the breadth of Canada might attend the General Assembly, expenses paid. Some of these men and their wives hadn't been out of the woods in years. Ralph Connor knew what this meant.

iv

Then, when the Great War came thundering, our sky pilot stood up and said Canada must send a half million men. Many scoffed at him; but he was right, and we sent the half million and over sixty thousand didna come back. From St. Stephen's there was an enlistment of close on four hundred, including the minister and five members of the Session. The dominie went in the spring of 1915 after the congregation had confirmed his leave of absence—Major Charles W. Gordon, chaplain to the Forty-third Battalion Cameron Highlanders of Canada. Many St. Stephen's men were enrolled in this battalion and one of the members of the Session, Robert McDonald Thomson, was their first colonel. It was the Western Front—from the Ypres Salient, Sanctuary Wood, the bloodshed of the Somme and back again to Arras. In that time Ralph Connor saw the regiment shrunk from full strength to two officers and sixty-five men. He knelt down amid the roar of guns and the hailing of machine gun bullets to do last rites for his own men and comrades. Among them was Colonel Thomson. On the eighth day of October, 1916, the outfit stormed the Regina Trench on the Somme. Unable to advance, they wouldna retreat. So they died where they stood.

V

The Major and *The Sky Pilot in No Man's Land* are books ye'll verra well recollect; likewise the novel of twa years back, *To Him That Hath.* Since ye hanna read it, it's the new novel from the pen of Ralph Connor, I'll just speak a word of to ye. He calls it *The Gaspards of Pine Croft* and explains it is "a romance of the Windermere Valley." A story of the life and moulding of Paul Gaspard, it is. Here's a mon with two powerful strains mixed and fighting for mastery of him. From his mither, Paul inherits a rare sense of the presence of God; his father gifted him with a fine artist sense, and a bounding spirit, a passion for life to the full. The clash of the two men in the boy grows with him to manhood, so that after the death of his mither he stands between two women, who beckon different ways. Then when a great decision is put before him the mon takes upon himself a burden and a responsibility that test him body and soul. 'Tis a life and death struggle set in the grand country Ralph Connor makes his own. There's the valley of the Windermere before you with the Gaspard ranch, Pine Croft, flanked on one side by a great bend of the Columbia River and on the other by a mountain wall of virgin forest. In this mysterious wilderness, the figures of Indians do come and go, touching the lives of the white people with disaster, with dread—with an unco beauty as well.

Books by Ralph Connor

Beyond the Marshes
1898 *Black Rock*
1899 *The Sky Pilot*
Ould Michael
1901 *The Man from Glengarry*
1902 *Glengarry School Days*
Breaking the Record
1904 *The Prospector*
The Pilot of Swan Creek
Gwen
1906 *The Doctor of Crow's Nest*
The Life of Dr. James Robertson
1909 *The Foreigner; A Tale of Saskatchewan*
The Angel and the Star
The Dawn by Galilee
The Recall of Love

1912 *Corporal Cameron of the North-West Mounted Police: A Tale of the MacLeod Trail*
1914 *The Patrol of the Sun Dance Trail*
1917 *The Major*
1919 *The Sky Pilot in No Man's Land*
1921 *To Him That Hath*
1923 *The Gaspards of Pine Croft*

Sources on Ralph Connor

Ralph Connor, the Well-Beloved. Booklet published in 1914 by George H. Doran Company. Now out of print.

Silver Jubilee, 1895-1920, of St. Stephen's, Winnipeg. Booklet published by the congregation of St. Stephen's Presbyterian Church, Winnipeg, Manitoba.

11. Here, There and Everywhere

i

IN his new book, *The Humanizing of Knowledge*, the author of that fascinating study, *The Mind in the Making*, James Harvey Robinson, says: "Personally I have reached the conclusion, after many years of teaching, that one should choose for instruction, whether one be dealing with young or old, *some phase of human interest rather than some field of scientific investigation*"—and he goes on with force and plainness to point out the defect of an educational scheme in which knowledge is imparted by going in and out of great numbers of pigeonholes. He is really pleading for methods of instruction that shall take account of the ordinary man's interest in his world, and shall proceed by the natural process of mental associations instead of by artificial and arbitrary tetherings to the post of this and that "subject." Seldom has the difficulty been put with more brevity, simplicity and general sweetness of temper, or in a way to give such decent courage to individual self-respect. "We are not many of us interested in isolated scientific facts of any kind. That species of interest, as we have seen, is reserved for the few. But all of us are open to the effects of such new knowledge as gets under our skins. And the great art is not to exhibit our own insight and learning but really to influence those whom we are aiming to influence." There could be no better text or opening for a chapter devoted to books of many varieties, inasmuch as books have always taken, except where restricted by school formulas, the lines of human interests and the path of some natural association of ideas. In this sense, though teaching may need to be humanised, knowledge has never been without its humanisation. A James Harvey Robinson cannot write about science without being led into the absorbing history of the mind that is slowly achieving science. A Camille Flammarion, discussing astronomy, finds it above all things natural to relate his knowledge with man's religious ideas. An L. P. Jacks, analysing religious doubts, moves directly over the border of so-called psychology into the sphere of conduct and behaviour, because the answer lies over there. A George Santayana employs poetry to state those portions of his philosophy which prose can scarcely embody with sufficient expressiveness; bases criticism on his philosophy and distils or re-distils philosophical ideas from all the varieties of his learning.

To take M. Flammarion, for example. His new work, *Dreams of an Astronomer*, could without any essential inaccuracy be styled "A Humanisation of Astronomy." Here is a book produced in this French scientist's eighty-first year, at an age where "isolated scientific facts" had lost all fanciful meanings and were seen only in their warm and present human significance. The point with M.

Flammarion was not that we live on a poor little world in a vast universe composed of worlds within worlds and flaming suns and revolving planets, nor that this universe so immense is but an item of larger immensities. The point was in the significance of these facts to the heart and mind of a man or a woman. What does it mean as regards our attempt to know God? In what perspective does it place our aspirations and our efforts toward what we sometimes call "righteousness"? Flammarion gives the richness of his physical knowledge in untechnical language; in words that summon the imagination he constructs pen pictures of other worlds than ours. That we may have the value of comparison, he describes Venus and Mars—the latter possibly inhabited by creatures millions of years ahead of us in their development. This moving and inspiring book ends with a sentence that might serve as the quiet challenge of science to much of philosophy and religion. Says M. Flammarion: "Let us not be personal, like infants or the aged, who see only their own room, let us know how to live in the infinite and in the eternal."

But this lofty idea needs translation into the terms of our finite existence and our character of religious beliefs. It finds it in such a book as L. P. Jacks's *Religious Perplexities*. Like *The Humanizing of Knowledge*, this is a slender book that can be read through in about an hour and it is equally a book that is likely to influence a lifetime. It is beside my point that Professor Jacks is one of the greatest living philosophers and religionists; but it is a fact of the highest relevance that he writes as no one writing on these subjects has written since William James. The same power to pierce to fundamental questions—and answer them; the same lucidity of thought and expression are characteristic of the two men. Jacks exhibits the same tolerance of the forms of religious belief; and it is only after a discussion of "Religious Perplexities in General" that he closes with a talk about "Perplexity in the Christian Religion." He says: "Far be it from me to set up an exclusive claim for Christianity. Anyone who does that goes a long way towards forfeiting his title to be called a Christian. Let each of us look for truth where it is most accessible and where it speaks the language he best understands." He begins with the two ultimate questions that man asks himself: "Why are we here?" followed by, "Why am I—I, and not John Jones or James Smith—here and now?" The answer to the first is the need of the One to differentiate itself into the Many, proving its universality and its power to integrate and raise up the good. But, he shows, the answer to the second question is in the conduct of the individual. Insofar as I by my courage in the face of life justify my particular existence, I supply the reason why myself, rather than Jones or Smith, exists in my place, here and now. Faith is not a new faculty added to us, it is simply our reason grown courageous. As Carlyle repeated, we all must answer the alternative: "Wilt thou be a hero or a coward?" Professor Jacks adds: "No philosophy can relieve us from the responsibility of having to make that choice"—and religion, telling us our choice must be the heroic one, strengthens us in making it.

It is religion, I think, that George Santayana represents—Santayana who contrasts for me with that rooted countryman of his, Miguel de Unamuno. I have a love for both, the one tenacious of his soil and its traditions, the other early detached, flung into the New England of Harvard and William James, now lodged in Paris, and always with his roots feeding orchid-like on the air. It is inevitable that one like Santayana should bear his blossom in poetry and criticism and his fruit in philosophy-religion, or religious philosophy. Thus he calls his *Scepticism and Animal Faith*, "an introduction to a system of philosophy," but it is so only in the literal sense probably necessary to secure the proper recognition from a too unimaginative world. The book, which has a charm unbecoming a philosophical overture, can be read independently of the volumes that are to follow it; but who reads it may be trusted to put independence on one side and "follow, follow." Santayana as poet is possibly matter to consider in a later chapter of our book, but since, as he says in the preface to his *Poems*, their subject "is simply my philosophy in the making," we should be privileged to a passing consideration here. "I see no reason why a philosopher should be puzzled. What he sees he sees; of the rest he is ignorant; and his sense of this vast ignorance (which is his natural and inevitable condition) is a chief part of his knowledge and of his emotion. Philosophy is not an optional theme that may occupy him on occasion. It is his only possible life, his daily response to everything"—call it religion, if you please, and regard its expression:

O world, thou choosest not the better part!
It is not wisdom to be only wise,
And on the inward vision close the eyes,
But it is wisdom to believe the heart.
Columbus found a world, and had no chart,
Save one that faith deciphered in the skies;
To trust the soul's invisible surmise
Was all his science and his only art.
Our knowledge is a torch of smoky pine
That lights the pathway but one step ahead
Across a void of mystery and dread.
Bid, then, the tender light of faith to shine
By which alone the mortal heart is led
Unto the thinking of the thought divine.

And to all who care for fine intellectualism neither arid of inspiration nor robbed of beauty and emotion I commend Santayana in all his books, those named and, of course, *The Life of Reason*, *Winds of Doctrine*, *The Sense of Beauty*, and *Character and Opinion in the United States* and the *Soliloquies* as well. For those unacquainted with the man, *Little Essays Drawn from the Works of George Santayana*, by Logan Pearsall Smith, may offer the readiest approach.

ii

The task to which James Harvey Robinson calls us has already been undertaken with the highest success by himself and some others. Among these has from the first been Edwin E. Slosson who now, with Otis W. Caldwell, the botanist and educator of Columbia University, has edited an admirable volume, *Science Remaking the World.* This book is so good and represents so intelligent a collaboration, that I hope it is only the forerunner of a number of similar volumes. In the dual editorship, Dr. Caldwell's contribution was his working familiarity with every field of modern science while Dr. Slosson lent his magic touch of the born populariser. The fifteen chapters, eleven of which are contributed by specialists in various fields, deal directly along the average person's lines of interest with such subjects as gasoline power, coal tar products, the modern idea of the atom, what we know of "infantile paralysis," our present knowledge of tuberculosis, the lengthening of human life, the world's health, botanical science, evolution, warfare against insects, forestation, the chemistry and economy of food, and those two basic foods, bread and the potato. Dr. Caldwell writes the general opening chapter and the chapter on lengthening human life with its special reference to Louis Pasteur's work; as was desirable in view of the great popular success of his *Creative Chemistry,* Dr. Slosson contributes the discussions of gasoline power and of the miracles wrought from coal tar.

Our quest shuttles back and forth between the discoveries of man and man the discoverer. At every stage we have to consider not only what man has gained in the way of knowledge but his potentialities in respect of all knowledge. That is why we have such a succession of books as Madison Grant's *The Passing of the Great Race*, those books by Lothrop Stoddard which are brought to attention in Chapter 22 of this volume, and, now, Roland B. Dixon's *The Racial History of Man.* The professor of anthropology at Harvard treats impressively and from a broad point of view the whole question of race. His account of race distribution and historical development is divided geographically. Beginning with Europe and a general outline of its racial history, he then takes up the separate countries or areas. In the same way he deals with Africa, Asia, Oceania, North and South America. His interesting conclusions, in some respects original and without the dogmatism that vitiates much writing on the subject, are given in a final chapter. But the best part is that this book is simply the first in a group of probably ten volumes, each to be written by a leading American authority, which is to describe, in the light of the latest investigation and discovery, the formation of worlds, the evolution of species, and the emergence and development of man.

Such books are desperately needed, to resume James Harvey Robinson's argument, if science is to save itself. Such is the present situation that "if no precautions are taken to bridge the gap between scientific knowledge and popular prejudice it may grow so wide that the researcher himself may be engulfed." It would not be the first time in human history when light was swallowed up in darkness. How dense that darkness can be, how persistent, how ironical and, perhaps, pathetic may be learned from the slightest perusal of Dr. James J. Walsh's astonishing and engrossing new book, called *Cures*. This is a history of new remedies of every sort in all ages which have cured for a while and then have failed. It will scarcely surprise us, although it may make us rather uncomfortable, to know that not Europe with its ancient and superstitious peoples but modern America has supplied the greatest number of cure delusions. Dr. Walsh puts the explanation on a charitable ground: "Americans are more enterprising and as a result we have had ever so many more successful discoveries of new"—but less permanently successful —"remedies." The subject is not without its humorous aspects. Insofar as Dr. Walsh has occasion to treat of some forms of curing which are still much adhered to, with or without correlated religious beliefs, his book treads on live and resentful toes. As a Catholic avoiding the discussion of Lourdes and other shrines, he invites reprisals; as a physician of very distinguished service and high standing, he is well-qualified to counter them. But aside from any possible controversy, what an amazing history of human credulity and ignorance he exposes—Dowie, rattlesnake oil, magnetic iron, metallic tractors, sympathetic powders, hypnotism, mesmerism, electric belts, plasters, pads, chest protectors, psychoanalysis and spiritualistic healing along with the various forms of "New Thought" come under review. It will be observed that as a rule Dr. Walsh gives credit for cures to even the most impossible notion or contraption—at first. A cure is a cure, perhaps only the more so if the actual curative agent is suggestion.

Suggestion! Is it possible that, on a subject so

bedevilled, a book could now appear of genuine usefulness, sanity and popular value? Personally I should have inclined to answer emphatically, "No!" But I cannot, for the book is before me. Dr. Louis E. Bisch, a physician practising in New York, lecturing on psychology at Columbia and directing the treatments given in mental and nervous cases at the large sanitarium in the North Carolina mountains, has been known to me hitherto by his *Your Inner Self*—without exception the best popular account of psychoanalysis and modern psychology I have ever seen. Now he has written *The Conquest of Self*, in which he expresses with the same directness and accuracy all that body of actual truth which the "How to Succeed" books build into such amazing forms of lies and nonsense. There is, of course, a certain power of accomplishment in each of us; there is a general direction for each of us to take; there are personal obstacles to overcome, and there is a power of progression to be developed. A better comprehension of one's self, as of others, can definitely be arrived at. All these facts Dr. Bisch translates into practical detail and illustrates with concrete instances, avoiding the claptrap with which the whole subject is now so heavily overloaded. In that general enterprise of the humanisation of knowledge to which (I hope) we are all fully committed, such a book as *The Conquest of Self* has a special merit; for where ignorance is thickest, it lights a clear and modest path, and where pseudo-science has done and is doing the greatest havoc, it puts truth in armour for the hardest part of a difficult journey.

iii

If, as some contend, the purpose of fiction is entertainment—an assertion we need not either attempt to refute nor deny—then the mark of good fiction is that, while perhaps entertaining us, it does something else. And about the "something else" I should think we need not be narrow in definitions. Maybe the entertaining novel we are reading adds its unobtrusive item to our understanding of this or that; maybe it tunes up our emotional natures. Or it may accomplish its bye-purpose in other directions. We may or may not be conscious of the additional result, or, if conscious of it, we may continue (perhaps wisely) to read for the sole purpose of being entertained. I do not believe one should read fiction with the something else in mind, nor, in a brief account of some new novels, would I attempt to suggest what the something else—differing, it is likely, with the individual reader—may turn out to be. If one asks me for bread, I will not offer him a loaf of vitamins, but palatable bread from which his body may take the elements it pleases.

For examples, you may derive from John Buchan's *Midwinter* your clearest idea of Dr. Samuel Johnson, or your greatest knowledge about the affections of a young lady; your own mind will satisfy its proper need. From Compton Mackenzie's *The Altar Steps* and its sequel, *Parson's Progress*, certain temperaments gain religious and ecclesiastical satisfactions. The modern, intimate taste for sensory impulses can be gratified in reading

John Dos Passos's unusual novel, *Streets of Night;* just as the correlative instinct for a fresh and daring idealism is fed by such a fine first novel as Cyril Hume's *The Wife of the Centaur.* Arnold Bennett's *Riceyman Steps*, with its story of a young charwoman who works for a miserly bookseller and his wife, renews the heart in its assurance of our common humanity, and offers the rich nourishment which rejoiced us in *The Old Wives' Tale.* And so it goes with fiction.

We think of Brand Whitlock now as the author of *Belgium*, but a further thought recalls him, and with pleasure, as a writer of fiction. His new novel, *J. Hardin & Son*, was planned ten years and more ago and discussed with the late William Dean Howells, whose interest in it was keen. The actual writing had begun in the summer of 1914 at a small country place near Brussels when the catastrophe of war began its pre-emption upon all of the American Minister's time and energy. Except for intervals of thinking about it and occasional notes, Mr. Whitlock could do nothing but protect the manuscript on journeyings to and fro—until the end of 1918, when, after the armistice, he resumed writing as opportunity offered. The book was progressing in earnest at Biarritz and Spa in 1922, and was completed in New York in the spring of 1923. Mr. Howells's interest will be understood when it is explained that *J. Hardin & Son* takes place in a little Ohio town. The story begins when Paul Hardin, the son, is ten and accompanies him to middle age—perhaps one should say to that point in or at the beginning of middle age where, as with

Sinclair Lewis's Babbitt, a man's character takes its final determining shape in some act or decision which controls the rest of his life. For Paul Hardin this moment comes when he recognises one of the buggies made forty years before by his father, takes hold of one of the spokes and finds it as solid, as resistant as on the day it was made. Paul had hardly liked his father, whose sternly-held and sternly-expressed views and whose passion for moral reform in the shape of prohibition seemed like a life-long and perverse obstinacy, embittering all the preludes to affection, sympathy or even understanding. Yet now! Something comes out of that spoke, something out of his father's life that settles his behaviour toward the two women who are for him to deal with in regard to himself. Mr. Whitlock has aimed, however, at the reconstruction of a period in American life. His momentous personal problem in the life of Paul Hardin is simply the foreground for a study of American ideas in a certain kind of community in the years within his own recollection, say from 1880 on pretty well into our century. Over a hundred characters, many of them of more than passing importance, are involved in the extremely varied but entirely naturalistic incidents of the novel.

J. Hardin & Son, the work of an American at fifty, makes a contrast with the work of a Norwegian of fifty, the age at which Jonas Lie wrote his *The Family at Gilje*. The Norwegian novelist, whose story is just offered in a careful translation, uses a much simpler scheme. His tale opens with a picture of a home in the mountains of Norway where a father and mother are anxious to get their children married off. It ends when each child has solved his or her problem. If environment conquers in one child, individuality is sure to come out on top in another. Jonas Lie's book, I am told, makes Norwegians feel that they are living again the scenes of early life; and at the same time the novel is full of the most modern ideas about marriage, the home and the management of children, introduced not by main strength and the hazard of fictional illusion but subtly, by an artist who shared Ibsen's supply of "social dynamite" but whose artistry was paramount. Lie is called a realist, as, I suppose, Bojer and most of the Scandinavians would be (except Jens Jacobsen in *Marie Grubbe*); but what is the white magic in these writers of the white snow-countries that makes their realism so unfailingly poetic? Is it indigenous? Cannot we acquire it here in America? Shall we exile our artists to Canada, whence now comes little but the worn-out stories of strong men and their uniform primitiveness with women?

I do not know the answers to these questions, nor do you; but I do know that certain writers are *simpatico* in certain provinces of society—Frank Swinnerton, for example, in the stratum whence he drew his *Nocturne* and his *Coquette* and in the somewhat different middle-class level on which we meet the characters of his new story, *Young Felix*. Here is a satisfactory representative English novel in the mode called realism to contrast with our American and our Norwegian. I say "contrast"—for I don't think comparisons will get us very far.

What we are better employed in doing, in my opinion, is a species of addition rather than subtraction; we shall find a difference in the attitude as well as the art of Brand Whitlock, Jonas Lie, and Frank Swinnerton. Is not each worth our while? I think so. I think such a novel as Jay William Hudson's *Nowhere Else in the World* is worth the while of most readers, who may, however, be a bit puzzled at first to discover how different it is from his *Abbé Pierre.* Mr. Hudson may possibly have written the Great Chicago Novel as Carl Sandburg is sometimes thought to have written the great Chicago hymn or chant. At least, his *Nowhere Else in the World* is in its essence apocalyptic. Stephen Kent, who had been enchanted by Paris after a youthful rebellion against Chicago and its blatant commercialism, lives to look upon the city of his birth as "like Rodin's 'Thinker,' primitive, powerful, with mighty sinews," as "the spiritual capital of America," as a place where he and others will join in "moulding, not paintings and statues, but a civilisation destined to be the summit of all art, of all dreams." There is incidentally in this tense story a competent picture of American academic life which will cause squirmings. Mr. Hudson's knowledge of American colleges is derived at first hand.

Much first hand knowledge, I happen to know, has gone into the writing of George Looms's second novel, *John-No-Brawn.* The action of this rather terrible but certainly impressive piece of fiction takes place in Louisville, Kentucky, the author's home town, and in and near Denver, Colorado. The book is one of an intensity that has already occasioned extremely divergent opinions. The story is that of a sick man, an indeterminate character trapped by the horrible and inescapable fact of disease. He comes to the conclusion that he is a hopeless drag on his young wife. Against the warnings, protests and threats of doctor and nurse, he walks out of the hospital. "They watched him near the stairway, saw him reel slightly and then reach out his hand and take hold of the banister—saw him steady himself. He paused for a moment . . . and then he passed around the partition corner, out of sight." Such an ending is exalting or deadly in its depressiveness, as you please; just as the story itself is a thing of magnificence or of utter drabness. Like the powerful war novel by Thomas Boyd, *Through the Wheat*, a violent reaction in one direction or another is to be expected of the reader. It is probably an advantage in Mr. Boyd's novel over Dos Passos's *Three Soldiers* that *Through the Wheat* is almost entirely a story of fighting in the front line. All agree that this was war, at least, and something is gained at the outset by the setting aside of various prejudices and preconceptions. *Through the Wheat*, far more than *Three Soldiers*, contrasts with high effectiveness with Henri Barbusse's *Under Fire*. Again may I plead that if the two novels, the French and the American, are to be entered in a fight by rounds, there can and should be no decision. *Through the Wheat* is a wonderful thing to have been plucked in Belleau Wood, at Soissons and Saint Mihiel by a boy not yet twenty.

While Mr. Whitlock is going back of our day

for his Middle Western picture, Meredith Nicholson, slightly his senior, has been busy with the immediacy not only of the present day but the very hour. Mr. Nicholson's new novel, *The Hope of Happiness*, like its predecessor, *Broken Barriers*, reckons with a social life in which, if they have not been entirely swept aside, American standards of conduct have been very much altered. The young woman who drinks too hopelessly much is put before us, but the essential story is one of a situation between father and unacknowledged son with the probable complications of men's business and women's love. There is an ability of characterisation and a temper and evenness in the writing which make the reader feel that Mr. Nicholson writes for a much ampler purpose than would be served by a novel of changing manners and enlarged social license. These are mere appurtenances of the story he has to tell.

Not to have a story to tell is to forfeit the best claim to consideration at the hands of most readers of fiction; and among those Americans who have never made the forfeiture I would have no hesitation in naming Irvin S. Cobb. The award of the O. Henry Memorial Prize for 1922 to the title story in Cobb's *Snake Doctor and Other Stories* seems to me more or less of an irrelevance; Cobb has written so many capital stories and the award, if it had then existed, might so easily have gone to him years ago. The tales collected in *Snake Doctor and Other Stories* exhibit, perhaps, a greater variety than some of the earlier collections, and there is a Judge Priest story without which, I am certain, a majority of Cobb's readers would consider the book incomplete. "Snake Doctor" itself has been criticised as being altogether mechanical. My suggestion to those who advance that criticism would be conveyed in the form of a question, or two questions: Did they get no thrill from reading the story? And if they did, was that thrill a purely mechanical effect? For the point is not whether the thing producing an effect is a mechanism, but the nature of the effect itself. Nothing is more mechanical than the theatre, but a good play is not made the less art thereby. Actors, you may say, or acting; but a scene has been "made" or destroyed more than once by that utterly mechanical detail, the stage setting. . . . If as has sometimes been predicted, a machine will be invented to produce upon us all the effects of good fiction, we shall none of us quarrel with the inventor nor will anyone try to destroy the device unless it be our fictioners. In the meantime, I advise no one to neglect them, lest the day of the obvious and unconcealed machine never arrive.

iv

To blaze a trail for the reader through the rich forest of books educational, philosophical, scientific, and withal "popular" is no easy task. I have not attempted to do more than put down the titles of some new and recent "general" books, with the authors, and sometimes a note upon the volume. But should these not be classified? Dear reader, if you will give me the classification of the things you are interested in, I will classify the books. . . .

Christ or Mars? by WILL IRWIN. A passionate but documented indictment. Mr. Irwin says we do not want peace hard enough; the mood of man must be changed before peace can come about. He believes it can be done. "We are trying to hide in squirrel-holes from God. And the church, which purports to interpret to our world His intentions, is hiding too."

NICHOLAS MURRAY BUTLER'S *Building the American Nation* is a series of lectures on Samuel Adams, Benjamin Franklin, Washington, Hamilton, Madison, Jefferson, John Marshall, Webster, Jackson and Lincoln.

The Ideals of Theodore Roosevelt, by EDWARD H. COTTON. The book deals especially with Roosevelt's religious beliefs and his creed as expressed in a life of action. Theodore Roosevelt's sister, Corinne Roosevelt, writes the preface.

The Spirit of Islam, by SYED AMEER ALI. Recognised as the one authoritative work in English for use in Moslem centres of instruction. Of especial interest in connection with Lothrop Stoddard's *The New World of Islam.*

Man and the Attainment of Immortality, by JAMES Y. SIMPSON. After a careful outline of biological evolution, the author interprets Christianity as the most important stage in the evolution which, from being physical, is tending more and more to become a mental and spiritual process.

G. STANLEY HALL'S *Jesus, the Christ, in the Light of Psychology*, an interpretation of what we know of Christ in the light of present-day psychological knowledge, is now procurable in one volume.

A new and useful introduction to the study of philosophy is JOSEPH A. LEIGHTON'S *The Field of Philosophy*.

JAMES HARVEY ROBINSON'S *The Humanizing of Knowledge*, discussed above, is one of the volumes of the Workers' Bookshelf series, books primarily planned for use in American trades union colleges but of varying general interest. Other books in the series are *Joining in Public Discussion*, *The Control of Wages*, *Women in the Labour Movement*, etc. (by various authors).

The Greek View of Life, by G. LOWES DICKINSON, a book of charm and permanence, should possibly rather be assigned to Chapter 15 of this book.

The Making of the Western Mind, by F. MELIAN STAWELL and F. S. MARVIN. A short survey of the leading elements of the European cultural inheritance from the days of classical Greece to our own day.

Suggestion and Mental Analysis, by WILLIAM BROWN. Takes into account Coué and Badouin and psychoanalysis, and culminates in an exposition of Bergson's philosophy.

The Dominant Sex, by MATHILDE and MATHIAS VAERTING, translated by Eden and Cedar Paul. Argues that there are no distinctively "masculine" traits but that the traits so-called have been characteristic of either sex when dominant in a particular society; with evidence to support the theory.

The Mechanism and Physiology of Sex Determination, by RICHARD GOLDSCHMIDT, translated by W. J. Dakin. Remarkable breeding experiments carried out with insects; intersexuality; a subsection deals with man. A book of importance to biologists.

How to Sing, by LUISA TETRAZZINI. Practical advice by the great coloratura singer.

The Art of the Prima Donna, by FREDERICK H. MARTENS. Discussions by Bori, Calve, Easton, Farrar, Galli-Curci, Hempel, Homer, Jeritza, Schumann-Heink and others are the feature of the book.

Public Speaking, by FRANK H. KIRKPATRICK. Those interested in this subject will probably want also ALFRED DWIGHT SHEFFIELD'S *Joining in Public Discussion.*

The Process and Practice of Photo-Engraving, by H. O. GROESBECK, JR. There has hitherto been no handbook and manual.

Construction of the Small House, by H. VANDERVOORT WALSH. For the architect and the layman alike.

As an example of the finest type of book in one of many special fields, there may be mentioned ARTHUR T. BOLTON'S *The Architecture of Robert and James Adam*, in two volumes with about 700 illustrations, folio size, $60.00.

The Book of Building and Interior Decorating, edited by REGINALD T. TOWNSEND. Practical advice from experts.

Interior Decoration, by FRANK ALVAH PARSONS. A standard work.

The Psychology of Dress: Life Expressed in Clothes, by FRANK ALVAH PARSONS, is a history of costume made still more interesting by illustrations.

The Amateur's Book of the Garden Series, edited by LEONARD BARRON, offers:

The Vegetable Garden, by ADOLPH KRUHM
Planning Your Garden, by W. S. ROGERS
Lawns, by LEONARD BARRON
House Plants, by PARKER T. BARNES
The Flower Garden, by IDA D. BENNETT

For the owner of the greenhouse there is *Gardening Under Glass*, by F. F. ROCKWELL; SYDNEY MITCHELL's *Gardening in California* is a guide for the amateur on the Pacific slope; and *Adventures in My Garden and Rock Garden*, by LOUISE BEEBE WILDER (author of *My Garden* and *Colour in My Garden*) is the descriptive history of a piece of land hardly more than an acre in size.

The Plain Sailing Cook Book, by SUSANNA SHANKLIN BROWNE. Simple recipes for beginners.

A Handbook of Cookery for a Small House, by JESSIE CONRAD. With a preface by her husband, Joseph Conrad. This was the meat on which our Cæsar fed and grew so great.

A Pocket Bridge Book, by WALTER CAMP. For those who must have their daily dummy.

Modern Auction, 1923, by GRACE G. MONTGOMERY. The new edition of a standard work.

Singles and Doubles, by W. T. TILDEN, 2D., world's tennis champion, 1920, 1921.

The Gist of Golf, by HARRY VARDON. Vardon writes most readably and gives a chapter to each club. Pictures.

Field Soccer and Hockey for Women, by HELEN FROST and HAZEL J. CUBBERLEY. Pictures and diagrams.

Ski-ing Turns, by VIVIAN CAULFIELD. With card diagrams that can be removed from the book.

How to Box, by NORMAN CLARK. With 61 photographs.

Training for Power and Leadership, by GRENVILLE KLEISER.

The Making of an Executive, by A. HAMILTON CHURCH. Personal qualifications and the special knowledge required.

Creative Selling, by CHARLES HENRY MACKINTOSH. Making and keeping customers.

The Law of Sales, by JAMES BURTON READ. The law relating to the transfer of personal property for considerations.

Advertising for the Retailer, by LLOYD DALLAS HERROLD. Complete information on every type of advertising used by the retailer. Illustrations of layouts, window decorations, show cards, letters, etc.

The Leadership of Advertised Brands, by GEORGE BURTON HOTCHKISS and RICHARD B. FRANKEN. Successful advertising and marketing methods.

EDWARD H. SCHULZE's *Making Letters Pay* covers business letters from the viewpoint of "better results, in less time, at lower cost"; while CARL A. NAETHER's *The Business Letter* offers thoroughgoing practice in making good business letters a habit. SALLIE B. TANNAHILL's *Ps and Qs: A Book on the Art of Letter Arrangement* is concerned with personal letters.

Funds and Their Uses, by FREDERICK A. CLEVELAND. Now available in a revised edition. Methods, instruments and institutions of modern financial transactions. The revision adds chapters on the United States Treasury, commercial banks, the Federal Reserve system, trust companies, investment bankers and agricultural credit institutions.

Cotton and the Cotton Market, by W. HUSTACE HUBBARD. Production, marketing, the future contract system, the speculative factor; a pretty complete survey.

Reminiscences of a Stock Operator, by EDWIN LEFEVRE. The chief appeal of this book is the appeal of fiction, although it is obviously founded on the facts of one or more Wall Street careers. Much market wisdom.

Co-operative Marketing, by HERMAN STEEN.

Historic Textile Fabrics, by RICHARD GLAZIER. More than 200 varieties are illustrated.

The Business of Writing, by ROBERT CORTES HOLLIDAY and ALEXANDER VAN RENSSELAER. A trustworthy book on marketing the writer's product.

Writing to Sell, by EDWIN WILDMAN. What will be marketable and why, from short pieces for household periodicals to special feature articles for monthly magazines.

The Community Newspaper, by EMERSON P. HARRIS and FLORENCE HARRIS HOOKE. Developing the newspaper to the community's benefit and the owners' profit.

Readers interested in the subject of JAMES HARVEY ROBINSON'S *The Humanizing of Knowledge* will be interested in ABRAHAM FLEXNER'S new book, *A Modern College and a Modern School.*

Modern Industrialism, by FRANK L. MCVEY, presents in very full outline and from the examples of many countries present-day industrial organisation.

Trade Unionism in the United States, by ROBERT F. HOXIE. A revised edition is ready.

Everybody's Business, by FLOYD PARSONS. A readable survey of America's natural resources and the story of the development of our major industries.

The Great Game of Politics, by FRANK R. KENT.

Too Much Government—Too Much Taxation, by CHARLES NORMAN FAY.

NOTE: The list of every publishing house has its special characteristics and the reader of books will naturally associate certain types of books with certain imprints; it is desirable that he should, aiding the bookseller, when possible, in the quest for publications of a special sort. I have tried to name below, as a general guide supplementing the fragmentary list above, the chief types of publications of the four houses associated in the production of this book:

D. Appleton & Company, whose long history has given them the honour of publishing important works by Charles Darwin, Haeckel, Froebel, Thomas Huxley, John Stuart Mill, Max Nordau, G. Stanley Hall, Muensterberg, Flammarion, Florence Nightingale and L. Emmett Holt, publish many scientific, business, educational, technical and industrial books, military and naval textbooks; books on the Spanish language and many translations into Spanish from English, including fiction; medical books; fiction by Zona Gale, Joseph C. Lincoln, Harold Bell Wright, Edith Wharton, Brand Whitlock, etc., and general literature.

George H. Doran Company publish many books of historical importance, memoirs, biographies, etc.;

contemporary politics; travel; sport; belles lettres; a very large list of religious books; spiritualistic books by Sir Arthur Conan Doyle and others; poetry; plays; and a remarkable fiction list including Walpole, Mary Roberts Rinehart, W. Somerset Maugham, Arnold Bennett, etc.

Doubleday, Page & Company are noted as the publishers of many garden and nature books; of important biographies and historical works; travel; poetry; belles lettres; general literature and fiction by Joseph Conrad, Booth Tarkington, Gene Stratton-Porter, Edna Ferber, Kathleen Norris, etc. They publish the works of Rudyard Kipling (except the Outward Bound Edition: Scribner).

Charles Scribner's Sons publish works on architecture; historical and biographical books and memoirs; letters; belles lettres; books dealing with problems of race and society; sociological works; poetry; plays; books on sports; works on art and decoration, philosophy and religion; many books illustrated in colour; and fiction. In a long career the house has had the distinction of publishing the works of J. M. Barrie, Thomas Carlyle, Edmund Gosse, W. E. Henley, Maurice Hewlett, James Huneker, Henrik Ibsen, Henry James, George Meredith, Theodore Roosevelt, George Santayana, Robert Louis Stevenson, etc.

All four houses publish books for boys and girls.

Fiction.

In addition to the fiction already discussed attention may be invited to the following new and recent books (for new fiction by Galsworthy, Conrad, V. Sackville West, Arthur Train, Harold Bell Wright, Ralph Connor, Booth Tarkington, Zona Gale, Gene Stratton-Porter, Joseph C. Lincoln, Edith Wharton, Christopher Morley see respective chapters on these authors; also see Chapters 3, 15, and 18):

Cross-Sections, by JULIAN STREET. Short stories.

Butterfly, by KATHLEEN NORRIS.

Rufus, by GRACE S. RICHMOND.

Miss Bracegirdle and Others, by STACY AUMONIER. Short stories.

The Motherless, by BENGT BERG, translated by Charles Wharton Stork. The story of a motherless boy and a motherless bear cub.

The Shadowy Third, by ELLEN GLASGOW. Short stories.

The Middle Father, by ANTHONY M. RUD. Norwegian settlers in the Middle West.

Conquistador, by KATHARINE FULLERTON GEROULD.

The Orissers, by L. H. MYERS.

Four of a Kind, by J. P. MARQUAND. Four little novels.

The Love Legend, by WOODWARD BOYD.

The Marriage Verdict, by FRANK H. SPEARMAN.

The Really Romantic Age, by L. ALLEN HARKER.

Broken Barriers, by MEREDITH NICHOLSON.

Timber Wolf, by JACKSON GREGORY.

Colin, by E. F. BENSON.

Eris, by ROBERT W. CHAMBERS.

Pandora Lifts the Lid, by CHRISTOPHER MORLEY and DON MARQUIS.

The House of Helen, by CORRA HARRIS.
The Gay Year, by DOROTHY SPEARE.
The Middle of the Road, by SIR PHILIP GIBBS.
La Parcelle 32, by ERNEST PEROCHON.
North of 36, by EMERSON HOUGH.
Fires of Ambition, by GEORGE GIBBS.
Madame Claire, by SUSAN ERTZ.
Corduroy, by RUTH COMFORT MITCHELL.
The Public Square, by WILL LEVINGTON COMFORT.
The Ground Swell, by ALFRED B. STANFORD.
The Song of the Dragon, by JOHN TAINTOR FOOTE. Short stories.

12. Totalling Mr. Tarkington

i

IN the interesting procession of his work, Booth Tarkington has pretty well paralleled the somewhat vacillating development of popular literary taste in his country. This, there is every reason to believe, has resulted from no conscious intention. The fashion, in considering Mr. Tarkington, has usually been to contrast what are called his two natures—the romanticist who wrote *Monsieur Beaucaire* and the realist (more or less) who wrote *The Gentleman From Indiana* and *The Turmoil*. Very sensibly has it been pointed out that the two strains are manifest side by side in a number of his novels, such as *The Conquest of Canaan*, where the realism of character is sadly impaled on the rocks of plot. But, if I may advance the idea with due diffidence, such as Tarkington always shows in any discussion of his work, the much more instructive comparison lies deeper in the man and is the result of an unrelenting pressure of environment on a personality endowed with most exceptional talent and even unmistakable genius. One can say, I think, although with a great deal of hesitation over its unavoidable crudeness, that Mr. Tarkington in some sense repeats what Mr. Van Wyck Brooks conceives to be the tragedy of Mark Twain, only in Tarkington's case it has no air of tragedy. The common view of the author of *Alice Adams* is that he is a lucky fellow who deserves all his luck. Only in a narrow, godlike perspective would he appear tragic. And such a conclusion might easily be premature. When *Monsieur Beaucaire* appeared Mr. Frederic Taber Cooper declared it certain that we knew the extent of the author's capabilities, adding that it was unthinkable that he should ever again essay the realism of *The Gentleman From Indiana.* A couple of years ago plenty of persons qualified to have and to express an opinion asserted that Tarkington would never overcome his propensity toward a pulled-together and "happy" ending in a novel; and in the same year appeared *Alice Adams.* As Mr. Tarkington is only fifty-four, and may easily have a dozen years and a half a dozen prime novels directly in front of him, to be dogmatic is to run a perfectly unreasonable risk of stultification. I shall try to avoid that.

ii

"An unrelenting pressure of environment on a personality endowed with most exceptional talent . . ."

Newton Booth Tarkington was born in Indianapolis, 29 July 1869, the son of John Stevenson Tarkington (died 1922, aged ninety) and Elizabeth (Booth) Tarkington. The father, a Civil War soldier and a lawyer, was for some years in politics; the son was a member of the Indiana Legislature

BOOTH TARKINGTON

in 1902-3. The mother's family is not traceably connected with those Booths celebrated as actors. In his study of *Booth Tarkington* which is and will for a long time remain the chief resource and delight of those considering the novelist, Robert Cortes Holliday points out that the Indianapolis of Booth Tarkington's youth was a town, and that B. T. is neither a city nor a country boy, but a town boy. For a while in his childhood the boy was affected by nervous disorders resembling St. Vitus attacks. At about the age of eleven, he became a friend of James Whitcomb Riley, who was a neighbour. In his teens, Tarkington had the behaviour of a normal boy and a spirit of deviltry showed itself that was to last him until he was thirty. He went to Phillips Exeter, then to Purdue University, and finally to Princeton, where he "made" Ivy, than which, in the way of social success, Princeton offers nothing more beautiful. Much on the sentimental side is made to this day of Tarkington's singing of "Danny Deever" at class gatherings and reunions. After leaving Princeton, Tarkington returned to Indianapolis and pursued the busy social life possible to a young man of the town while at the same time he read a good deal and tried various styles of writing. Mr. Holliday intimates that, like Stevenson, Tarkington "played the sedulous ape" to a succession of literary masters, to find out how the thing was done. The interesting point is that the beginner kept this activity quite strictly to himself. "It was probably a consciousness of the foolish look which his unrewarded activities may have had outside that caused Mr. Tarkington at that time modestly to describe the serious schooling which he gave himself as 'fussin' with literachoor,' " Holliday tells us. The fact that the young man earned only $22.50 gross, or $62.50, or whatever it was, by his first five years of literary effort has since been as widely published as Joseph Hergesheimer's fourteen years without a single acceptance.

The junior Tarkington was under no necessity of earning his living and a notebook kept at that time by his father records the repeated return by publishers of his first novel, *The Gentleman from Indiana*. *Monsieur Beaucaire* was a long time getting accepted. The whimsical *Cherry* was bought by Henry Mills Alden for Harper's Magazine, pigeon-holed as a mistake and then unearthed and printed when *Monsieur Beaucaire* had made Tarkington "valuable." Forty thousand words of an early draft of *The Gentleman from Indiana* had had to be discarded because, having got his hero out for a walk, Tarkington could carry neither him nor the story any further. After an interruption of some length, *The Two Vanrevels* was resumed and wound up only with the greatest difficulty.

Mr. Tarkington was married in 1902 and again in 1912. He lived for a while in France and Italy (Capri). His summer home, at Kennebunkport, Maine, is usually spoken of with some reference to the study, where models of vessels of every rig, a valuable collection, are displayed. This is sometimes spoken of as "the house that *Penrod* built" and the ship models are perhaps natural to a home overlooking a New England harbour. It is also to be recollected that certain of Mr. Tarkington's ancestors hailed from Salem. Perhaps any other significance in those ships is merely fanciful.

No one who meets Booth Tarkington is insensible to the personal charm of the man. He is absolutely without affectation, and the perfect host, the staunch friend, the sympathetic listener and the contained and modest talker. Whatever the vicissitudes he has undergone, whatever the pressures put upon him, he has weathered them all with a steady helm. It seems an astonishing, unwarranted and probably an impudent thing to suggest that this man has been to a deplorable extent the victim of circumstances (largely comfortable circumstances); and that, with a less winning personality —if some outward expression for the thing must be sought—the chances are he would have been a much greater writer than, on his record, he is today.

iii

You see, of course, how handicapped he was from the start by being "a good fellow." The extent of that handicap can only be realised, I think, by knowing that to this day "nothing, apparently, so much gives Mr. Tarkington the horrors as the idea of the 'literary.' He does not want to be 'caught,' he declares, writing 'prose.' " I quote Mr. Holliday, who adds: "Some literary editor in New York told him that some of the passages in *The Turmoil*, in particular (I think) the cemetery scene, were noble English prose, worthy, I suppose, of the author of *Urn Burial*. 'He liked them,' says Mr. Tarkington with a wry face, as though, if he knew just how, he would cut those passages out." But why should Tarkington be horrified by the thought that he may have written "literature"? What black curse lies upon "literature"? The only one I know is the contempt of "good fellows" and other philistines for an affair they know nothing of and self-defensively profess to despise. And if Mr. Tarkington thinks, as perhaps he does, that he spent painful years of reading and practise writing without the secret hope that he would some day write a piece of literature, then, I suspect, he is much mistaken. But what is it, this mental process? Why should he be "very quick to insist" that none of his family have been "offensively" literary? Who is offended by literature? "Good fellows" have been known to be very much annoyed by the presence among them of one whose possession of a taste they did not share seemed to impugn their own completeness. There is more than a suspicion that "Tark" has jekyllhyded others so long as to have concealed something very precious to him from himself. There could be no greater contrast, for example, than between Joseph Hergesheimer and Booth Tarkington (in this matter). Both are persons of some taste and genius who follow the profession of letters. I reveal nothing when I say that Hergesheimer, of whom personally I am fond, is considered by many people to be most conceited. Mr. Hergesheimer would be the first to uphold such a statement. One of the universally-praised traits of Mr. Tarkington is his utter lack of self-conceit. What is the explanation?

Nobody lacks self-conceit, least of all a person

with Tarkington's endowment. It may not be detectable, but any psychologist will tell you it exists. Hergesheimer was just as "conceited" in the days when no editor would take his stuff as he is today; only the quality wasn't visible, there being (practically speaking) no one to observe it. And the quality itself was fully engaged and enterprised in sustaining Joseph Hergesheimer, until such time as a measurable success, some rounds of applause, should sustain him. When that hour has struck in an artist's life, fortunate the artist if he can turn the "self-conceit" (which is really self-sustention) into the direct channel of his work! But to return to Booth Tarkington: The environment of the Indianapolis of the 1880s (a pleasant town), was perhaps not the most favourable for a boy of a specially nervous constitution and that excessive sensitiveness so frequently found in company with a fine imagination. It isn't to be wondered at that he was "precocious" until about the age of four, and "slow" after he began going to school. Phillips Exeter, like all such places, is devoted to finding the highest common social factor in the boy. What Purdue may have been when Tarkington went there, I have no idea; but it cannot possibly have exceeded Princeton as a place where self-disguise was imperative for self-preservation. There are plenty to remember those Princeton days, when students wore paint-stained corduroys and drank constructively, innocently mistaking eccentricities of dress and conduct for the achievement of personality. The real Tarkington underneath was forcing itself up at this time; he was writing for the college magazine such stuff as college magazines are made on. He went back to Indianapolis to continue writing; but the long era of good fellowship had done its work, a certain "self-conceit" and with it a decent open dignity had been put under battened hatches, and the young man was preparing to pay the fairly serious penalty—the penalty of an inability to take himself seriously enough, the penalty of wasted time, vitiated effort, delayed arrival, deferred achievement.

iv

Little wonder, then, that Mr. Tarkington told Mr. Holliday in 1917 that he was writing a book (*The Magnificent Ambersons*) that he didn't think anybody would read; and a year or so later he was talking in the same strain about *Alice Adams*. The last remaining vestiges of an attitude which has crippled him are perceptible in such utterances. He was ready, in 1917, to admit that he couldn't read Stevenson any longer, to confess that the stories of American politics called *In the Arena* were about all of his early work he "could stand to re-read." Popularity and unpopularity, he thought, had always been an accident with him; his idea seemed to be that "anybody can write a popular story"—of course, anybody can't—and, as for himself, he had never "played the goat to entertain anybody." And devices in his books that might have the air of being bids for popular favour were there simply because, when he wrote, he didn't know any better. As for putting them in to please an editor or reader: "Really, I'd as soon have forged a check."

Holliday quotes him further: "I've written things only as I thought they ought to be written. I thought in my youth that life could be got into books with prettier colours and more shaping than the models actually had; and I fell in with a softer, more commonplace and more popular notion of what a *story* should be. Where that acceptance definitely stopped in *me* (though the book may not show it) was *Beauty and the Jacobin.* It was at that time that I was painting with my old ornamental picture framer. Until then, I thought they were the 'cheese,'—not for sales, but the *right* 'cheese.' "

Perfectly honest! If there is anything else, and I think there is, it is hidden from Mr. Tarkington himself, or was. We may look upon the melodrama and sentimentalism of *The Gentleman from Indiana*, or *The Conquest of Canaan* and feel less distaste for them than does Tarkington who, at their mention, looks pitifully unhappy. He is suffering the acute reaction of the years after, whereas it is possible for us to note the simple fact that what now seems conventional and cheap in those novels was much less conventional, and not nearly so cheap, in 1899 and 1905. The fact remains—doesn't it?—of Tarkington having written an essentially realistic novel, his first, when we were all wild about *Richard Carvel* and *Prisoners of Hope* and *When Knighthood Was in Flower*—that sort of thing. Although, to be sure, there was *The Honorable Peter Sterling*, there had been the earlier novels of William Dean Howells, and Theodore Dreiser was putting on paper *Sister Carrie.* Another fact that remains is the co-existence (1905) of *In the Arena* and *The Conquest of Canaan* and the fixed, large achievement, in 1912-13, of the novel called *The Flirt*.

It is easy to agree with Mr. Holliday that the efforts at invention in the story surrounding Cora Madison are "childlike," but I am convinced that *The Flirt* is a novel for which a place must be reserved in any list of twenty distinguished American novels. The portrayals of Cora and her brother, the boy Hedrick, seem to me to settle that. Thackeray's picture of Becky Sharp is, I feel, no more biting than Tarkington's delineation of Cora; Hedrick has as much gusto as any character of Dickens; and in both cases Mr. Tarkington has accomplished the thing with less than half the effort Thackeray and Dickens brought to bear. Of Tarkington, as they would say in golf, it is all in the wrist. The same undemonstrative precision, skill and force which went into the porcelain perfection of *Monsieur Beaucaire*, which fumbled so badly in such a mixture ("the rough") as *The Two Vanrevels*, is felt on every page of *The Flirt* where Cora or Hedrick are "in play." Unfortunately, the inspired suggestion of the present Mrs. Tarkington which was responsible for the existence of Hedrick Madison is also responsible indirectly for the boy Penrod. Those Penrod stories which, Tarkington admits, cost no effort to write! Toward this variety of work several attitudes are possible. The strictest condemns it, and because of it rates down the author. Obviously, such a view is just only where the author has held his writing throughout as a sacred vocation.

The severe, exalted standard of judgment cannot very well be applied to anyone like Arnold Bennett or Booth Tarkington, both of whom, for quite different reasons, have a lively sense of what I would call the amenities of living. A more tolerant attitude holds the author justified for one or several excuses—he may have his living to make, he may have the thing in him and need to get it out of his system, the demand for Penrodism may carry its vox-populi-vox-Dei conviction, there may be nothing else to write. . . . Between the smashing drive and the perfect strokes on the putting green, one is not allowed to intermit the bad brassy or the futile iron shot; one is required to play.

The Flirt appeared in 1913, *Penrod* in 1914, *The Turmoil* in 1915, *Penrod and Sam* in 1916, *Seventeen*, an outgrowth of *Penrod*, in 1916 also; *The Magnificent Ambersons* in 1918, and *Ramsey Milholland*, the last wring-out of Tarkington's Bad Boy in 1919. Even those who declare the creation of Penrod and William Sylvanus Baxter, Jr. (in *Seventeen*) to be "great work"—and they are numerous and their opinion is respectable—will perhaps feel, as they contemplate the prolonged attack of Penroditis, that this adolescent in literature gave his fashioner a distinct setback. They may look with admiration at a photograph of the study in The House That Penrod Built and witness all those ships, and the thought may occur to them that these beautiful toys took too long the place of ampler vessels, which, with rich cargoes, with the help of the stars and in spite of weather, might have been worked home.

V

One such fine vessel, richly-freighted, made port at last, in 1921, the *Alice Adams.* To praise this novel, the first in which Mr. Tarkington made an entirely successful passage, is easy; to discriminate in regard to it is difficult, for the simple reason that Mr. Tarkington's past work has made such a performance incomparable. Here was a man who in his greatest feats had always shown corresponding blemishes. *The Flirt* had been spotted with melodrama (as if the drama of Cora and the mordancy of Hedrick did not serve to tarnish any artificial sheen). *The Turmoil*, more skilfully constructed than *The Flirt*, suffered an entire loss of the detachment which Tarkington preserved toward Cora Madison; and instead of a pitiless portrayal we had a modern morality play. *The Magnificent Ambersons* was afflicted with a pulled-around ending. But in *Alice Adams* all of these defects were met and adjusted; the movement was natural and not "plotted"; no moral underlay the exposed incidents; Mr. Tarkington was impartial without being in the least unsympathetic. Then why discriminate? Surely, *Alice Adams* has everything! Not at all. No author's one book ever has, I suppose; and in finally achieving the symmetry and truth and grace of *Alice Adams* there was the sacrifice of a nervous force which animated, in a varying extent, all three of the earlier novels. One must learn, in criticism, to value above all else what can only be called "vitality," whether in painting, or sculpture, music or literature. This mysterious but indispensable flame burns with a different intensity in individual writers. In Mr. Galsworthy, for example, it is low in novels, somewhat higher, at times, in plays; but relatively low throughout his work. In Mr. Tarkington, I cannot help feeling, it is higher in *The Flirt* than in anything else he has written; for savage and powerful as are the stories of *In the Arena*, the material is something that the author touches with his foot, rather than shapes with his hands. Indeed, this instinctive repugnance in Mr. Tarkington, as inveterate in him as in so many American writers, is one of the strictest limitations on his art. In older cultures than ours in America, where it is well understood that admission to the human race cannot be denied by some to others, a Balzac or a Conrad or even a Dickens can write with the same manifest vitality of almost anybody, however inhumanly horrible—as, for example, the "incorruptible" Professor and mad anarchist in Conrad's tale of *The Secret Agent*. In the case of Tarkington, Mr. Holliday has cleverly observed the type of material in which our writer's vitality is most evident—the memorable procession of drunkards in his stories, the unmatched darkeys of the stable alleys, the large number of Tarkington characters vocal with song.

As to plays: the man doesn't regard them as his "real trade." All the earlier ones were written in collaboration, usually with Harry Leon Wilson; and Tarkington, with an engaging candour, admits at once that the great cost of a theatrical production must be met, if possible, by filling the house. Writing alone, he has given the stage such utter ineptitude as *Poldekin* and such delicious comedy as *Clarence.* He now writes a play, usually, because a particular producer wants one with a particular actor in mind. In his book-length fiction he is unrestricted, unless the engagement in advance of the next couple of novels for serial publication may have its oblique effect. After all, it must be very difficult, knowing that your next two books are first to be placed before a certain large constituency of women readers, not to select your material "according" and not to mould it imperceptibly somewhat nearer the—supposed, suspected, or ascertained—hearts' desire of all those ladies.

vi

Booth Tarkington's home in Indianapolis, at 1100 North Pennsylvania Street, is a plain brick house, far from new. Business creeps into the street, but there is some "lawn" still about the house, a hedge, Virginia creeper on the brick walls. Six winter months are spent here, the other six in the house at Kennebunkport, which, being newer, is furnished with more simplicity and taste. Tarkington's workshop is upstairs—a tilted drawing board beside an east window, a flexible electric lamp, plenty of large-size sheets of yellow paper, two dozen pencils kept sharp by two pencil-sharpening machines. Tarkington has never used a typewriter and dictates only letters and not all of those. His sister-in-law, Miss Louise Keifer, copies his pencilled yellow pages of manuscript on the typewriter. Spectacles of all sizes and weights lie on a table.

The man breakfasts between nine and ten, works until 1.30, and then pauses to eat a slender lunch brought to his study on a tray. He continues working until 3.30, and sometimes writes in the evenings, although the habit of writing pretty regularly at night has been abandoned. Even so it is a longer working day than most writers can keep. Mrs. Tarkington intercepts all interruptions; no telephone call can break in, nor any thought-distracting piece of news. On evenings when there is no engagement and Tarkington is not writing, he will play double-deck solitaire for an hour, read until about one o'clock, then go to bed. In Maine the day's programme is a half-hour earlier throughout; work stops around noon; a short motor ride and a quick dip in the ocean follow; and the afternoon is most likely to be spent in a motorboat. The Maine evening frequently includes a walk of a mile to and from the movies; this is mainly for the sake of the walk, although the worse the picture is, the more restful Tarkington is likely to find it.

Notes, sometimes covering several dozen pencilled pages and undecipherable by anyone else, precede the composition of a play or novel. They are vague ideas and suggestions, the writer endeavouring not to crystallise his story too suddenly. When this occurs, it is sometimes necessary to write the next to the last chapter or scene and then go back to the general plan or the beginning. Work proceeds every day, Sundays included, and averages about 1,400 words a day of fresh output, preceded by correction of the previous day's writing. In addition to this day by day revision, Tarkington revises a story or book as a whole; it is then typed, and after that is seldom altered.

"He has never resorted to neurotic realism or the much over-exploited nastiness of high life to give zest to his fiction," says a recent utterance in praise of Mr. Tarkington. And the author is quoted as himself saying: "The problems of youth had been interesting me for some time, more than I realised"—when he turned to *Penrod*—"except the one problem that most people who call themselves realists feel that they must deal with—that is, in an untrammelled fashion—the problem of sex, which I have never felt was a subject for exploitation."

"Neurotic realism" is a phrase of wabbly connotation, but if a study of neurotic characters and tendencies be meant, there are plenty of those in Tarkington fiction. Most of the Tarkington drunkards are neurotic, Cora Madison is a victim of the narcism complex, and, as Mr. Holliday has pointed out, "*The Turmoil* is remarkable as a book of nervous diseases." One of the most unlifelike things about Penrod (still more, William Sylvanus Baxter, Jr., he of *Seventeen*) is the absolute erasure of that contact with "the facts of life" which constitutes one of the indubitable facts of boyhood. And though as many crimes have been committed in the name of realism as in the name of liberty, the painfully sincere purpose of some of our most "untrammelled" writers in their treatment of sex cannot justly be called "exploitation." One thinks of Sherwood Anderson. The analysis of Holliday, in a final quest for the secret of Tarkington's popularity as an author (not invariable, but abundant), is perhaps as good as we shall get:

"He is very much like most people. There is nothing, except its energy, peculiar about his mind; it has no strong idiosyncratic bias, no strange, abnormal quality. At first, as in *Cherry*, he may have been excessively belletristic. That was not only not odd, but quite natural in a well-educated, young writer. But, just for the joke of the thing, think for an instant of Mr. Tarkington in connection with such a writer as, let us say, George Moore. In this wearer of the literary ermine you find laid bare a soul compacted of nearly everything that is detestable to the mind of a plain citizen going about his business in the marketplace. He has confessed consuming egotism, quivering sensibility, fastidiousness, vanity, timidity coupled with calculating shamelessness, sensuality, a streak of feline cruelty, and absolute spiritual incontinence. Or try to think of Mr. Tarkington coming along with some such perverse thinking (however shrewd) as Samuel Butler's: 'the worst misfortune that can happen to any person is to lose his money; the second is to lose his health; and the loss of reputation is a bad third.' Mr. Tarkington admires all those things which every decent, ordinary, simple-hearted person admires: dash, courage, honesty, honour, feminine virtue and graciousness and beauty, and so on. He hates precisely those things hated by all honest, healthy 'American' people: sham, egoism, conceit, cruelty, affectation, and so forth. In short, though he is a red hot artist (and most Americans 'don't care a nickel for art'), he believes in all those things which make up the creed of the average sane, wholesome person in this country. He has infectious humour, and (though savage in attack upon what he feels to be vicious) abounding 'good humour.' Added to all this, he has a most winning and rich, though not at all complex, personality. He is in his own person, indeed, what most of us would like to be. In a word, doubtless his books are popular because of the same qualities that made their author popular as an undergraduate."

There are compensations of all kinds on this earth, and one of Mr. Tarkington's—the most enviable of all, I think—must be knowledge of a certain occasion in which he was of the utmost possible service to another American writer. The course he took at that time, the energy he displayed, would have been very improbable in one whose natural vanity of himself as an artist was in the least like George Moore's. If it was for too long a literary misfortune that Mr. Tarkington's "self-conceit" lay in the direction of being a good fellow, at least he made of good fellowship, in this instance, the minted gold of personal greatness. No! Now it can*not* be told; but there will be those alive to tell it.

Books by Booth Tarkington

1899 *The Gentleman from Indiana*
1900 *Monsieur Beaucaire*
1902 *The Two Vanrevels*
1903 *Cherry* earlier, in composition, than *The Gentleman from Indiana*

1905 *In the Arena*
1905 *The Conquest of Canaan*
1905 *The Beautiful Lady*
1907 *His Own People*
1908 *The Guest of Quesnay*
1909 *Beasley's Christmas Party*
1911 *Beauty and the Jacobin*
1913 *The Flirt*
1914 *Penrod*
1915 *The Turmoil*
1916 *Penrod and Sam*
1916 *Seventeen*
1918 *The Magnificent Ambersons*
1919 *Ramsey Milholland*
1921 *Alice Adams*
1922 *Gentle Julia*
1923 *The Fascinating Stranger and Other Stories*

Plays by Booth Tarkington

1901 *Monsieur Beaucaire* with E. G. SUTHERLAND
With HARRY LEON WILSON:
- 1906 *The Man from Home*
- 1907 *Cameo Kirby*
- 1908 *Your Humble Servant*
- 1908 *Springtime*
- 1909 *Getting a Polish*
- 1916 *Mister Antonio*

1917 *The Country Cousin* with JULIAN STREET
With HARRY LEON WILSON:
- 1919 *The Gibson Upright*
- 1919 *Up from Nowhere*

1919 *Clarence*

1920 *Poldekin*
1921 *The Wren*
1921 *The Intimate Strangers*

Sources on Booth Tarkington

Booth Tarkington, by Robert Cortes Holliday. DOUBLEDAY, PAGE & COMPANY. Authoritative, honest, delightful; especially sound in its detailed criticism of the books up to and including *The Turmoil* and *Seventeen*. When Holliday's book was written, Tarkington was at work on *The Magnificent Ambersons*, for an estimate of which see Holliday's *Broome Street Straws*.

Contemporary American Novelists, 1900-1920, by Carl Van Doren. THE MACMILLAN COMPANY.

Booth Tarkington at Home, by John R. McMahon, LADIES' HOME JOURNAL, November, 1922 (page 15).

Private Information.

Articles, reviews, etc., are plentiful and the reader is advised to consult the READERS' GUIDE TO PERIODICAL LITERATURE for the years since 1914.

13. A Parody Outline of Stewart

i

ABOUT two years ago, when Donald Ogden Stewart had just abandoned the bond business for the pursuit of a literary career, he was asked to write a brief account of his life, with the following result:

"Donald Ogden Stewart was born in Columbus, Ohio, on November 30, 1894. In his early years he gave manifold evidences of his gift for humour, and many of his bright childhood remarks are still related by his proud mother upon the slightest provocation, or in fact, upon no provocation at all. There were others, however—principally among the guests at the hotel where Donald lived—who did not think that this child prodigy was so funny. Mr. Stewart bears a long red scar on his head—such as might be made by a brick or other missile—as mute evidence of one little red-headed girl's particular lack of appreciation of his early humorous efforts.

"At the age of 14 he was sent to the Phillips Exeter Academy because it was a good preparatory school for Harvard. In the fall of 1912, Mr. Stewart entered Yale. While at New Haven, Mr.

Stewart went out for all the athletic teams possible, and was always among those of whom it was said in the college paper at the end of the season, 'And we also wish to thank those members of the third and fourth teams who have worked so faithfully without reward—and yet we cannot say without reward—for they are rewarded with the knowledge that they have worked for old Yale,' etc.

"Mr. Stewart was graduated in 1916 and selected a certain large public service corporation as the scene of his future success. It was his desire to start at the bottom and work up; the first half of this wish was readily granted him. After a brief, inspiring visit with the head of the corporation, Mr. Stewart was sent to the Birmingham, Alabama, office which was about as far away as the head of the corporation could possibly send Mr. Stewart. While in Birmingham, Mr. Stewart took a keen interest in his job and read the complete works of Anatole France, George Moore, Fyodor Dostoievski, Henrik Ibsen, Gustav Flaubert and many others. He also intended to read the Alexander Hamilton business course, but did not quite get around to it before he was sent to the Pittsburgh, Pennsylvania, office.

"In Pittsburgh, Mr. Stewart took a keen interest in his job and read the works of Leo Tolstoy, Friedrich Nietzsche, G. B. Shaw, Thomas Hardy, Joseph Conrad and others. He also started to take piano lessons and got as far as 'The Happy Farmers.' He was just on the point of reading the Alexander Hamilton business course when he was sent to Chicago. After ten months in Chicago, Mr. Stewart joined the Navy. Having never been on

Photo by Nickolas Muray

DONALD OGDEN STEWART

a ship or the ocean in his life, he was at once appointed an instructor in Practical Navigation, Seamanship, Naval Ordnance, and Signals. This experience was invaluable and Mr. Stewart came out of the Great War a deepened man.

"His old position with the great corporation awaited him and Mr. Stewart went back to the work of the world in the spring of 1918. He was sent to the Minneapolis office, where he took a keen interest in his job and read the works of H. G. Wells, Havelock Ellis, and H. L. Mencken; met F. Scott Fitzgerald, and led two cotillions. He was also preparing to take up the Alexander Hamilton business course when he accepted an offer of employment in Dayton, Ohio, with a financial organisation.

"Mr. Stewart spent a delightful year in Dayton where he learned to play golf, and read the works of Max Beerbohm, Sainte-Beuve, Casanova, Swift, James Branch Cabell, James Huneker, and William Congreve. He also renewed his piano lessons, getting as far as the Bach three-part inventions and 'Easy Classics.' On December 30, 1920, he read the first volume of the Alexander Hamilton business course, after which he decided that he wanted to go in for literature. In January, 1921, Mr. Stewart came to New York City to find a job (literary if possible), but there were so many symphony concerts that month that he didn't get a chance to look around until the middle of February.

"The idea for the *Parody Outline of History* came to Mr. Stewart in March, while hearing Mr. Mengelberg conduct the National Orchestra in the Pathetique Symphony.

"Mr. Stewart is unmarried and very near-sighted. He is fond of Beethoven, Scotch, and Max Beerbohm."

ii

So much for Mr. Stewart's life up to the publication of *The Parody Outline of History*. In the following year (1922)—but let Mr. Stewart again speak:

"After the appearance of the *Parody Outline* Mr. Stewart, having heard a great deal about Europe in the course of his naval war service in Chicago, decided to go abroad. Many of his friends recommended Paris as a pleasant city in which to work, so Mr. Stewart went to Paris, which he found indeed very pleasant but not for work. So after a brief period of recuperation he journeyed to Vienna where he grew a splendid red beard and wrote *Perfect Behavior*.

"Finding, however, that the beard was exhausting too much of his creative energy, Mr. Stewart shaved and went to Budapest, where he enjoyed himself immensely at the rate of 700 Hungarian crowns to the dollar.

"But in the middle of October he began to feel strangely uneasy, and as his condition grew steadily worse he consulted an authority and learned, to his surprise and delight, that he was going to have another book.

"Bidding a hasty farewell to the gay life of Budapest, which now seemed all too empty and frivolous, Mr. Stewart journeyed with his precious secret to Capri, there, under the ever-blue Italian skies, to await the happy event. He prayed with all his heart that it might be a novel, for he had never had a novel, although he had wanted one all his life. But early in February, 1923, Mr. Stewart discovered that the 'little stranger' was to be another satire, and although it was a bit of a blow at first, after a few days he got over his disappointment at not having a novel; and when, in June, Mr. Stewart returned to America he took with him, proudly, his little third book, which he had christened *Aunt Polly's Story of Mankind*."

iii

Alexander Woollcott speaking in "Shouts and Murmurs" in the New York Herald of March 18, 1923:

"Stewart is a preposterously tall, blonde man, with an enviably large amount of his twenties still to squander. His profile is faintly reminiscent of that most delightful and fantastic of all creatures, Winsor McKay's Gertie. He knows more about the music than he does about the books of the world, and has, we suspect, gone in for reading so recently that he probably thinks all novels are like Joyce's *Ulysses*. We ran across him here and there in France last summer, starting out on one pilgrimage together from the Café Valterre, in the Place Stanislas at Nancy, that celebrated restaurant which set forth marvellous dishes even when the bombs were dropping on Nancy every evening and there was not another good meal to be found anywhere else in Lorraine. Up the street somewhere was M.

Coué, healing away for dear life, and on the outskirts of the town an imitation Oberammergau was in full swing. But the two of us were minded rather to move on to the battlefields, and for the purpose engaged a morsel of a French car, driven by a youngster who spoke a horrible dialect he had picked up three years before from the Americans stationed at Neufchateau. The memories of that rambling excursion into a cheerless countryside, still littered with the rusted snarls of barbed wire and still gashed with the trenches no one has had time or strength to obliterate, are brought flooding back by the inscription in the copy of *Perfect Behavior* lying open here on the desk. It is inscribed: 'In memory of terrible days and ghastly nights on the battlefields of France,' and winds up with this disconcerting proclamation: ' "It shall never happen again."—Stewart.'

"Marc Connelly was agitated the other day by the receipt of a cablegram from Stewart in Capri which read thus:

" 'The Queen of Sweden is here. What shall I do?—Stewart.'

"Connelly's cabled reply must be admired equally for its sagacity and its thrift. It was: 'Compromise.' "

Books by Donald Ogden Stewart

1921 *A Parody Outline of History*
1922 *Perfect Behavior*
1923 *Aunt Polly's Story of Mankind*

A PARODY OUTLINE OF STEWART

Sources on Donald Ogden Stewart

The Making of a Humorist, by DONALD OGDEN STEWART, suppressed by the author, 1921.

My Naval Career, by DONALD OGDEN STEWART (Privately unpublished, 1921).

14. Miss Zona Gale

i

NO one any longer doubts that Zona Gale belongs in the very small company of American women novelists whose work is of the first artistic importance. Her history is interesting. Of old New England parentage, she was born in Portage, Wisconsin, where she now lives. She wrote, at thirteen, a novel "which almost simultaneously came back to me from a publisher." At sixteen, just after she had entered the University of Wisconsin, she submitted a 3,000-word short story to the Milwaukee Evening Wisconsin, which paid her $3. When she finished college she went to work for that newspaper. "I secured a position by attrition. I presented myself every morning at the desk of the city editor. At the end of two weeks the city editor let me write about a flower show. I have never put such emotion into anything else I have written." She was another month getting on the staff. Later, by offering a list of suggestions based on the day's news, she succeeded after many weeks in getting on the staff of the New York World.

An anonymous writer in The Bookman has pictured Miss Gale in New York: "When she was a reporter on the World, and as beautiful as any girl could be, she was put on difficult assignments that might well have terrified one as fragile and flower-like and feminine as she; but she never winced. . . . She covered murders and robberies—anything given her to do she did, at any hour of the day or night. But all the while she was writing exquisite poetry; and every day of her life she sent a letter to her mother, who was back in Wisconsin. If she was waiting for an interview with some financier of the hour, she did not dawdle her time away in the corridor of his hotel. Instead, she pulled out a pad and pencil and wrote as many pages as she could on a short story; or she dashed off a lyric; or she made copious notes for future work. I think she was about the most ambitious girl in New York at that time—too ambitious, some said; her praises were being sung—too much sung was a common rumour; her picture—how lovely she was, and is!—was published repeatedly—too repeatedly, dear enemies whispered; and everyone was waiting to see just how long it would take her to make good."

ii

It took some time. Not until the year in which she was 29 did she land anywhere "to speak of," though for ten years previous to that acceptance, by Success Magazine, she had constantly submitted stories. That was in 1903. Then, in 1911, the Delineator held a short story contest in which over 15,000 stories were received. Miss Gale took first prize with a tale called "The American Dawn." It was $2,000 and in addition her other two entries (each person was allowed to submit three stories) were deemed good enough to be purchased. But meanwhile she had written stories about Pelleas and Ettare, two old lovers, and stories about Friendship Village—some forty of the first and, ultimately, about sixty of the second—and the process of collecting her Friendship Village fiction into books had begun. Said Miss Gale, in 1919: "The first editor to whom these Friendship Village stories were submitted declined them with the word that his acquaintance with small towns was wide but that he had never seen any such people as these. . . . I am still not sure that he was not right."

She was the author of ten published books before she produced anything constituting a lien upon general attention. But then, with an effect of extreme suddenness to the world outside of Portage, there came from her pen the 402-page novel, *Birth*. Its length is a point of interest in view of the brevity of *Miss Lulu Bett* and *Faint Perfume*, both of which are so decidedly under the average novel in length. And yet *Birth* exhibits the same conciseness of phrase, the same avoidance of unnecessary words so noticeable in the two later books. It is the story of a poor little man, Marshall Pitt, who comes to an insignificant Western town as a pickle salesman and remains there as a paperhanger, a husband and a father. The book's comments on life have been aptly described as "piercing"—it is a fine needlework of satire—but there are lovely lyrical moments and the tragic action is touched with majesty. Altogether a great novel. Miss Gale considers it the finest thing she has done and for once her judgment of her own work, generally as untrustworthy as most authors' or slightly more so, is right.

Then came *Miss Lulu Bett*, read with the enthusiasm of discovery by the publisher, who telegraphed his congratulations—a thing publishers infrequently do! Except in England, where its merit was quickly noted, *Birth* had not sold at all well. Six magazine editors had rejected *Miss Lulu Bett* as a serial. Happily, all signs failed. The crisply-told little novel of the household drudge and her fortunes went into one edition after another; a play from the novel was sought and Miss Gale fashioned it herself; the annual Pulitzer prize was awarded to the play. Whether the concision of style practised so effectively in *Birth* was not carried a bit too far in *Miss Lulu Bett* must always remain a matter of opinion. The most interesting point, I think, is the change of ending which the requirements of the theatre forced upon Miss Gale. As she observed, an audience in a playhouse could not reasonably be expected to swallow the spectacle of a woman marrying two men in the space of three hours, even though the indicated lapse of time was much longer than that; she therefore, to make the play, caused Miss Bett's first marriage to turn out to be valid after all. In this matter Miss Gale was not guilty of "sweetening" her story, as has been charged. She simply was up against a limitation as definite as that which restricts the number of scenes possible in a play.

iii

And this year she has given us *Faint Perfume*, a study of a finely sensitive feminine personality stifling in the atmosphere of a quite usual sort of American family. Leda Perrin, forced to make her home with the Crumbs, is brought into a fleeting contact with Barnaby Powers, a writer with a temperament of the same response. They meet, together face the defeat of their desire, and go separately apart. At the close there is the briefest possible second meeting and a hope is held out for their eventual happiness together. This theme, of the utmost delicacy, is the occasion for a considerable display of virtuosity by Miss Gale. By means of deft and distinct individualisation of her characters—each Crumb, for instance, standing out as a complete fiery particle—she orchestrates the melodic fragment of Leda and Barnaby in a sort of free treatment (but with careful working out), as a composer might do in setting a quartette for strings. May this musical simile be helpful! The clipped style of *Miss Lulu Bett* is here carried a step further, until Miss Gale almost seems to out-Sinclair Miss May Sinclair. The style has been called precious, which is the technical word for what the ordinary person calls "affected"; and, on the other hand, one able critic has declared that it is not the style that is precious but Miss Gale's material. One thing is certain, the treatment is as far removed as possible from the literalness of such a novel as *Main Street*, and this is natural to expect when we remember that Miss Gale is, after all and perhaps fundamentally, a poet. Her poems published in book form are to a great extent inferior to her best poems, which, so far as I know, still repose in some old files of the Smart Set magazine.

The point, however, is not the merit or demerit of *Faint Perfume*, nor the relative values of Miss Gale's three books here discussed. The point is Zona Gale, her undeniable artistry, her literary maturity and her manifest power . . . and the importance of her work to come.

Books by Zona Gale

1906 *Romance Island*
1907 *The Loves of Pelleas and Ettarre*
1908 *Friendship Village*
1909 *Friendship Village Love Stories*
1911 *Mothers to Men*
1912 *Christmas*
1913 *When I Was a Little Girl*
1914 *Neighborhood Stories*
1915 *Heart's Kindred*
1917 *A Daughter of Tomorrow*
1918 *Birth*
1919 *Peace in Friendship Village*
1920 *Miss Lulu Bett*
1920 *Neighbors* (play)
1921 *Miss Lulu Bett* (play)
1923 *Faint Perfume*

Sources on Zona Gale

The Women Who Make Our Novels (second or third edition, 1919 or 1922). MOFFAT YARD & COMPANY.

The Literary Spotlight, XVIII: Zona Gale, in THE BOOKMAN for April, 1923. This article now forms a chapter in the book, *The Literary Spotlight*, with an introduction by John Farrar.

Zona Gale, An Artist in Fiction, by WILSON FOLLETT. Booklet published by D. Appleton & Company.

15. *For the Literary Investor*

i

AS in the world of finance there are varieties of investment, so in reading. A delicate parallel would be between individual authors and, let us say, the mortgage field; whereas the reader who chooses books included in undertakings like the Lambskin Library, the Murray Hill Library or the Modern Student's Library is like the man adventuring among well-seasoned bonds. The individual author is the bolder risk, less easily to be abandoned, lacking (usually) the element of diversification; the certainty of interest from those carefully selected Library volumes is somewhat greater and the investment in them is more readily marketable in the discovery that your commitment is shared with the other fellow, who also knows and has read them. Then there is among books that type of investment for which men constantly seek when trying to place their money—the unlisted and almost unheard-of, lonely, isolated enterprise which one may, and probably will, have all to himself. . . .

What follows is a series of what, in the money world, would be called "offerings." These literary offerings are not necessarily in the least related to each other, although here and there you may find features in common. Each stands on the foundation of its own "attractiveness" to you as an individual; but there is none which has not given a good return to some group of readers, large or less large. Some are well-seasoned; others, although new, show their intrinsic worth for such time and attention as you may commit to them.

ii

J. C. Snaith, novelist. John Collis Snaith, born in 1876, in Nottinghamshire of Yorkshire stock. Athletic in his youth, before his health became impaired, playing cricket, football and hockey on county teams. Always in the middle of a novel, either at Skegness or in London, where he may with difficulty be tracked down at the Garrick Club, hidden among W. J. Locke, W. B. Maxwell, A. E. W. Mason, Hugh Walpole, Arnold Bennett, E. Temple Thurston, etc. His novels exhibit constant variety. Richard Mansfield was always hoping for a play from Snaith's *Broke of Covenden* so that he might act as Broke. *The Sailor*, supposed to have been suggested by John Masefield's career, was a great popular success (1916) and is read and remembered widely today. *The Coming*, an exquisite and powerful story in which the reappearance of Jesus Christ in present-day England is suggested, made an extraordinary impression. On the whole it is perhaps Snaith's own favourite. *The Undefeated*, a story of England in wartime, had a large sale and gives promise of more permanence than any similar book, including H. G. Wells's

Mr. Britling. A recent novel, *The Van Roon*, is a lighter story written around the theft of a famous painting. Snaith's *Araminta*, which is being freshly brought out this year, is a whimsical romance of a country girl who comes to London and is sued for by two noblemen. Snaith says: "Each novel I write is in the nature of an experiment. To me a good novel is a mental tonic, exhilarating, educative, humanising." He is both versatile and in the quality of his work of unusual excellence.

W. B. Maxwell, novelist. English. A writer who has reached undeniable greatness at times and who, when possessing the finest material, need ask no odds of any living novelist. His most recent story, *The Day's Journey*, is a beautifully-conceived and beautifully-written story of the friendship between two men enduring throughout their lives. The differences in character, the obstacles arising in the course of that friendship, the antagonisms and fallings-apart and the renewals of these two old comrades are put on paper with a fidelity of observation, a tenderness and an avoidance of sentimentality that would be difficult to overpraise. Maxwell's novels are of great variety; attention is particularly called to *In Cotton Wool*, the story of a weakling. *Mrs. Thompson*, *The Devil's Garden* and *Spinster of This Parish* are also highwater marks in his writing.

Hugh Walpole. Perhaps no living novelist has shown so uniform a quality or so progressive an excellence. He resembles a stock which, starting at a modest price and unfailingly paying dividends, has gone steadily upward to par and is now .quoted at a premium. His great success, *The Cathedral*, is now followed by *Jeremy and Hamlet*, which, although not a "sequel," is a companion volume to *Jeremy* (most popular of all Walpole's stories before the appearance of *The Cathedral*). As *Jeremy* dealt with the history of a little boy—most singularly resembling the Hugh of Mr. Walpole's own boyhood—so *Jeremy and Hamlet* presents the adventures of that boy accompanied by the only proper companion for a small boy, a dog.

Rudyard Kipling. For a discussion of Kipling's new work, *The Irish Guards in the Great War*, see Chapter 8. The best exposition of Kipling, the poet, will be found in Andre Chevrillon's *Three Studies in English Literature: Kipling, Galsworthy, Shakespeare* (translated by Florence Simmonds). Katharine Fullerton Gerould, in her *Modes and Morals*, in the essay on "The Remarkable Rightness of Rudyard Kipling," offers a brilliant justification for Kipling as a prophetic and moral influence in English affairs. The literary investor should not let these aspects take his attention from the Kipling of *Plain Tales from the Hills*, of *Kim* and of such short stories as "The Brushwood Boy" and "They." A collection of rich, remarkably diversified, "gilt-edged" securities possessing the widest possible market and an almost universal currency.

Selma Lagerlöf, Swedish novelist, the only woman so far to receive the Nobel Prize for Literature. The quality of her work is best conveyed by the words of various critics. Edwin Björkman: "She has revived not only the courage but the ability to feel and dream and aspire that belonged to the scorned romanticists of the early nineteenth century. But this . . . she has achieved for us without surrender of that intimate connection between poetry and real life which was established by the naturalists in the latter half of the same century." J. B. Kerfoot, in Life: "The wise cannot find bottom nor the child get beyond its depth." Attempted comparisons with George Eliot fail because Selma Lagerlöf has the fine Swedish folklore to enrich the roots of her work. "She is as national," says Walter Prichard Eaton, "as a song by Grieg or a play of Tchekov. And like all deeply national art, it is therefore universal." Hugo Alfven, the Swedish composer: "Reading Selma Lagerlöf is like sitting in the dusk of a Spanish cathedral. . . . Afterward, one does not know whether what he has seen was dream or reality, but certainly he has been on holy ground." The best approach is possibly through *The Story of Gösta Berling*. Her other great novels are *Jerusalem*, woven from the actual experience of Swedish colonists in the Holy Land, and *The Emperor of Portugallia*. Her *Nils* stories for children are mentioned in Chapter 9. Complete works are best procured in the Northland Edition.

iii

A convenient size and a beautiful binding are more than desiderata. Who, wishing Bram Stoker's grim masterpiece, *Dracula*, would not now prefer a new copy in the handy leather of the Lambskin Library? If one is out to acquire a copy of W. Somerset Maugham's *The Moon and Sixpence*, will he not choose it in its plum-coloured leather and gilt top of the Murray Hill Library? If I go forth to buy *Pride and Prejudice*, I am as certain as anything to ask for it from the volumes of the Modern Student's Library, because this will give me William Dean Howells's introduction to the novel.

There is a further advantage of these collections in that they give ready and inexpensive access to exceptional books that are otherwise out of print. I might have excessive trouble, for example, to get hold of *Dracula* elsewhere. Yet the commonest advantage of such sets is probably as a guide in reading. A publisher does not put a book into his Lambskin Library, or his Murray Hill Library, or his Modern Student's Library unless the book is one of proved worth and established permanence and continuing popularity. The Library, therefore, offers a convenient and trustworthy solution to those who, among books not freshly published, are unable to see the trees for the forest. A word about these collections is in order.

The Lambskin Library at present comprises nearly fifty volumes, chiefly fiction, although Lawrence F. Abbott's *Impressions of Theodore Roosevelt*, Helen Keller's *The Story of My Life*, Booker T. Washington's *Up From Slavery* and Franklin's *Autobiography* lay a massive foundation for biographies. Conrad, Frank Norris, Selma Lagerlöf, O. Henry, Dumas, Scott, Tarkington, Edna Ferber, Ellen Glasgow, Zola and Rider Haggard are some of the authors represented. Many of the books have interesting prefatory notes and among the contributors of these are William Lyon Phelps, Christopher

Morley, William Allen White, John Macy and William Dean Howells.

The Modern Student's Library is ultimately to include as many as possible of the books one would wish to read in a comprehensive survey of English and American literature. Both the general reader and the student have been held in mind; the books represent a sane departure from the heavily annotated texts of a few years ago. The books have been edited, and introductions to them have been provided by such authorities as William Dean Howells, Stuart P. Sherman, William Lyon Phelps and Carl Van Doren. Bacon's *Essays*, Boswell's *Life of Johnson*, Browning, Carlyle's *Sartor Resartus*, Emerson's *Essays*, Hardy's *The Return of the Native*, Hawthorne's *The Scarlet Letter*, Meredith, Ruskin, Scott, Stevenson, Thackeray, Thoreau and Whitman are among those already included.

The Murray Hill Library, commencing with modern fiction, will probably enlarge its scope to include some of the best modern non-fiction. Its very handsome binding now covers twelve books, picked works by Arnold Bennett, Somerset Maugham, Mary Roberts Rinehart, Irvin S. Cobb, Walpole, G. A. Birmingham, John Buchan, Stephen McKenna, Swinnerton and Richard Dehan.

Of an entirely different character but not less valuable are the very large volumes of the Nature Library—those volumes by Neltje Blanchan, Julia Ellen Rogers, Nina L. Marshall and others called (for the most part) *The Butterfly Book*, *The Shell Book*, *The Tree Book*, and so on. Fairly expensive books, these, but cheap at any price with their many and wonderful colour plates and photographs from life. In their outdoor field they are not to be surpassed.

iv

Books of a biographical character we have considered already (Chapter 8) but it ought to be emphasised that, for the investor in literature, they hold a position quite as enviable and altogether desirable as does the class of securities known as municipals for the investor of moneys. Time will not match for us a book like Booker T. Washington's *Up From Slavery*, nor will literature furnish us with a more strangely suggestive career than that related in Raymond Weaver's *Herman Melville: Mariner and Mystic*. It was C. Alphonso Smith's *O. Henry Biography* that first gave the world the facts on which to base a true understanding of that extraordinary writer. The tale of unwearied courage in Edward Livingston Trudeau's *Autobiography* cannot lose either its freshness nor its strength of inspiration. To read P. P. Howe's *Life of William Hazlitt* and then to turn to his little book of selections called *The Best of Hazlitt* is to enter into a permanently valuable share of the English literary inheritance. *The Letters of Henry James*, selected and edited by Percy Lubbock, and James's own *Notes of a Son and Brother;* Sir Sidney Colvin's *John Keats* and his *Memories and Notes of Persons and Places;* the *Letters of James Huneker* and Huneker's autobiography, *Steeplejack;* and the *Letters and Papers of John Addington Symonds*, edited by Horatio F. Brown, are all of the class of books whose content is a permanent acquisition, an actual "property" of which the reader, in legal language, becomes seized and possessed.

One's investment in an ample author should be allowed to ramify in all directions natural to the lines of human interest. About Walt Whitman, for example, there is by now a cluster of books which the reader of *Leaves of Grass* or of Whitman's prose cannot afford, in their entirety, to neglect. Whether he will want one or all, or what ones he will want, will depend upon the relation he establishes with Whitman himself. The best brief biography is *Walt Whitman: The Man and His Work*, translated from the French of Leon Bazalgette by Ellen FitzGerald. Personally I do not think one can feel himself acquainted with Whitman unless he has read, or read in, the three massive volumes of Horace Traubel's *With Walt Whitman in Camden. The Letters of Anne Gilchrist and Walt Whitman*, edited by Thomas B. Harned, form an unusual and engrossing chapter in the lives of both. Those keenly interested will explore further yet in the two volumes of the *Uncollected Poetry and Prose of Walt Whitman*, edited by Emory Holloway, who is now at work on a long and comprehensive biography of the poet.

The book with beautiful illustrations is a true investment, since now such illustrations are seldom if ever wasted on a second-rate text. To a great extent these illustrated books are ones appreciable by children as well as by their elders—things like *Westward Ho!* and *The Last of the Mohicans*—and came up for our consideration in Chapter 9.

But there are certain classics, like the editions of *A Midsummer Night's Dream* and Milton's *Comus* with pictures by Arthur Rackham, which are adult throughout. One of the most splendid is the Vierge Edition of *Don Quixote*, in four volumes, illustrated with 260 drawings by Daniel Vierge and provided with an introduction by Royal Cortissoz. The same work, illustrated by Jean de Bosschere, may be had in one large volume; and other treasures of the sort are *The Rubaiyat of Omar Khayyam* and Shakespeare's *The Tempest*, both illustrated by Edmund Dulac. I must not omit the edition of Scott's *Quentin Durward*, with illustrations in color by the American artist, C. Bosseron Chambers.

When, in Chapter 2, we discussed books of essays, it was with the thought of their beguiling qualities pretty much forward in our minds. I hope I do not derogate the essay, a literary form raised to the highest eminence by Bacon, Emerson, Lamb and so many others, when I say that its widest and most useful office resembles the form of investment known as short-term notes. Investors of money are constantly in receipt of funds for which, at the moment, they have no suitable repository; and investors in literature are frequently in the same fix. The man with money buys high grade commercial paper with an early maturity and watches for his long-term investment. The reader with time on his hands may often most profitably do likewise. But in one respect he is the more favoured person. If his brief-lived investment is well-chosen, the chances are great that it will lead him to some author or some group of books to which he can gladly commit his reading hours for a month or several months or a year.

Such, among literary profit-producers, are books like Stuart P. Sherman's *The Genius of America* and his *Americans*, the first devoted to "studies in behalf of the younger generation" of such subjects as Puritanism, shifting morals, popular education and American critical writing; the second a series of presentations of individual figures—Roosevelt, Emerson, Whitman, Carnegie, Paul Elmer More, Franklin, and others. Either his *On* or his fictional satire, *The Mercy of Allah*, should lead the chance reader some ways further in the conquest of Hilaire Belloc. Dr. Joseph Collins's *The Doctor Looks at Literature* has, in a very few months, created and aborted some thousands of readers of James Joyce, Fyodor Dostoievski, Marcel Proust, D. H. Lawrence, May Sinclair, Rebecca West, Stella Benson, Katherine Mansfield and the other contemporary writers whose pathology it inquires into. Books about books have all the range from Jesse Lee Bennett's invaluable reader's Baedeker, *What Books Can Do for Me* (with priceless reading lists of every variety) to Maurice Francis Egan's delightful *Confessions of a Book-Lover* and Henry van Dyke's *Companionable Books.* What will you try? John Corbin's *The Return of the Middle Class* with its impulsion toward other social studies? J. H. Gardiner's *The Bible as English Literature* or William Lyon Phelps's *Human Nature in the Bible* with their lights upon ancient thinking and racial character? Corbin's book may lead you back to Edward Carpenter's *Civilization: Its Cause and Cure.*

Gardiner and Phelps may send you to Horace G. Hutchinson's *The Greatest Story in the World*, which is the story of mankind from the beginnings of history to the time of the firm establishment of the Roman Empire. From that picturesque history of the civilisations that succeeded each other in the Mediterranean lands would you be led in the direction of Henry Fairfield Osborn's *Men of the Old Stone Age* and Madison Grant's *The Passing of the Great Race*, or toward the recent books by Lothrop Stoddard, or into the fascinations of Edwyn Bevan's *Hellenism and Christianity* and G. Lowes Dickinson's *The Greek View of Life*, I wonder? As one wishful of your enjoyment and satisfaction, I hope you wonder, too.

Here, of all things, is *A History of Chinese Literature*, by Herbert A. Giles, professor of Chinese in the University of Cambridge (you didn't know they had one, did you?). It begins with Confucius (born B.C. 551) and is divided into eight parts according to dynasties. One sees easily that while each age had its poets and writers, the drama and the novel did not develop in China until the Mongol Dynasty (A.D. 1200) and the famous Ming Dynasty (A.D. 1368-1544). From all the important writers Dr. Giles quotes at length in excellent translation; he summarises plays and explains the curious technique of the Chinese theatre. The book is rounded off with examples of Chinese wit and humour.

Here is George H. McKnight's *English Words and Their Background*, with facts only recently recognised about the relation and differences of American English and British English; with a good chapter on slang; with new light on the changes word meanings have undergone, and why; with stuff about personal names and place names.

The general reader has perhaps tried to find out about Dante, and found, on the one hand, some work by the scholar and for the scholar, on the other, books full of technical and controversial idiom. Behold, here is Mary Bradford Whiting's *Dante: The Man and the Poet* with its simple and memorable account of the student, lover and statesman, the exile and wanderer, the poet and seer. Or he has wondered if it were impossible for anyone to write about sex with beauty and sanity—and then has had the miracle of getting hold of Havelock Ellis's *Little Essays of Love and Virtue* wrought in his behalf. He has been the victim all his life of such stuff as Freudians are made on, and some benignant fate has put into his hands Basil King's convincing account of *The Conquest of Fear*. He has wearied over the Younger Generation and been comforted as he read Brander Matthew's *The Tocsin of Revolt;* contemporary criticism—too contemporary—has set his teeth on edge until he found a more ripened wisdom in the books of W. C. Brownell. A sense of futility and a dark brown taste of boredom have resulted from the perusal of the usual kind of book on How to Live; and the sparkling and nutritious antidote has proved to be Arnold Bennett's *How to Make the Best of Life*. For that condition in which one cannot endure concentration on a single topic for the duration of a book—what? Perhaps either volume of Bennett's *Things That Have Interested Me*, or some such book as Basil Anderton's *Sketches From a Library Window*, in which one may read about a French gourmet, a sixteenth century humanist, holiday joys in Northumberland, the art of the translator, the adventures of an English seaman in the Napoleonic wars, or Sir Thomas Browne.

V

"I never read fiction."

The next time I meet him I shall not place in his hands a novel, not even one of the great masterpieces among the novels. I shall hand him *My Best Story*, to which thirty-one English authors have contributed (though we may claim John Russell for America). Here in a single book are such perfect tales as Stacy Aumonier's "The Great Unimpressionable," one from Ernest Bramah's *Kai Lung's Golden Hours*, Quiller-Couch's "Statement of Gabriel Foot, Highwayman," Galsworthy's "Courage," Perceval Gibbon's "The Connoisseur," Cunninghame Graham's "The Lone Wolf," Elinor Mordaunt's "The Gold Fish," John Russell's "The Price of a Head" and Rebecca West's "In a City That Is Now Ploughed Fields." Arnold Bennett, G. K. Chesterton, W. W. Jacobs, May Sinclair, H. G. Wells and Israel Zangwill are some of the others who furnish stories for the collection. Such a book, by its variety as well as from its superlative quality, ought to win him to fiction more readily than any long tale, however distinguished.

He is rare, but you do sometimes meet him, that type of literary investor who cannot trust himself to range over the whole field . . . like one whose fortune, however great, must needs be kept strictly in savings bank accounts. I grant you that one needs to know his fiction, both in itself and in relation to his possible profit. But I personally would not for the world be one of those who have never heard of Charles De Coster's *Legend of Ulenspiegel*, that classic of the Lowland countries which Hendrik Van Loon named recently as one of the ten books he has enjoyed the most. I should not be willing to be ignorant of "Elizabeth," whose *Vera* had such grim power and whose *The Enchanted April* made a good many enchanted Mays, Junes, Julys, Augusts and other months for its readers. Of what avail to have read novels by Kathleen Norris and to have missed *Certain People of Importance*, I should like to know? Who thinks he has any acquaintance with the work of Edna Ferber if he has omitted to read *The Girls* or such tales, in *Gigolo*, as "Old Man Minnick" and "Home Girl"? Yet there are unfortunate persons who read *One Man in His Time* and who will read the stories in *The Shadowy Third* and innocently suppose they have "read" Ellen Glasgow, that competent and admirable novelist whose earlier novels, like *The Deliverance*, have such surprising vitality when you read or re-read them today.

Opportunities lost? Ah, but one of the grand advantages of the literary investment over the money opportunity is right here: Your new and worthwhile book and your old and seasoned book are, alike, always offering.

16. Naturalist vs. Novelist: Gene Stratton-Porter

i

WITH Gene Stratton-Porter, the quality of enthusiasm is not strained, it droppeth as torrential rains from the heaven of her state of mind. Anyone acquainted with Mrs. Porter and regarding her with positive affection is certain to be subject to the recurring notion that she has, after all, confused heaven with earth. It is not that she finds nothing on earth to contemn, but that she finds the same objects for perpetual glorification. The rest of us live our wavering lives in a flux of emotions, which we commonly mistake for accomplishments of our intellects. We glorify this at one age, and that at another. Mrs. Porter, from the beginning, has worshipped the same pantheon.

A pantheon it is, owing to her possibly inherited passion for the works of nature. Her idea of art is as clear-cut as the ordinary mortal's notion of property. Perhaps clearer, since the ordinary mortal often finds difficulty in distinguishing the forms of property, whether real, personal, or mixed (as lawyers say). To Mrs. Porter, art is any human effort that encourages, or even possibly forces, nature to grow. It is art when you handle flowers with the deftness and astonishing results achieved by Mrs. Porter's mother; it is art when you write a story that tends to stimulate or fortify the natural (i.e., usual) impulses of the average man or woman to live and learn, to seek and engage in interesting work, to mate, to beget or bear children. Any art that does not tend directly toward these primary social and personal ends isn't art to her; she regards it with heavy suspicion.

Some years ago it was suggested to Mrs. Porter that she furnish autobiographical material for a booklet which should satisfy the eager requests of her readers for personal facts. Mrs. Porter assented. The result was a booklet largely in her own words, and remarkable for an accent that some would call boastful and others, refreshing. We may defer for a few moments the details that Mrs. Porter set down, but the question of her personal tone and temper is one to be considered at the very outset. Is she merely naïve? Is she self-assertive, conceited, boastful? What does she embody, and what is the secret—if it is a secret—of the enormously wide appeal of her work? To attempt an answer isn't easy. But let us see. . . .

ii

Gene Stratton-Porter is a self-made woman, with all the drawbacks that self-manufacture entails. Certain definite advantages, too! It is not meant that she owes nothing to her parentage, wifehood, motherhood—she owes much to these, and her great indebtedness to her father and mother she has herself proclaimed. And yet, in the rôle in which the world views her, she owes nothing to anybody except herself. For although the late Richard Watson Gilder gave her encouragement with her first book, and although others encouraged her with the famous *Freckles*, she would undoubtedly have gone on with no encouragement whatever and would have become what she is today. Why? The explanation inheres in that phrase, "self-made." Self-made people, whatever they may lack, are obviously people with a capacity which we don't ordinarily bother to distinguish except by the result they achieve with it. That is, perhaps, typical of the mental laziness of the rest of us. But if we ask ourselves what the capacity is, in terms other than the easily-named result, the answer may be extremely surprising.

Who are the persons who are so happily independent of the encouragement, the approval, the applause without a tiny measure of which the rest of us couldn't go on? They divide into the two great classes of mankind, if we consider psychology and temperament. There are the mystics—the saints, the martyrs, and some artists. There are the non-mystics—many artists among them, to be sure. The mystical mind isn't the secret. The mental make-up of those who walk (who are able to walk) by themselves, is. They have, either from birth or by hard-wrung conquest, a kind of self-sufficiency more precious, for living purposes, than fine gold. It may be the bright, unconscious self-sufficiency of a Gene Stratton-Porter, or the admirable fortitude of a Joseph Conrad or the diffident charm of a Booth Tarkington—the manner is nothing; it is there. The mode of acquisition, except as it bears on work and affects personality, whether birthright or painful purchase, is nothing, either. The thing is there, like driven piles or bedrock. He who lacks that foundation must take his chance of his house, built on sands, being washed away.

With Mrs. Porter this invaluable element of personality has existed from the time of her earliest childhood. Nor is the faculty in question a superficial matter, like self-confidence. It was with a considerable lack of self-confidence that Mrs. Porter began writing; but notice that she began. How many others who had the self-confidence when they started have had to acquire the self-sufficiency, the power of self-sustention? How many have failed to do that? Self-confidence, indeed, is the most perfect of traitors. But there is a reservoir in the Self. . . .

Like every other prize, this one has its penalty. What will carry one to the top of a high rock will also, unimpeded, carry one over the rock's edge. The balance in egoism always trembles; when it comes to rest, one dies. And here is Mrs. Porter, who had in her a capacity that could have overcome mountains and that found only moderately difficult hills in its path. She must have burst into a thousand pieces if it hadn't been that she was a naturalist first and a novelist afterward, that she underwent the preoccupations of a wife and mother, that she toiled in swamps and wrote books, kept other people alive with her money as well as her courage and vitality, launched forth on self-pinions as a poet, corresponded with innumerable readers, did this and that and the other and then hit upon something else. She was one of twelve children. "To this mother at forty-six and this father at fifty, each at intellectual topnotch," she was born, the Minerva of mature and remarkable parents, a child who kept, in her own words, "thinking things which she felt should be saved," so that she frequently tugged at her mother's skirts and begged her to "set down" what the child considered stories and poems —generally some big fact in nature that thrilled the child, usually expressed in Biblical terms. Whom have we here? An incarnation as extraordinary as the Florence Nightingale whom Lytton Strachey put on paper? I think so.

iii

Mark Stratton, the father of Gene Stratton-Porter, described his wife, at the time of their marriage, as a "ninety-pound bit of pink porcelain, pink as a wild rose, plump as a partridge, having a big rope of bright brown hair, never ill a day in her life, and bearing the loveliest name ever given a woman —Mary. God fashioned her heart to be gracious, her body to be the mother of children, and as her especial gift of Grace, He put Flower Magic into her fingers."

From tiny seeds found in rice and coffee, Mary (Shellenbarger) Stratton started little vines and climbing plants. Rooted things she soaked in water, rolled in fine sand, planted according to habit, and they almost never failed to grow. When, intent on growing a tree or shrub from a slip or cutting that appeared hopeless, she cut the slip diagonally, inserted the lower end in a small potato and planted as if it were rooted, she was nearly always successful. Being of Dutch extraction, bulbs were her favourites—tulips, daffodils, star flowers, lilies, dahlias, little bright hyacinths that she called "blue bells." From these she distilled perfume by putting clusters, at the time of perfect bloom, in bowls lined with freshly made, unsalted butter, covering them closely, and cutting the few drops of extract thus obtained with alcohol. In Ohio a man gave her two tiny cedars of Lebanon which she brought with her to the farm in Wabash County, Indiana, planting one in her front yard and one in the small cemetery on the corner of her husband's land. It stands, thirty feet tall or over, two feet in circumference, guarding her grave.

All twelve of her children lived to be eight; an attack of scarlet fever joined with whooping cough was fatal to two of them a little over that age. The house, "Hopewell Farm," was an oblong box kept speckless. The liberal table and appetising food were known by all who travelled that way. She made the clothing for her brood. In the house that she kept so faultlessly clean, at the table she heaped with hearty dishes, Mark Stratton, conscious of his worthy British blood, praised her "tidiness" and accepted responsibility for the mental and spiritual welfare of his wife and children. It was understood that he had been named for a Mark Stratton who lived in New York and married a beauty, Anne Hutchinson. It was misunderstood that the first Mark and his wife settled on Stratton

Island, "afterward corrupted to Staten." From this point back for generations across the ocean, we are told that Mrs. Porter's father "followed his line to the family of Strattons of which the Earl of Northbrooke is the present head (1913). To his British traditions and the customs of his family, Mark Stratton clung with rigid tenacity, never swerving from his course a particle under the influence of environment or association." Perhaps, after all, he was British. "All his ideas were clear-cut; no man could influence him against his better judgment. He believed in God, in courtesy, in honour, and cleanliness, in beauty, and in education. He used to say that he would rather see a child of his the author of a book of which he could be proud than on the throne of England, which was the strongest way he knew to express himself." It is not too highly imaginative, I am sure, to believe that Mr. Stratton also planted slips and cuttings successfully; but they were slips of his own tenacious mind and they were planted most successfully in the receptive mind of his daughter, Gene.

We must note Mr. Stratton rather carefully. "His very first earnings he spent for a book; when other men rested, he read"—toiling upward in the night, in that time of Longfellowship, that has since been abandoned for fifteen minutes a day, in this era of Eliotry. The memory of Mr. Stratton enabled him to quote paragraphs at a time from Hume, Macaulay, Gibbon, Prescott and Bancroft—he was perhaps fondest of history—while as for the Bible, he could repeat it entire, his daughter says, except for the genealogies, and give chapter and verse. The genealogies were "a waste of grey matter to learn." Mrs. Porter confesses: "I was almost afraid to make these statements, although there are many living who can corroborate them, until John Muir published the story of his boyhood days, and in it I found the history of such rearing as was my father's, told of as the customary thing among the children of Muir's time."

Sermons, lectures, talks on civic improvement and politics, delivered without thought of personal fatigue or selfish inconvenience at the end of journeys of many miles were Mark Stratton's contribution to the cause of Good. It seems unkind to examine such performances dispassionately. "He worshipped beauty: beautiful faces, souls, hearts, beautiful landscapes, trees, animals, flowers. He loved colour: rich, bright colour and every variation down to the faintest shadings." Mrs. Porter keeps a cardinal silk handkerchief that he was carrying when stricken with apoplexy at the age of seventy-eight. "Over inspired Biblical passages, over great books, over sunlit landscapes, over a white violet abloom in deep shade, over a heroic deed of man, I have seen his brow light up, his eyes shine." He used especially to thrill his young daughter by the story of John Maynard, who piloted a burning boat to safety while he slowly roasted at the wheel. That he should tell it was natural, since the telling gave him opportunity to reproduce, with many inflections, the captain's cry of "John Maynard!" and the answer, "Aye, aye, sir!" echoed until it sank to a mere gasp, a whisper. . . .

iv

Gene Stratton was only a few years old when her mother, who had once nursed three of the children through typhoid fever, contracting it herself, broke down. Mrs. Stratton lived for several years, suffering continually, frequently tortured by pain. The youngest child was therefore allowed to follow an impulse and escape the training given her sisters. She followed her father and brothers outdoors, sleeping on their coats in fence corners, awakening, sometimes, to find shy creatures peering into her face. "I trotted from one object which attracted me to another, singing a little song of made-up phrases about everything I saw while I waded, catching fish, chasing butterflies over clover fields, or following a bird with a hair in its beak; much of the time I carried the inevitable baby for a woman-child, frequently improvised from an ear of corn in the silk, wrapped in catalpa leaf blankets." She made special pets of birds. She had been taught that they were useful and had "a gift of Grace in their beauty and music, things to be rigidly protected. From this cue I evolved the idea myself that I must be extremely careful, for had not my father tied a 'kerchief over my mouth when he lifted me for a peep into the nest of the humming-bird, and did he not walk softly and whisper when he approached the spot? So I stepped lightly, made no noise, and watched until I knew what a mother bird fed her young before I began dropping bugs, worms, crumbs, and fruit into little red mouths that opened at my tap on the nest quite as readily as at the touch of the feet of the mother bird."

All this life became a thing of memory just before the mother's death. Then they left the farm and went to town, to the city of Wabash, that Mrs. Stratton might have constant medical attention. The ninety-pound bit of pink porcelain, plump as a wild partridge, the little Dutch woman who had borne twelve children and kept a spotless farmhouse and heaped up good things on the long dinner table, lay with her head on a pillow, a cinnamon pink or a trillium placed where its fragrance would reach her with every breath she drew. She was dying. She had helped Mark Stratton with the bush- and vine-covered fences that crept around the acres they owned in a strip of gaudy colour; she shared the achievement of that orchard, lying in a valley, with its square of apple trees in the centre, so that at the time of blossoming it appeared as if a great pink-bordered white blanket had been let down on the earth. To her equally with her husband was due the presence on shale, which they might have drained, of sheets of blue flag, marigold and buttercups. All this was going out of her children's life and she was going out with it. The youngest child, in particular, had been leading a harum-scarum existence; if she reported promptly three times a day when the bell rang at meal times, with enough clothing to constitute a decent covering, nothing more was asked of her until the Sabbath. Mary Stratton was perhaps about to be released, to receive the benefit of a freedom in which, if her hands were not busy, it was not likely she would be happy or know what to do. Gene Stratton, whose father permitted his youngest to idolise him, was to be taken from outdoor freedom, her feet shod, her body restricted by the burden of Sunday clothing, her active legs stilled to a shuffle beneath the desk of a close schoolroom, and her mind set to droning over books. Unfortunately she came to the ordeal with no purely feminine resources of inattention, preoccupation or indifference. Her father had seen to that. It was he who was responsible for the child that revelled in *Paul and Virginia*, *Undine*, *Picciola*, *The Vicar of Wakefield*, *Pilgrim's Progress* —"exquisitely expressed and conceived stories" that "may have done much in forming high conceptions of what really constitutes literature, and in furthering the lofty ideals instilled by my parents." Mrs. Porter adds: "One of these stories formed the basis of my first publicly recognised literary effort." She was assigned to write a class composition on "Mathematical Law." She postponed, rebelled, wrote a paper retelling the story of *Picciola* and in fear and defiance read it aloud in class. After one page the teacher halted her while she summoned in the superintendent of city schools to hear the sixteen foolscap pages from the beginning. "One instant the room was in laughter, the next the boys bowed their heads, and the girls who had forgotten their handkerchiefs cried in their aprons. Never again was a subject forced upon me." She was her father's daughter, and her father was Mark Stratton.

"My mother went out too soon to know, and my father never saw one of my books; but he knew I was boiling and bubbling like a yeast jar in July over some literary work, and if I timidly slipped to him with a composition, or a faulty poem, he saw good in it, and made suggestions for its betterment. When I wanted to express something in colour, he went to an artist, sketched a design for an easel, personally superintended the carpenter who built it, and provided tuition. On that same easel I painted the water colours for *Moths of the Limberlost*, and one of the most poignant regrets of my life is that he was not there to see them, and to know that the easel which he built through his faith in me was finally used in illustrating a book.

"If I thought it was music through which I could express myself, he paid for lessons and detected hidden ability which should be developed. Through the days of struggle he stood fast; firm in his belief in me. He was half the battle. It was he who demanded a physical standard that developed strength to endure the rigours of scientific field and darkroom work, and the building of ten books in ten years, five of which were on nature subjects, having my own illustrations, and five novels, literally teeming with natural history, true to nature. It was he who demanded of me from birth the finishing of any task I attempted and who taught me to cultivate patience to watch and wait, even years, if necessary, to find and secure the material I wanted. It was he who daily lived before me the life of exactly such a man as I portrayed in *The Harvester*, and who constantly used every atom of brain and body power to help and to encourage all men to do the same."

No further illumination should be needed on the most extraordinary personal influence in Mrs. Porter's life.

V

Gene Stratton was married in 1886, at the age of eighteen, to Charles Darwin Porter, of Wabash, Indiana. Marriage, a home of her own, and a daughter were successively brought to bear upon a nature already powerful; none of them succeeded in eradicating the impress of Mark Stratton. The new home was a cabin of fourteen rooms (at first), standing on some fifteen acres near the Limberlost Swamp. The familiar address runs: "Limberlost Cabin, Rome City, Indiana." Red, white, pink, blue, lavender and yellow flower-beds of an acre apiece were laid off in the deep woods running down the shore of a lake; the cabin stands in the middle of the yellow bed, a dwelling of large rooms and four fireplaces, two of which Mrs. Porter built, to a large extent, herself. One is of pudden stone, red and blue pebbles; another, in the living room, is constructed of field boulders split to expose their quartz crystals that sparkle under artificial light. The windows were built with broad, deep casements especially to furnish feeding-tables for birds. On the open, cement-floored porch may stand in winter wheat, apples, cabbage and celery bunches. Chickadees, titmice, nuthatches, sapsuckers, flickers, song sparrows, jays, cardinals and squirrels come to the sills to eat the chopped wheat, ground corn and suet put out for them.

But this is to mix past and the comparative present. It was not long before Mrs. Porter's daughter was old enough to go to school. "I knew how to manage life to make it meet my needs, thanks to even the small amount I had seen of my mother. I kept a cabin of fourteen rooms and kept it immaculate. I made most of my daughter's clothes, I kept a conservatory in which there bloomed from three to six hundred bulbs every winter, tended a house of canaries and linnets, and cooked and washed dishes, besides, three times a day. In my spare time (mark the word, there was time to spare else the books never would have been written and the pictures made) I mastered photography . . ." but we need not go with her into the details of this one among many of her personal triumphs. She was for two years editor of the camera department of Recreation, for two years on the natural history staff of Outing, for four years specialist in natural history photography on the Photographic Times Annual Almanac. She had a dread of failure and, at first, carried on her special work as secretly as possible. "My husband owned a drug and book store that carried magazines, but only a few people in our locality read these, none were interested in nature photography or natural science; so what I was trying to do was not realised even by my own family. I did not want to fail before my man person and my daughter and our respective families." She was further afraid of ridicule in a community "where I was already severely criticised on account of my ideas of housekeeping, dress and social customs." When she first attempted "nature studies sugar-coated with fiction" she proceeded with the same furtiveness. "I who waded morass, fought quicksands, crept, worked from ladders high in air, and crossed water on improvised rafts without a tremor, slipped with many misgivings into the postoffice and rented a box for myself, so that if I met with failure my husband and the men in the bank"—Mr. Porter was president of the Bank of Geneva—"need not know." Through loss of her address at the New York end, she waited unanswered until one day, months later, when she went into "our store" on an errand and the storekeeper said: "I read your story in the Metropolitan last night. It was great! Did you ever write any fiction before?" Mrs. Porter relates: "My head whirled, but I had learned to keep my own counsels, so I said as lightly as I could, while my heart beat until I feared he could hear it, 'No. Just a simple little thing! Have you any spare copies? My sister might want one.' "

The appearance of her first story led to an order for a second, to be illustrated with her own photographs. She had a day, or less, to fill the request for photographs, and kept a number of persons up all night to pose for her. The genesis of *Freckles*, her second book, was the discovery by lumbermen of a nest of the black vulture in the Limberlost Swamp. Her husband, whose business had compelled him to allow her to work alone but who was also a natural history enthusiast, insisted that he must go with her. "A Limberlost trip at that time was not to be joked about. The swamp had not been shorn, branded, and tamed. There were most excellent reasons why I should not go there. Much of it was impenetrable. Only a few trees had been taken out; oilmen were just invading it. In its physical aspect it was a treacherous swamp and quagmire filled with every plant, animal, and human danger known in the worst of such locations in the Central States.

"A rod inside the swamp on a road leading to an oil well we mired to the carriage hubs. I shielded my camera in my arms and before we reached the well I thought the conveyance would be torn to pieces and the horse stalled. At the well we started on foot, Mr. Porter in kneeboots, I in waist-high waders. The time was late June; we forced our way between steaming, fetid pools, through swarms of gnats, flies, mosquitoes, poisonous insects, keeping a sharp watch for rattlesnakes. We sank ankle deep at every step, and logs we thought solid broke under us. Our progress was a steady succession of prying and pulling each other to the surface. Our clothing was wringing wet, and the exposed parts of our bodies lumpy with bites and stings. My husband found the tree, cleared the opening to the great prostrate log, traversed its unspeakable odours for nearly forty feet to its farthest recess, and brought the baby and egg to the light in his leaf-lined hat.

"We could endure the location only by dipping napkins in deodorant and binding them over our mouths and nostrils. Every third day for almost three months we made this trip, until Little Chicken was able to take wing."

The idea of *Freckles* came one day when they were leaving the swamp. A big feather with a shaft over twenty inches long came spinning and swirling earthward, and fell in Mrs. Porter's path. It was an eagle's feather, but although she instantly looked aloft, Mrs. Porter's well-trained eyes could not catch sight of the bird. She has always regretted that to her story the title *Freckles* was given; her wish was for "The Falling Feather"—that tangible thing drifting down out of Nowhere, just as the boy came in the story of her fashioning.

The insertion of marginal drawings of nature subjects in *Freckles* made a distinct impression get abroad that it was simply a nature book, with the result that three long years were required for the novel to attain its enormous popularity. Published in 1904, the book had sold, ten years later, 670,733 copies in the regular edition.

vi

Mrs. Porter as an author is now fairly before us and may be considered profitably before we take a look at her newest novel, *The White Flag.* So familiar a phenomenon calls for incisive comment. She writes her stories "exactly as they take shape in my mind" and the excisions are sometimes—as in the case of *Her Father's Daughter*, which yet remained overlong—quite heavy. The edited and published fiction is of itself remarkable for an unrestraint, a vigorous emphasis, a masculine zeal, with which there is generally combined freshness of feeling and a transparent sincerity. It is this sincerity, proceeding as it so often does from a total unconsciousness of what lies behind it, that the popular instinct detects at once in the pages of a work of fiction. It has, of course, nothing whatever to do with literary art, it is never shamed or enriched by the processes of introspection, and in this it conforms to the wilful egoism fundamental with the Northern races in a new country and exploitable environment. The student of psychology may be interested, for more reasons than the inheritance of Holland ancestry, to compare the late Theodore Roosevelt and Gene Stratton-Porter in personalities and characters. Each has swayed the millions; each, beyond all possible question, has influenced human lives. Neither was oppressed by the enormous responsibility attached to such a rôle. I would not say that the one had more education than has the other, but their educations were different.

"To spend time writing a book based wholly upon human passion and its outworking I would not," exclaims Mrs. Porter, to whom art is an expression of flower-beds and children a-plenty, censored books and human lives lived on sober and industrious models. And she compromised on a book "into which I put all the nature work that came naturally within its scope, and seasoned it with little bits of imagination and straight copy from the lives of men and women I had known intimately, folk who lived in a simple, common way with which I was familiar." In simple justice it should be pointed out that she insisted upon alternating nature books and novels, although far more money could be earned by writing only fiction.

Just as the child was taken from the fields, shoed and harnessed in "Sunday clothes" and put into school, so the naturalist was torn, though somewhat more gently and gradually, from her proper enjoyments and placed in the trammels of book-length fiction. What wonder that she revolted?—but the rebellion of *Picciola*, though ending in personal triumph, was not the end of school; and the rebellion of the novelist, though rewarded with a tremendous personal triumph, did not end her ordeal of novel-writing. What people like Mrs. Porter never achieve is a successful rebellion from, within, themselves. Something more powerful than they quells their self-insurrections; they go on; money seems worth while for what can be done with it to give happiness and widen opportunity for others; the task is good—why? It is a task; something that must be done very thoroughly. The father, Mark Stratton, to whom his daughter was so observably devoted, gave her a set of ideals that were to lift her up, like strong links of iron, and then to turn into rigid chains. She who owes so much to him owes to him more than she has ever suspected, a compulsion put upon her from within herself, the final reward or fate of every worshipper.

She has tried to escape. She has written poetry. There was *The Fire Bird;* and lately there has been *Euphorbia*, a long narrative published serially to the astonishment of readers of Good Housekeeping. The subject of *Euphorbia* is interesting—a woman to whom marriage brings non-fulfilment, whose husband tramples and uproots the red-and-white wild flower she loves. When at length the man dies, the mother has one fearful moment in which her child reaches toward a bit of euphorbia with she knows not which intention. But he loves it. Escape! It is not necessary to make as much of this as the psychoanalyst would make of it, nor, perhaps, to miss the mark so widely. "My life has been fortunate," Mrs. Porter admits, "in one glad way: I have lived mostly in the country and worked in the woods. For every bad man and woman I have known I have met, lived with, and am intimately acquainted with an overwhelming number of thoroughly clean and decent people who still believe in God and cherish high ideals, and it is *upon the lives of these that I base what I write.*" There is a puzzling fierceness in the attacks she launches on those who write otherwise; she is vulnerable somewhere in this connection or she would show less heat and animosity. And, to some extent, her active resentment is justified, for she has had a heavy experience of misleading praise and some experience of hypocrisy. I remember an occasion upon which she wrote to me, with scornful inflections, to lay before me the evidence in the case of a certain well-known writer who had enthusiastically praised her work, though "not for publication." It was a course which, like herself, I should join in condemning; but was it so much of a matter? Did, could, the voice of a single one, count for much where she had heard already the open voices of praise from so many thousands? And if it was so, then why?

Who answers that will make possibly the largest single contribution to the psychology of literature, for this identical question finally arises in the case of writers great and small.

vii

Never, perhaps, has Mrs. Porter been more herself than in her latest book, *The White Flag;* although *Her Father's Daughter*, as originally written, was overgrown. Both these books are autobiography—*Her Father's Daughter* of the heart, *The White Flag* of mind and memory. If Mrs. Porter has but one story to tell, no one has succeeded in telling it so often with such freshness of feeling or such repeated success in the matter of readers. *The White Flag* is the story of Mahala Spellman, daughter and only child of Mahlon and Elizabeth Spellman. The opening scenes are laid in the Indiana of the 1880s. The village is called Ashwater. For what seems an excessive time our attention is concentrated upon Elizabeth as a little girl and Junior Moreland as a little boy. Nothing could be more typical of Mrs. Porter than the attention she bestows upon her heroine in childhood—the exact detail of Mahala's dress, the recorded precision of her unfailingly correct behaviour. If there is something unnatural about the child, there is everything natural to a child in Mrs. Porter's fiction. In picturing the richest man in the village Mrs. Porter blackens his villainy to a pitch where Mr. Moreland is neither more nor less credible than some of the characters in, let us say, *Way Down East.*

Mahala, in ensuing chapters, refuses Junior Moreland in the face of the fact that his father could save her father from ruin. Her father fails, and, broken, dies. Her mother becomes an invalid. When finally Mahala can truthfully say that all is lost except self-respect and courage, a deadly blow is levelled at her self-respect. Some money is stolen. Circumstantial evidence accuses Mahala, and Ashwater shuns her.

It will not be supposed that Mrs. Porter fails to raise up a champion in her heroine's hour of need. All along we have been in touch, in close touch, with Jason. We knew him as a boy, apparently the washerwoman's son. We know him as a young man, springing to Mahala's relief. There is no real reason why, in such a situation and with two such principal characters, Mrs. Porter should not work miracles. She does. . . . Of course her point is that the virtue, goodness and courage of Mahala and Jason earn their own ample rewards; and the thousands who are reading *The White Flag* will accept this as so.

Books by Gene Stratton-Porter

1903 *The Song of the Cardinal*
1904 *Freckles*
1907 *What I Have Done With Birds* (republished, 1917, as *Friends in Feathers*)
1908 *At the Foot of the Rainbow*
1909 *A Girl of the Limberlost*
1909 *Birds of the Bible*
1910 *Music of the Wild*
1911 *The Harvester*
1912 *Moths of the Limberlost*
1913 *Laddie*
1915 *Michael O'Halloran*
1916 *Morning Face*

1918 *A Daughter of the Land*
1920 *Homing With the Birds*
1921 *Her Father's Daughter*
1922 *The Fire Bird*
1923 *White Flag*
Euphorbia appeared as a serial in Good Housekeeping: January, February, March numbers, 1923.

Sources on Gene Stratton-Porter

Gene Stratton-Porter, A Little Story of Her Life and Work. This is the booklet, now out of print, published some ten years ago by DOUBLEDAY, PAGE & COMPANY, based upon the long self-account written by Mrs. Porter and prepared by Eugene F. Saxton.

"An American Bird-Woman." Anonymous article in CHAMBERS'S JOURNAL (London and Edinburgh. New York: International News Company), Part 46, October 1, 1914: page 636.

Private Information.

17. *Poetry and Plays*

i

IF you look at the poets as they move in their procession before your eyes, you will see that each is dressed after the manner of his age—the Elizabethans in starched ruffs; the men of the Eighteenth Century in knee-breeches; the men of today in Homburg hats. And if you listen to their verses you will hear that each composes, too, after the manner of his age. For there have been fashions in poetry as there have been fashions in dress, and you can tell the period of a poem not only by the name and date of the poet but by the style and flavour of the poetry." From this thought J. F. Roxburgh has written "a beginner's introduction to English poetry" with the charming title, *The Poetic Procession.* His brief review of the poets from the Elizabethans to the men now writing is felicitous enough. But although I am sure his intention in the sentences quoted was not literal, the image of present-day poets in Homburg hats is very disconcerting. Don Marquis has probably worn one, thus inviting the visitation of insurance agents. But I am sure some of his poems have been written with the wind blowing through his hair. Such poems as "The Name," in his *Dreams and Dust*, for example, or those "Premonitions" in his *Poems and Portraits.* It is as difficult to say, with Marquis, where the humourist stops in his poetry and the thinker steps in as to mark the same exit-entrance in the man's prose. *Sonnets to a Red-Haired Lady and Famous Love Affairs* and a part of *Poems and Portraits* are supposed to belong to Marquis the jester; but, of the second-named book, which part? "The man who has laughed lest he should weep, the clown of the seven times broken heart" is Richard Le Gallienne's apt characterisation of Marquis. I am not sure that "The Tom Cat" in *Poems and Portraits* is a bit less "serious" than such a poem as "Inhibition" in the same collection.

> Behind the placid front of use
> The baffled whims move to and fro;
> We fear to let these genii go. . . .

Sober-faced, we carry hidden within us something for which the poet has found one of those rare things in the language, the perfect phrase; it is

> The golden nonsense of the heart.

Perhaps we also are like the Tom-cat and, on our occasions, "chant the hate of a million years."

> He will lie on a rug to-morrow
> And lick his silky fur,
> And veil the brute in his yellow eyes
> And play he's tame, and purr.
>
> But at midnight in the alley
> He will crouch again and wail,
> And beat the time for his demon's song
> With the swing of his demon's tail.

I am as certain that Marquis admires and condones the Tom-cat as I am that he has sought the troubling and elusive "Name" which has variously seemed, as he tells us in his fine poem, to be Love, and Beauty, and God.

The Boston Evening Transcript spoke not long ago of "the unhurried ascent of John Hall Wheelock to the highest rank among contemporary American poets." The statement seems to me free from any exaggeration; and it is encouraging to think that Mr. Wheelock is in a way to reach the height more conspicuously than did Edwin Arlington Robinson, of whom, until his unveiling a few years ago by fellow poets, the larger public seems to have remained in a lamentable ignorance. Mr. Wheelock's *Dust and Light* (1919) and his *The Black Panther* (1922) have a beauty and sentience best illustrated by quotation. Here are some lines from "Earth," in *Dust and Light:*

> Deftly does the dust express
> In mind her hidden loveliness,
> And from her cool silence stream
> The cricket's cry and Dante's dream;
> For the earth that breeds the trees
> Breeds cities too, and symphonies.
> Equally her beauty flows
> Into a saviour, or a rose—
> Looks down in dream, and from above
> Smiles at herself in Jesus's love.
> Christ's love and Homer's art
> Are but the workings of her heart;
> Through Leonardo's hand she seeks
> Herself, and through Beethoven speaks
> In holy thunderings around
> The awful message of the ground.

The thought is Emersonian, but with Emerson lyricism was a doubtful and an inconstant capture. Here is "The Lion-House," from *The Black Panther*, a poem, I cannot but think, that any poet would be proud to sign:

Always the heavy air,
  The dreadful cage, the low
Murmur of voices, where
  Some Force goes to and fro
In an immense despair!

As through a haunted brain—
  With tireless footfalls
The Obsession moves again,
  Trying the floor, the walls,
Forever, but in vain.

In vain, proud Force! A might
  Shrewder than yours, did spin
Around your rage that bright
  Prison of steel, wherein
You pace for my delight.

And O, my heart, what Doom
  What warier Will has wrought
The cage, within whose room
  Paces your burning thought,
For the delight of Whom?

The black and silver of cover and jacket on Elinor Wylie's second book of poems, *Black Armour*, were not so much to match the title as to convey the colour impression of a number of readers who had studied the book in manuscript. The poems, grouped under the names of the parts of a suit of armour—Breastplate, Gauntlet, Helmet, Beaver Up, Plumes—perhaps require study, not in the sense of textual analysis (though they will repay that) but in the sense of returning to them several times, so that their compressed emotion may fully expand itself. I had almost said, explode itself. Indeed, it may sometimes produce nothing short of an explosion of feeling in the sensitive reader. I am thinking now of such works as "Now That Your Eyes Are Shut" (which opens the section called Plumes). I have heard the poem "Peregrine" called the best in the book, the dryly concise account of a

> Liar and bragger,
> He had no friend
> Except a dagger
> And a candle-end

and whose career, the narration of which includes a dozen feats of rhyming, was summed up when

> He spoke this sentence
> With a princely air:
> "The noose draws tighter;
> This is the end;
> I'm a good fighter,
> But a bad friend:
> I've played the traitor
> Over and over;
> I'm a good hater,
> But a bad lover."

But "Fable," with its effects in twenty-four lines as powerful as Coleridge's in his *Ancient Mariner*, and "Lucifer Sings in Secret" are to me finer than "Peregrine" because more individual. I mean that I could imagine a later Browning writing "Peregrine," but cannot imagine anyone but Elinor Wylie writing "Lucifer." Much stress has been laid on Mrs. Wylie's gift for bright, strange images in her poetry, and this is no small item in her genius; but the steeled emotion, the unearthly cry that is heard under the burnished and metallic surfaces, sometimes in not instantly intelligible words, is her voice as a poet. In "Now That Your Eyes Are Shut," which I quote, there is one stanza that might have been written by a poet of a long-past century—I leave you to name him—but there are two stanzas, the most important, which I can imagine no one but Elinor Wylie writing:

Now that your eyes are shut
Not even a dusty butterfly may brush them;
My flickering knife has cut
Life from sonorous lion throats to hush them.

If pigeons croon too loud
Or lambs bleat proudly, they must come to slaughter,
And I command each cloud
To be precise in spilling silent water.

Let light forbear those lids:
I have forbidden the feathery ash to smutch them;
The spider thread that thrids
The gray-plumed grass has not my leave to touch them.

My casual ghost may slip,
Issuing tiptoe, from the pure inhuman;
The tissues of my lip
Will bruise your eyelids, while I am a woman.

ii

The title poem in Amanda Hall's book, *The Dancer in the Shrine*, tempts to quotation, but there seems to me something unfair in reprinting it complete and to cut lines from it is to mutilate both what is taken and that which is left. There is a good deal of the life of the countryside in the book; Miss Hall's New England is that of Thoreau but her lyrical gift is distinctly personal. A characteristic mood and treatment is shown in "I'll Build My House of Sticks and Stones," from which the following couplets are taken:

I'll build my house of sticks and stones,
Of lollypops and herring bones,

None other than myself to please—
Of fine, fresh straw or green sage cheese;

I'll build my house of this and that
To suit my pleasure and my cat—

I'll clothe myself in cast-off rags,
In cobwebs or in barley bags,

The shabbier I am encased
The fruitier my joy will taste.

I'll set my two lips to the air
And carol to the birds' despair. . . .

Some musing morning as I sing
Perhaps I'll catch God listening,

In soft enchantment at His sill.
He'll tell His angels to be still,

He'll say to them in tones discreet
That there is singing in the street. . .

The pagan quality keeps its joyousness while transmuting it into something reverent and beautiful in such lines as "The Dancer in the Shrine." The religious note, differently accented, may be found in the work of Alice Meynell, whose complete verse is now available in *The Poems of Alice Meynell.* Mrs. Meynell's death has brought a sharp emphasis upon the rare character of her poetic gift. Alfred Noyes says she has left to the world a volume "containing only masterpieces," but I like better the words of J. L. Garvin: "Not one of her poems but was the music of a thought as most of her essays were the fruit of perception." Let me not quote "The Shepherdess," so widely known and so self-expressive, but "Chimes" with its changing image and its "music of a thought" sung to perfection:

Brief, on a flying night,
From the shaken tower,
A flock of bells take flight,
And go with the hour.

Like birds from the cote to the gales,
Abrupt—O hark!
A fleet of bells set sails,
And go to the dark.

Sudden the cold airs swing.
Alone, aloud,
A verse of bells takes wing
And flies with the cloud.

Mrs. Meynell was one of a group of contemporary Catholic poets of whom, it may be, Aline Kilmer is the most widely known and read in America. Of the others of that group I should like especially to mention two whose new books of verse have just appeared—Sister M. Madeleva, a nun in the congregation of the Holy Cross at Holy Rosary Academy, California, and Wilfred Rowland Childe, who is English. Sister M. Madeleva's collection called *Knights Errant* contains verse highly spiritual in type, clear and strong in emotional expression, and admirable for the manner in which the author has adhered to subjects and thoughts strictly within the limits of her clearly defined experience. Mysticism is natural to these Catholic singers, and will be found strongly in Mr. Childe's *The Gothic Rose*, a book of poems quite Gothic in spirit, sometimes wistful, sometimes marked with melancholy and obviously the outgrowth of a loving adoration. Although such poems as "The Dirge for Westminster" and "The Virgin of Flanders" are the body of *The Gothic Rose*, there is a range including an Oxford poem ("Idylle Oxonienne"), one or two classical subjects, such as "Daphne," and the modern verse of "The Austrian River."

Like Amanda Hall, Josephine Daskam Bacon is both novelist and poet, but it is as a poet that Mrs. Bacon will arrest our attention for her *Truth o' Women*, which has been described as a *Spoon River Anthology* for women. The book consists of a group of "Epitaphs for Women" in free verse; this one being characteristic:

> I was sorry to leave you,
> Because I knew you needed me.
> But are there no women who are sorry to die
> Because they need their husbands?
> I wanted, dying, to be one of them!

Forty of these "Epitaphs" are followed by a series of dramatic monologues under the general title,

"Truth o' Women." The monologues are spoken by the mother of Joan of Arc, Lincoln's mother, Dante's wife, Milton's daughters, the wife of Judas, one of Bluebeard's wives, the mother of Mary and Martha and the wives of Columbus, Sir Isaac Newton, Cadmus, Adam, Shakespeare, Socrates, Pilate and Julius Cæsar.

No, evidently realism in poetry is not through! Look, here is "an epic of insignificance" called *The Life and Death of Mrs. Tidmuss*, by Wilfrid Blair. Pursuing the Spoon River comparison for Mrs. Bacon's book, one is on the verge of calling Blair's work a *Main Street* of England in verse. In subject matter it is more like John Masefield's *Widow in the Bye Street*, I should say. We start with Selina as the young daughter of a greengrocer, see her as a slow and bashful girl leading a drab existence and wooed finally by Tom Tidmuss, who is interested in poultry-raising. He is a printer by trade. They plan to marry and get a cottage. Then, for the first time, Selina lives:

She had a ring, and roses in her cheek.

A year's wait reaps the reward of her wedding day.

She had no wedding bells. Her well-oiled sire
Led her in tribal veilings up the aisle
To where a curate, impatient for his hire,
Hovered, and Tom in his stiff Sunday style.
Things went through quick. It mattered not. She moved
In a mazed phantasmagoria all the while.

Thereafter births, deaths, a subdued drudgery, old age, the selling of the house and furniture and the going to live with her daughter, where she is not very happy. The poet concludes on a swift crescendo, *maestoso:*

> Death sets free: it is Life that holds in thrall . . .
> Blow up, O trumpets of eternity!
> Shout, souls of God, from starry sea to sea!
> Stars, clash your shining shields—a soul is free!

iii

Of George Santayana as a poet I have incidentally spoken in Chapter 9, quoting one of his superb sonnets, but I think I neglected to call attention to the preface he has recently provided for his *Poems.* It is an omission that must be repaired. I can scarcely give an idea of the preface's excellence as vigorous and beautiful prose, but aside from Santayana's explanation that the subject of these poems is "simply my philosophy in the making," it is just to quote this passage: "A Muse—not exactly an English Muse—actually visited me in my isolation; the same, or a ghost of the same, that visited Boethius or Alfred de Musset or Leopardi. It was literally impossible for me then not to re-echo her eloquence. When that compulsion ceased, I ceased to write verses. My emotion—for there was genuine emotion—faded into a sense that my lesson was learned and my troth plighted. . . ." I cannot resist quoting from the closing poem, the lines on Art that count as a translation from Theophile Gautier but are actually so much more than that:

All things are doubly fair
If patience fashion them
    And care—
Verse, enamel, marble, gem. . . .

—All things return to dust
Save beauties fashioned well.
    The bust
Outlasts the citadel.

The gods, too, die, alas!
But deathless and more strong
    Than brass
Remains the sovereign song.

How W. E. Henley would have loved this! (But perhaps he saw it, and was not silent). Henley, whose *Poems* in my copy are the nineteenth edition—and my copy is far from new. Henley and Francis Thompson and Kipling go on; few of us need any urge or even any reminder to re-read them; their poetry gains its fresh recruits with every season of the young men, and old men have been known to resume their youth over the pages. . . .

Youth! That is the cargo that sails on those perilous seas forlorn we looked upon from John Keats's casements opening on the foam. What a frank title for a first book of verse is Robert Roe's *Here You Have Me!* The title poem and a few others in the Whitmanesque tradition are followed by a group of poems derived from experiences as a sailor, verses that break free of any tradition known to me; and by poems ripened out of an intimate contact with the Arizona desert. I have liked some of these greatly, just as I like, for another reason,

Vachel Lindsay's *Going-to-the-Sun*, which is suitably fantastic. Some way must be devised for everyone to hear Lindsay recite or chant his verses, since in no other way can the reader possibly get more than half their effect. I think if all could hear him in a half dozen, the awakened instinct and quickened imagination in most of us would accomplish the rest. We should then be able merely to read him and feel the elixir.

In a later chapter of this book devoted to Christopher Morley there is mention of his poem, "Parson's Pleasure," which gives title to his new and by all odds best collection of verse. The remarkable change and growth in Morley as a prose writer has been attended by chemistries in the poet, and I expect the large popularity gained by his poems in *Chimneysmoke* will accrue without delay to the poems in *Parson's Pleasure.* But are you familiar with the poetry of Franklin P. Adams? I only partly mean the F. P. A. of the daily breakfast table and occasional short lyric or bit of versification heading a newspaper column. I mean the author of *Tobogganing on Parnassus*, and *Weights and Measures*, and *Overset*, and *So There!* Light, satiric verse, most of it; but how finished and perfect in its form, how penetrating in its arrowy indirection! Whether he is penning the address of the passionate advertiser to his love or doing for Horace what Edward Fitzgerald did for a certain Persian singer, Mr. Adams is constantly curing the evils of civilisation, freeing those "baffled whims" Don Marquis tells about and generally making life more livable by making it more singable.

iv

Among studies of contemporary poets we have had none so valuable, I think, as Lloyd Morris's *The Poetry of Edwin Arlington Robinson.* The first and most important inspiration that came to Mr. Morris was undoubtedly the divisions of his subject, so that he brings us to the consideration of a difficult master under the headings natural to the poet, his "Men," his use of "History," and "Legend," his two prose "Plays," and as the crown, his "Ideas" or intellectual content. It is hard to see how any reader of poetry can do without this lucid discussion and exposition of one who may well be, and is by competent critics adjudged to be, the greatest living American poet. A biographical note, following the careful bibliography of Mr. Robinson's works by W. Van R. Whitall, rounds out the usefulness of the little volume.

The popularity of anthologies of verse is now proverbial, and I expect that there will be plenty of attention for the *Anthology of American Verse* which J. C. Squire, poet and editor of the London Mercury, has completed. The work shows the advantages gained by the onlooker's standpoint, who can bring to bear a sense of perspective better than our own. The selection also shows Mr. Squire's fine taste which, so far as I know, has no superior and very few equals among those whose knowledge of poetry would qualify them to be anthologists at all. Another collection of extreme importance but necessarily from a different angle has been completed by Margery Gordon and Marie B. King, and just published under the title *Verse of Our Day.* As the compilers had distinctly in mind school use of this book in a special edition, as well as the wide popular audience in an edition from which certain textbook features would be omitted, their aim was for inclusiveness and a highly representative quality above all else—though a rigid selection was inevitable, too. The result is a book presenting 347 poems, 225 by American poets and 122 by British. Ninety-two of the Americans and 42 of the British poets are modern—that is, they lie between Eugene Field and Amy Lowell on the one hand, between W. E. Henley and Alfred Noyes and John Masefield on the other. Biographies of the poets, reading lists and, in the school edition, certain guides to study have been included. The popularity of *Verse of Our Day* ought to be sure and of some permanence.

Henry van Dyke, assisted by Hardin Craig and Asa Don Dickinson, has edited *A Book of British and American Verse* rather from a standpoint like J. C. Squire's. "This is not an attempt to make another historical anthology of English verse," Dr. van Dyke explains. "I have looked only at the value and beauty of the poems themselves." If some poets were unrepresented, it was not to be helped. "Those that seemed the best have been chosen out of many, not to illustrate a theory, but for their own sake, because they are good to read." And for those who loved Roosevelt as well as for those who have the anthologist's interest, there is *Roosevelt as the Poets Saw Him*, edited by Charles Hanson Towne and containing poems by Kipling,

Edith Wharton, Richard Le Gallienne, William Watson, Edgar Lee Masters, Owen Wister, John Hay, Vachel Lindsay, Edwin Arlington Robinson and Robert Bridges.

V

Leaving aside all disputes on the score of the drama, one of the best moments of our contemporary literature came a few years ago when it was first known that J. M. Barrie had consented to the publication of his plays. And then when the published plays began to come along, the moment enlarged itself. Here was a man who was practically inventing something, a curious but felicitous compound of novel and drama, a mixture of narrative and dialogue, something that extended far beyond the irrepressible wit and satire of G. Bernard Shaw's stage directions, priceless as those had been. There was a feeling, with good reason, that by this step Barrie had done more to instate himself with posterity than by anything heretofore. For about the plays themselves, as plays, the controversy is already active; but about the success of the plays as published I know of no dispute or objection. *Dear Brutus* is the eighth volume in a series which already included *A Kiss for Cinderella*, *Alice Sit-by-the Fire*, *What Every Woman Knows*, *Quality Street*, *The Admirable Crichton* and two collections of the shorter plays, *Half Hours* ("Pantaloon," "The Twelve-Pound Look," "Rosalind," "The Will") and *Echoes of the War* ("The Old Lady Shows Her Medals," "The New Word," "Barbara's

Wedding," "A Well-Remembered Voice"). There are good things to come yet, including *Peter Pan*, and these are in preparation; but much of the best Barrie and best-agreed-to Barrie is now ready to go on the bookshelf (where it won't stay put very well)—and the best of Barrie is good in any company. For example, *The Admirable Crichton*, which even the most critical have found strong words to praise. The printed version avoids the fault of the 1918 stage revival in which, as has been said, Barrie dulled or allowed some one else to dull the edge of his perfect satire. For a short and appreciative yet discriminating account of Barrie the playwright, one could not do better than read the chapter upon him in John W. Cunliffe's *English Literature During the Last Half Century* (Macmillan: Revised Edition, 1923).

John Galsworthy, the subject of the first chapter of this book, will not, of course, be overlooked by anyone concerned in knowing the best plays of our time. His plays are to be had, complete at present, in five volumes (*Plays: First Series; Plays: Second Series*, etc.) and a supplementary volume, *Six Short Plays*. Or, with the exception of the six short plays, each may be had separately. Probably a consensus would select *Loyalties*, *Justice*, *Strife*, *The Silver Box*, *The Pigeon* and *The Skin Game* as his most important and representative dramas.

Arnold Bennett's new play, *Don Juan de Marana*, represents one fulfilment of a threefold ambition. Don Juan, together with the legend of the Wandering Jew and the story of Tannhäuser, had attracted him for years as great subjects for drama. A good deal of preliminary work on the Wandering Jew theme was wasted by news that somebody else had written a play on the theme and obtained a production. "I put the Wandering Jew aside for ten years," explains Bennett. "With regard to Tannhäuser, I am still wondering how to cure Elizabeth of her insipidity, and how to get into the heads of a twentieth century audience the surely obvious fact that music is not an essential ingredient of the tale." Don Juan Tenorio proved impossible as the basis of a play, but finally Bennett came upon the other, later version of the Don Juan story. "And then I discovered what I wanted in a work on my own shelves, the plays of Dumas *père* in twenty-five volumes. I ought to have divined that since Dumas wrote plays on everything, he must have written a play on the Don Juan de Marana variation of the Don Juan legend."

At last all of W. Somerset Maugham's plays are available for the reader, some ten volumes that include not only *The Circle*, but *Lady Frederick*, *The Explorer*, *Jack Straw*, etc. It should perhaps be noted here that the play *Rain* is not a Maugham play, but an adaptation of Maugham's tremendous short story, "Rain," included in his book of South Sea tales, *The Trembling of a Leaf*.

John Dos Passos in his *Rosinante to the Road Again*, in the chapter on "Benavente's Madrid," has conveyed with clearness and much picturesqueness the style and point, the character and perfection of taste in a certain style (*lo castizo*) with which Jacinto Benavente's dramas abound. It is this that from their Spanish viewpoint makes them of such distinction; but that would hardly account for their success outside Spain. Larger qualities—a gentle and deadly satire, a nervous vitality, wit—do that; and the visit of Señor Benavente to America a few months ago did much to attract attention to his work. Twelve of his plays, assembled in three volumes in the translations of John Garrett Underhill, are now accessible to the English reader. Benavente represents a more modern Spain than the Echegaray with whose *drame passionel* those who read plays are sufficiently familiar. He should be read for his own sake and as a Continental dramatist much more distinctly representative of something national, something Spanish in sensibility, than are the outstanding playwrights of other European lands—excepting Russia, no doubt. One can scarcely read Ibsen for Norway, or Strindberg for a little corner of the world; Tchekov is Russia but Andreiev is humanity. Jacinto Benavente, however, is Spain without the sacrifice of those elements which are of importance to a society in any country.

The impressive success of the Theatre Guild is known everywhere, and the Theatre Guild Library is very welcome for its addition of several of the finest of recent plays to the resources of the reading table. The series has been auspiciously begun with publication of Karel Capek's *R. U. R.*, Ernest Toller's *The Mass-Men*, and Elmer L. Rice's *The Adding Machine*. A particularly good pick of recent successes will be found in *Contemporary American Plays*, edited by Arthur H. Quinn and containing Jesse Lynch Williams's "Why Marry?"

Eugene O'Neill's "The Emperor Jones," Rachel Crothers's "Nice People," Gilbert Emery's "The Hero," and George S. Kaufman's and Marc Connelly's "To the Ladies!"

Of recent books on the drama, Stark Young's *The Flower in Drama: Papers on the Theatre*, has attracted wide attention and much deserved praise. Not much more than a year ago Mr. Young, previously a professor of English, began to write his papers on plays, actors, and the theatre in general in the New Republic. His articles and reviews attracted at once the attention of discriminating people interested in the theatre; their admiration was quickly developed by an attitude which showed a comprehending sympathy for what the younger men were trying to do and yet never lost sight of the drama as a developed art with certain inviolable principles. Moreover, he wrote with wit, precision and charm. There is no better reading of its sort, I think, than his "Dear Mr. Chaplin," his "Circus," or his "Letter to Duse," all contained in this volume. Perhaps a note should explain the title, which is based on a sentence: "If one aims only at the beautiful, the flower is sure to appear"—a phrase drawn from Seami, 1363-1444, who, with his father, stood at the head of the No of Japan.

18. *Lost Patterns*

COLLESTAMORE was showing me his library, but a summons to the telephone had drawn him from the room and I was standing before the set of shelves between the cases containing rarities and those which held fine bindings, frankly puzzled. There were not many books ranged here and I could not make out the distinction that grouped them together. It might have been no distinction but mere accident in the case of anyone less methodical than Collestamore. With him, no; some thought or queer intention must underlie the choosing. Fiction and non-fiction, new books and some old ones, some volumes of attractive format and design and others whose homely plainness was possibly compensated by the fact of their being first editions —it meant nothing. Alphabetical arrangement by authors hadn't been attempted and was, indeed, scarcely worth while until the little assembly grew larger. Then he returned and met my look of inquiry with:

"You've discovered my Lost Patterns."

"Lost Patterns?"

"Oh," he said, "there aren't many of them, as yet. The fact is, I only thought of it a week ago. It rained all afternoon, so I spent a couple of hours amusing myself with them—with a beginning of them."

" 'Lost'? But some of them are new enough."

"It's the only name I could think of that I rather liked," was his explanation. "A Lost Pattern—the idea I was trying to express—may be either old or new. It has nothing to do with the edition or the binding, but everything to do with the contents of a book. Novel or essay or biography, the text ought to represent something we have not had before or since and aren't likely to have again; something individual in the scheme or the style; something wholly personal in the flavour—in short, unique, I suppose. What James Huneker would have called a unicorn. By the way, *he* is a Lost Pattern, probably."

"Probably." I was not unsympathetic to his idea. "You are anxious to get together a collection for the collection's sake, I take it."

"No, for the reader's sake. It wouldn't have any value as a collection, other than the curious, and I swear it could have no value for the person of literary practices." I glanced at him but could detect nothing in his expression. I have always suspected Collestamore of secret literary practices, concealed efforts to put his freakish self into words. My idea is that he attempts essays and that so far he is like a fellow fond of cigarettes and learning to roll his own. He went on, more meditatively: "A fellow desiring to be a writer would waste his time if he aped these people." All the same, I thought, I will bet that you——

"I began with a few new books," he was saying.

"New or comparatively so. The thing that started me, I guess, was Elinor Wylie's novel." He fingered his copy of *Jennifer Lorn*.

"I haven't read it."

"She has made a replica of the eighteenth century novel, a suitably fantastic story about an English aristocrat and his bride who journey to the India of the East India Company and meet with bizarre adventures. It is what you would expect of a poet enamoured with the life of that glittering period. I wonder that Max Beerbohm hasn't done it long before this. Or Aldous Huxley."

"I see you have them both represented here."

"Yes, the thought of them sprang from Mrs. Wylie's book. I took down Huxley's *Crome Yellow* and his *Mortal Coils*. From Max I wanted the books of his caricatures—*Rossetti and His Circle* and that other one he calls *A Survey*. My collection of Lost Patterns was begun, then and there. The idea of what would constitute a Lost Pattern was formed—I don't say it didn't enlarge afterward nor that it won't enlarge or change shape again. But, essentially, I knew what I wanted."

"Nobody knows what he wants," I objected. "The thing is obviously impossible. You mean you knew that you wanted to add more books to the five you had assembled."

"Any way you like." Collestamore's indifference was polite, but profound. "I began looking over the other shelves. The next thing I came upon was George Moore's *Hail and Farewell*. We shall never have a writer like George Moore, not even George Moore." I thought to myself: With that nuance, with a phrase like that, he is deliberately imitating Beerbohm's prose; I had better take no notice of it. His next remark startled me.

"Literary style, distinction, in the enterprise I had embarked upon was of no consequence whatever." And seeing that this wasn't brilliantly intelligible, he continued:

"The thing was much deeper than that—the personal twist or wrinkle was what I was after, the fly in the amber. Not a perfectly preserved fly in the amber of a choice literary expression but a wriggling insect caught on the tanglefoot of unaccustomed words would do as well." He was fast throwing grammar overboard in the effort to lighten ship and bring his thoughts to port. "I have not, as yet, come upon an illiterate author who deserves inclusion among my Lost Patterns, but I shouldn't hesitate to put him in."

"I see." After a pause: "Here you've got George Meredith. He's very nearly illiterate, don't you think so? Sometimes literacy can go too far, as in Meredith and in Henry James, whom you've put alongside. Maurice Hewlett is another matter."

"Well," said Collestamore, "I stuck them in as a matter of course. Anybody would naturally have thought of them in such a connection. The things I really pride myself upon are my detections among these single and mostly more recent books. You take F. Scott Fitzgerald's *This Side of Paradise*, or William McFee's *Casuals of the Sea*, or C. E. Montague's very fetching *Fiery Particles*, or Ernest Bramah's *Kai Lung's Golden Hours*, or Don Marquis's *Hermione*, or Alfred B. Stanford's *The Ground Swell*"—he was half pulling them out and letting them fall back, as he enumerated them—"and tell me if I have not shown both enterprise and catholicity."

I thought he had, but I also thought he should attempt some justificatory remarks, and said so. His point in regard to *This Side of Paradise* was its vitality in spite of its having, as Edmund Wilson, Jr., observed, almost every conceivable fault. "It had all imaginable faults, but yet, in Wilson's words, 'it did not fail to live,'" Collestamore argued. I nodded, and he went on. *Casuals of the Sea*, it appeared, pleased him by a lack of anything self-conscious in the writing. He much preferred it to the too purposeful artistry of McFee's *Command*. The singularity of those tales in *Fiery Particles*, he thought, called for no special pleading in its behalf. *The Ground Swell* was a sea pattern unique in its simplicity; Don Marquis's heroine and her little group of serious thinkers were the apotheosis of the Great Inane. As for *Kai Lung's Golden Hours*, he was merely echoing G. K. Chesterton, Belloc and a dozen others whose judgment was respectable and might command my deference not given to his own.

"Oh, I defer," I assured him. "You are the Lord High Executioner in this series of literary beheadings. I consider that a reign of terror has begun."

It wasn't beheadings, he said. He wasn't going over the field of daisies like the Syracusan tyrant and with his sceptre, cane, stick or staff cropping off the heads of the taller blooms.

"Daisies? I thought it was a field of corn."

As to that, he didn't remember. It was no matter, anyway. He was not demolishing, but singling out for eminence. No whistling cane, but——

"The sceptre gently touching one here, one there, knighting him, commanding him to spring up——"

"You will observe," in a tone of patient tolerance, "the surprising variety one gets in the shortest possible space of time at this sort of thing. Of course I thought of Jane Austen, and rather than put in *Pride and Prejudice* I chose *The Watsons* as completed by Miss Oulton. After all, *The Watsons* is later work than either *Pride and Prejudice* or *Sense and Sensibility* and the conjecture as to why it was never finished gives it special interest. By that time I was running over my books more or less as they stand on the shelves, alphabetised by authors. The next thing, therefore, was Arnold Bennett, and I chose *The Truth About an Author*. You know, it is the one book of Bennett's that could not, imaginably, have been written by anybody else. H. C. Bunner was next. I really don't know whether anyone living besides myself and Franklin P. Adams now cares for Bunner; if not, so much the better!"

"I see. The more lost the Lost Pattern, the more to be prized."

"Why not? His *Stories* and his *Short Sixes* are as American as, perhaps more so than, O. Henry." He was quietly dogmatic.

"Is O. Henry here?" I looked. "Yes, to be sure. Also portions of Kipling and, I judge, Frank R. Stockton practically complete. But these were among the matter-of-courses. Let's see:

Shouldn't you put in Frank Norris? *The Pit*, I suppose. And there's W. W. Jacobs."

He looked so restive that I stopped. "It's really no way to go at the thing wholesale," he protested. "I haven't made up my mind as to which one or two books of Stockton's yet; he's there in bulk only temporarily. I suppose it had better be *Rudder Grange*."

"Make it *Salthaven* from W. W. Jacobs," I urged. "Unless you strongly prefer *At Sunwich Port*."

"I do. Probably it's just that I read it first. After Bunner I ran against George W. Cable's *The Grandissimes*. Then I laid hold of Stephen Crane's *The Red Badge of Courage*. Then John Dos Passos's *Rosinante to the Road Again*."

"Thomas Beer has just finished a biography of Stephen Crane. Joseph Conrad has written a preface for it," I said, but Collestamore paid no attention. He was across the room, picking something out, and came back in a moment holding up Edmund Gosse's *Three French Moralists*. "Just thought of Gosse. This will do to hold the place for him until I decide. Have you never read it? Then you don't know Rochefoucauld or La Bruyere as you should know them. And you've missed a singularly urbane and exquisite example of English prose style."

"You have both Compton Mackenzie's *Carnival* and his *Sinister Street* in here. Make it *Carnival*. Let's see: David Graham Phillips's *Susan Lennox: Her Fall and Rise;* John Ames Mitchell's *Amos Judd;* and that new illustrated edition of *David*

Harum. I guess I'd agree with your choice of each of those." His expression remained polite but I could see it would make not the least difference whether I agreed or not. "Did you see Rodolph Valentino in 'The Young Rajah'?" I asked, to tease him. He was good-natured about it. "I did. I have no objection to Valentino, but I much prefer the story as told in *Amos Judd.*" He was ruffling the pages of *David Harum.* "I like these text drawings, don't you?" I said I did, adding that *David Harum* was the kind of book that cried for illustration.

"About biography, or especially, autobiography," he said suddenly. "Should you say Booker T. Washington's *Up From Slavery*, for one? There'll never be another of that pattern." But I had a suggestion for him there. "Anyway, you must include Bouck White's *The Book of Daniel Drew.*" He said at once, "Oh, yes!"—adding, "Autobiographical in form, anyway. White always contended that he found an actual record left by Uncle Dan'l Drew. Semi-fictional, if you like; but a grand piece of satire. And now I rather think we're wanted to sit down to lunch. Er—how about a swallow of something first? Or is that among your lost appetites?"

19. Joseph C. Lincoln Discovers Cape Cod

i

ON 13 February, 1870, in the town of Brewster, Massachusetts, which is on Cape Cod, there was born to Joseph Lincoln and Emily (Crosby) Lincoln a son whom they named Joseph Crosby Lincoln. The child's father was a seaman, so had been his father's father and his father's father's father; and so were all his uncles. His mother's people followed the sea. For a mile in each direction from the plain little house of the Lincolns every house contained a Cap'n. When the boy was a year old, his father died of a fever in Charleston, South Carolina. Emily Crosby Lincoln had made voyages with her husband, whose death made it necessary to move up toward Boston. In summers, however, the boy got back to the Cape with its sand dunes and cranberry bogs, its chance to fish and swim. "He rode the old stage coach from Harwick to Chatham; he knew the lightkeepers, the fishermen, the life savers, and the cracker-box oracles in the village stores. The perfume of the green salt meadows, the pungent pines and bayberries . . . the fishing boats, the dripping nets, 'the mighty surge and thunder of the surf along the shores' were part of his very existence." The description is reminiscent of Walt Whitman's account of his young manhood. "I suppose if I had been born a few years earlier, I would have had my own ship," Joseph C. Lincoln says. But the day of steam had begun. He went to school at Brewster and Chelsea. As he grew up, college was seen to be out of the question. The youth and his mother went to Brooklyn and he entered a broker's office. This work he hated. "I have always felt that they were fully as glad to get rid of me as I was to leave them." Wishing to draw, he fell under the guidance of Henry Sandham ("Hy") and went to Boston where, with another fellow, an office was opened for commercial work. To make a picture sell better, Lincoln sometimes wrote a verse or joke to go with it. Sometimes the verse or joke sold when the drawing did not. It was the day of universal bicycling. The League of American Wheelmen Bulletin had a circulation of over 125,000 and Sterling Elliott, its editor, offered Lincoln a job as associate editor. His verses were thus brought to the attention of a considerable public. He married in 1897 Florence E. Sargent, of Chelsea, Massachusetts, and he was writing verse, mostly in the vernacular of Cape Cod, for a number of publications. In 1899 the passion for bicycling began to wane and Lincoln definitely moved from Boston to New York to try to make a living as a writer on his own. He had written a first short story, a Cape Cod narrative, and sold it to Saturday Evening Post. That magazine, Harper's Weekly, The Youth's Companion and Puck were taking his verse, which was sometimes in a swinging

JOSEPH C. LINCOLN

metre and sometimes humour tinctured with philosophy. In 1902 Albert Brandt, of Trenton, New Jersey, published Lincoln's *Cape Cod Ballads*, in a yellow-backed volume with illustrations by E. W. Kemble. It was Lincoln's first book. Now he was writing short stories in earnest and with some success and he began a novel which could only be written by labouring at it on a corner of the dining room table from midnight on Saturdays through Sunday mornings until the manuscript was completed. It was the story of three old sea captains who, despairing of their joint efforts at housekeeping, advertised for a wife. Published in 1904 as *Cap'n Eri*, this affair settled two large doubts in Lincoln's mind; first, that he could sustain the interest of readers through a long story; second, that he could make a living by writing, and by writing books.

ii

Many have been the editions of *Cap'n Eri* since its appearance, nineteen years ago. The outline of those nineteen years in Joseph C. Lincoln's life is only pleasantly eventful. A friendship with Sewell Ford led him to become a resident of Hackensack, New Jersey. There he has built a house of "Colonial" lines, the sight of which is not good for less successful writers. A very handsome summer home stands on a terrace at Chatham, Cape Cod. In 1912 the Lincolns lived for a while in England and travelled to some extent on the Continent, visiting Switzerland. Frequently Mr. Lincoln has gone to one or another part of the United States, even unto California, to deliver, before crowded houses, his lecture on "Cape Cod Folks" or to give readings from his own books. And every year since 1904 has seen the publication of one, sometimes two, Lincoln novels.

In Hackensack Mr. Lincoln attends the Unitarian Church—he is a member of its Board of Trustees—and he was at one time a member of the Hackensack Board of Education. He used to belong to the Salmagundi Club in New York but resigned because he used the club and its privileges so little. He still belongs to The Players in New York; but in any ordinary sense of the word he is not a clubman. The family usually goes to Cape Cod in a motor car and while there Mr. Lincoln fishes and swims and sails all he can. In Hackensack golf is his principal diversion and he tries to play daily, "although there are times, particularly in my brand of golf, when there seems to be more hard work and moral strain than amusement, by a good deal." The man is a red-cheeked, rotund and comfortable man, with a bright eye and a catching smile and a great fund of stories such as the following:

"An old salt of my acquaintance spent a recent winter in Florida and found in the fishing of the region a fascinating but pretty strenuous pastime. As a skipper of the old school he scorned modern devices for fishing, such as reels. In fact he went out to fish tarpons in good Cape Cod fashion with merely a fishing line and his own bare hands. He hooked a tarpon and for a couple of hours there was waged a terrific battle between the fish and the stubborn old Cape Codder, whose hands were torn and blistered. Proudly he exhibited his 79-pound catch to the natives. 'Not much of a haul,' was their comment. 'Why, a little woman, no size at all, just brought in a tarpon that tipped the scales at 100 pounds.' Would he like to see a real fish? 'Thunder, no!' roared the Cap'n. 'Show me the woman!' "

iii

Hamlin Garland, the author of some accounts of American life which have not omitted the sombre, the discouraging, the bitter scenes and places, has written:

"Joseph Lincoln is not only a novelist of wide reputation, he is a public benefactor. His success has in it something heartening and corrective. In the midst of work which appeals to the base and cynical in human life (American city life) his clean, wholesome, humorous stories of Cape Cod sea captains and their neighbours give evidence of the fact that there is a huge public for decent and homely fiction, just as the success of his play, '*Shavings*,' is evidence that there is a paying audience for a decent and homely drama. His books can be read aloud in the family circle with joy to all the members of it—I know, for I have myself read eight or ten of them to my wife and daughters. They make no pretense of being profound, or new, or 'smart.' They are filled with the characters and the humour which are native to the Cape. Lincoln knows these Cape towns and their inhabitants as Irving Bacheller knows his men of the North Woods, for he was raised among them and lives in their neighbourhood several months of each year. He looks like one of them, like an old skipper, hearty, unassuming and kindly. The task which he has set himself is one which calls for a keen sense of character, democracy of sentiment and a fancy which never—or very seldom—loses its hold on the solid ground of experience. His plots are sometimes negligible, but his characters, even when they seem a bit repetitious, are a joy. His prosperity is well earned."

This undoubtedly expresses a general sentiment, although it does not express it so vividly as a sentence that appeared in the Los Angeles Express:

"One enjoys a Joe Lincoln novel as one does a long, cool, thirst-quenching drink on a hot day."

However, before examining the novels themselves, it is proper to put down here some things that Mr. Lincoln has said, at one time or another, showing his attitude toward them. Of course his attitude toward other kinds of fiction is a part of his general attitude, and so:

"I read all sorts of books and at all times. I don't know that I can name any particular author who may be called my favourite. I am very fond of Stevenson, for instance—but then, so I am of Kipling, except his more recent stories, which have a bit too much British Empire in them to please me,—of Mark Twain, of W. J. Locke, and many others. I think I like a story for the story's sake. I like to like my characters or dislike them in the old-fashioned way. It is for this reason perhaps that the work of such writers as Arnold Bennett, William De Morgan, Joseph Conrad, and others, of the realistic school, so-called, does not appeal to me as much as—well, as Mr. Locke's work, for instance. I realise,—no one can help realising—the fine literary craftsmanship in a book like *Lord Jim*. It is a wonderful piece of character mosaic, and yet in reading it I am always conscious of the literary work. I say to myself, 'This is marvellous; see how the writer is picking his hero to pieces, thought by thought, motive by motive.' And being so conscious of the writer, I do not lose myself in the story. This is not offered as a criticism; certainly I should not presume to criticise Mr. Bennett or Mr. Conrad. It is more of a confession of something lacking on my part. I enjoy reading *Lord Jim*, or *The Old Wives' Tale*, but I do not return to them again and again as I do to *The Beloved Vagabond* or *The Morals of Marcus Ordeyne*. Perhaps this is, as some of my realistically inclined friends tell me, a childish love for romance on my part. Well, perhaps it is. If it is, I can't help it; as I said, this statement is not offered as an excuse, but a confession.

"This sort of thing shows in my own stories. It would be very hard for me to write a long story which should end dismally. It is only too true that stories in real life frequently end that way, but I don't like my yarns to do so. So it is fair to presume that in whatever books I may hereafter write, the hero and the heroine will be united, virtue rewarded and vice punished, as has happened in those for which I am already responsible. Perhaps this same weakness for a story, a cheerful story, makes me care little for the so-called problem novel. It doesn't mean that I am not fond of novels dealing with certain kinds of problems. Winston Churchill's *The Inside of the Cup* I liked immensely; but the sex problem, the divorce question, and all that sort of thing does not appeal to me. A morbid lot of disagreeable people, married or otherwise, moping and quarrelling through a long story seem to me scarcely worth while. To a specialist in nervous diseases such a study might be interesting, but I really doubt if the average healthy man or woman finds it so. Certainly we should not care to associate with such people were they living near us. We should get away from them if we could.

"Perhaps I *could* write a story with gloomy situations and an unhappy ending, but I wouldn't like to try it. I would much rather try to make people cheerful and keep myself cheerful at the same time. There's enough sorrow in this world without finding it in books."

So he spoke ten years ago; so, with possibly the change of an illustration or two, would he speak today. From nine in the morning until noon or one o'clock he disappears into his workshop, frequently a place known only to himself, and either writes (with a soft, stubby pencil, on large sheets of yellow paper) or thinks about characters and the very attenuated skeleton which, for Mr. Lincoln, constitutes the "plot."

"I know there are people who can turn out a short story in two or three hours and it will be good enough to sell, but I cannot help feeling that it would have been much better if the writer had devoted more time to it. In my case, doing work that is satisfactory to me in any degree means that I must fairly sweat it out, if I may use the expression." There usually comes a time when he gets "a letter about once a week asking how the thing is coming along. That has been a frequent experience, especially when there are a lot of characters in my story, and I'm having more or less trouble with them. The story keeps stretching itself out. I think I may have to adopt Mark Twain's method, and begin throwing my people down the well." There is a genial artifice about nearly all his tales. Some years ago an interviewer for the Boston Globe touched on the subject of "specialty" writing, which was a natural topic, as all of Mr. Lincoln's fiction is a highly specialised affair, not only in its general localisation on Cape Cod but in its characterisation and homely wit and humour. The author said:

"A man writes what he knows. If he tries anything else it must fall—show hollow. And I find that it is necessary to write to your audience—that one must consider that a large number of his readers are to be women, and he must write things that will appeal to the women of today."

"You don't mean that you would consider the women to the point of writing stuff that would be saleable, and refrain from writing stuff which appealed to you, but might not be saleable?"

"Well," said Mr. Lincoln, slowly, "I haven't any 'message' that I know of. I'm not much of a highbrow. I have standards, though. And if I am to do the thing I want to do, I must get my book printed. But I've never been satisfied—although I did like *The Postmaster* pretty well."

This was ten years ago, and Mr. Lincoln has gone on, unchanging. He has the most enviable record of any living American writer. No book of his has been a failure. Some have done better than others, but with no serious qualification of the statement it can be said that each book has added to his audience, so that he has for some years been an unfailing best seller. Perhaps there has been a noticeable increase in his popularity with and since *The Portygee* (1919), which was published serially and then surprised the publishers by beating Lincoln records as a book. Or the gain may be traceable to the preceding book, "*Shavings*," and its successful dramatisation. But in his sustained, unbroken and increasing popularity as a fictionist Mr. Lincoln has no competitor. There are others whose individual books have sold more heavily, whose total sales may be larger, but they have had lapses, and their popularity has either been impaired or lost. Even as I write the process known in the trade as "slipping" is observable, here and there, in the case of one of the most popular American authors, a person with a long record of immediate successes, one of whose work the American soldier, in 1917-18, could not apparently get enough. Time does this thing, but apparently it cannot touch, except to enhance, the passion for the work of this native of Cape Cod, who clips his words a little and sometimes says "hev" and "hed" for "have" and "had"—about whom there is even a suspicion of the Down East nasal twanging as he talks. A wholly lovable personality. He once wrote:

"Bless the children. They are the most convenient excuses in creation. Probably, if it were not for them, you wouldn't get to the zoological gardens or the aquarium or the fairy play oftener than once a year or so. And as for the circus—but that's an old story."

iv

We have not finished, though, with the man's own account of his relation to his work.

"You can't use actual people. People aren't as dramatic in actual life as you want them to be. Of course, you may hear a phrase, or a story—you may talk with a person and get an impression and build up your character from those things. But using an actual person wouldn't work. Besides, it would be rather mean.

"In writing of a Cape Cod town or village, although I purposely refrain from describing it as any one town in particular, I have tried conscientiously to give the characteristics of Cape Cod towns I am acquainted with. The promontories and inlets and hills and marshes in 'my' Cape Cod may not be found where I have located them, but I have tried very hard to make them like those which are on the real Cape. And so with the Cape Codders in my stories. I have never knowingly drawn the exact, recognisable portrait of an individual. I have of course, received hundreds of letters from readers who inform me, in strict confidence, that they know the original of 'Cap'n ——' and recognised him at once. Nevertheless they are wrong. I have endeavoured always to be true to type, and in writing of the old deep-sea captain, the coasting skipper, the longshoreman or the people of the Cape villages, I have done my best to portray each as I have seen and known specimens of his or her kind. And in attempting to transcribe the habit of language I have made it a rule never to use an expression or idiom I have not heard used by a native of the old colony."

The differentiation of the various types of seaman has been carefully made by Mr. Lincoln, and is perhaps valuable to a full appreciation of his fiction.

"The type of sea captain who figures in my stories has not necessarily an accurately corresponding type in my acquaintance. Going back to the Cape after having lived in New York and Boston, I was able to get varying angles on the lives of the men and women I had known in my childhood. The old sea captains that I remembered best as a child were of more than one character, classified according to their work. One was the dignified old man who had travelled to some far-away corner of the earth and returned prosperous, to spend the rest of his days as an autocrat among his own people. He had met strange peoples, he had been trusted with a ship, and, as in the days I write of there were no instantaneous means of talking across the oceans, he was shrewd at bargaining and, being one of the owners of the ship, he lost no chance to bring home a cargo that would bring rich returns. In other words, he was a shrewd trader as well as a sailing master. The same dignified bearing that he used in his trade followed him on land, and, though jovial in manner, he was developed in dignity and character.

"The other type of captain was more popular with the youngsters. He may have been as shrewd, and possibly made as much money, but he was filled with a greater sense of humour, and took life as a pastime. Men of this description would gather round the stove and tell wonderful stories, though all sea captains talk shop when they get together.

"Then too there were what are termed the 'long-shore captains.' These were mostly engaged in fishing, or in trading with coast towns and cities. They were necessarily more limited in their views, for they spent more time ashore, often working a good-sized garden, fishing when the spirit moved, and running a schooner to New York or Boston if the chance came.

"Of all the sea-captains, however, those that I knew best were those who were actually sailing in the 1870's and 1880's, and who were largely engaged in carrying oranges and lemons from Mediterranean ports. These men were really the last of our sailing captains. I have one friend in particular who was in the fruit trade, and his stories of how they crowded sail and took every risk to bring in their cargoes are many and thrilling. Fruit, of course, is highly perishable, and while it might be a valuable cargo one day, a week later it would be worthless; therefore the sea races and adventures."

In an article, "Some Samples of Yankee Shrewdness," appearing in the American Magazine, Mr. Lincoln has told stories of Cape Cod captains he has known. Acuity of observation, caution joined to a quality of going in head-first if one goes in at all, and a singularly dry humour are a large part of the "shrewdness," as Lincoln makes it out. In the course of the article he offers this admittedly serious statement:

"In all my forty-odd years of experience with Yankees I do not remember ever having met one who habitually whittled. I have, of course, known some who whittled occasionally, when they were making a 'bow 'n' arrer' or a boat for one of the children. But I never knew one who whittled when he was making a trade." *Sic transit* the "Yankee" of one species of "fiction" and drama. But it is time to look at Mr. Lincoln's own fiction; then, perhaps, we may revert for a closing glance at the puzzle of Yankee shrewdness.

V

The newest Lincoln novel (1923) is *Doctor Nye of North Ostable*—Mr. Lincoln has something of a gift in titles for his special kind of book. There is a comfortable assurance in knowing that one is going to read about Dr. Nye, or a place called Fair Harbour, or an individual named Keziah Coffin, or the sure-to-be-amusing process of *Extricating Obadiah.* That last has a music of the syllables; it is solitary in this respect among Lincoln titles which are also easily affected by climatic changes, so that *Galusha the Magnificent* had to be altered in England to *The Magnificent Mr. Bangs.* But to return to our fishing—

Ephraim Nye, M.D., a "sympathetic" hero,

self-sacrificing, a man with a deal of humour, has a black cloud over his past, as all North Ostable knows. The story opens with his return to that Cape Cod village. All that day Marietta Lamb ("Mary's Lamb") had been scrubbing away at a great rate in the old Dillingham house, so long untenanted, and Henry Ward Beecher Payson, in full working regalia of overalls and wooden leg (for "best" and Sundays he had a cork leg) was busy in the yard. Miss Althea Bemis, who lived across the road and missed nothing that went on among her neighbours, asked innumerable questions, learning nothing. Judge Copeland, Cyrenus Stone and Cap'n Mark Bearse, "natives," and "the three most influential men in North Ostable" appeared on the scene. The Judge and Stone were bitter political enemies, always flying at each other's throats. Stone, who owned the empty house, admitted to Cap'n Mark Bearse that the place was being made ready for someone whose coming would be a great surprise.

Then, at nightfall, Doctor Eph arrived in a ramshackle gig.

People sat up late that night in North Ostable. In the home of Shubal Bash discussion ran high as Shubal and his wife, Angelina, tried to tell deaf old Aunt Lidy the story of Ephraim Nye. After studying medicine, the young Ephraim had married Judge Copeland's sister, Fanny, and had returned to his native town to practise. Fanny was fond of clothes and jewels and the Doctor worked hard to give them to her. Respected and liked, everyone turned against him when it was discovered that $7,200 of the $10,000 in the fund for the new meeting-house, of which he was treasurer, had been stolen. The bank had exhibited a check for $7,200 signed "Ephraim Nye, Treasurer," and the Doctor admitted the check to be his. His wife was very ill at the time. After her death, which occurred shortly, Ephraim Nye was tried and sentenced to five years in State's prison. Later the money began to come back in instalments until it was all paid up. Always the sums were sent through Doctor Nye's lawyer.

The two enemies, Cyrenus Stone and Judge Copeland, have, respectively, a son and a daughter; and Tom Stone and Faith Copeland are young lovers.

The stage is now set for Mr. Lincoln's story. And immediately, in a backward glance, one gets the rapid impression that the plot consists entirely of typhoid fever. Such an impression, however, is quite unjust. *Doctor Nye* is one of the more carefully articulated (or more carefully complicated) Lincoln novels. In addition to the revelation forming the climax of the story and putting Ephraim Nye in a heroic light, there is a fully-constituted early love affair for the Doctor, brought back and actively developed; there is the pair of young lovers, Tom and Faith; there is the prolonged duel between Judge Copeland and the Doctor; there is a considerable variety of minor incidents essential to the movement of the tale and to its final outworking. All this, mind you, aside from the real end sought by most readers of Mr. Lincoln's work—the exposition of "characters" and the continuous oscillation into humour.

It is the humour, then, that most deserves our scrutiny; for many of the Lincoln novels, practically plotless beside such a tale as *Doctor Nye*, have only the assets of their "characters" and humour to sustain a popular interest which they have not failed to feed. If there is any question about this, a glance at the technical "descriptions" of half a dozen of the books ought to settle the matter. Here, in a sentence, is what some of them simmer down to:

Partners of the Tide. Cap'n Ezra Titcomb and young Bradley Nickerson go into the wrecking business and meet with a series of surprising adventures and difficulties.

Cy Whittaker's Place. Old Cy Whittaker, bachelor, adopted a little girl. He and an old crony form a "Board of Strategy" for her upbringing.

Keziah Coffin. Keziah Coffin, typical Cape Cod old maid, proves the good angel of the minister in his courtship. Incidentally, she turns out not to be incurably an old maid.

The Postmaster. Cap'n Zeb Snow is discontented with inactivity after retiring from the sea. As postmaster he finds all the activity he wants.

Thankful's Inheritance. Thankful Barnes and her helper Emily lose their boarders when the house proves to be "ha'nted," but they gain a Cape Cod sea captain and also a handsome young lawyer—for life.

"Shavings." The quaint, unbusinesslike windmill-maker has no success in posing as a bank robber, but his loyalty and shrewdness bring happiness to all his friends.

The Portygee. The temperament and "calf love"

of the son of a Spanish opera singer make difficulties with his Yankee grandfather.

vi

No plots, only complications; but there must be admitted to be, within somewhat narrow bounds, a considerable display of "characters." Although even here certain stock figures are (probably necessarily) much employed—the gossiping old maid, Mis' Somebody-or-Other; the village comedian, like Henry Ward Beecher Payson, who periodically lapses from good behaviour and goes on sprees. One of the most interesting of Lincoln's portrayals is Albert in *The Portygee*, a young fellow half Spanish, half New Englander, with poetic and artistic impulses. "Set there in the small hamlet, chafing at the restraints and humdrumness of the place, Albert makes a delicious contrast to the native population," says Hildegarde Hawthorne. "We understand the passionate, temperamental boy as well as his old Grandfather, with his fury against all that sort of 'foolishness,' because their author understands them." I cannot go so far as Hildegarde Hawthorne in praise of the variety or depth of Mr. Lincoln's characters, while cheerfully granting, as I do, their frequent colour and whimsical charm. Often and inevitably, I suppose, in the work of one who has written two dozen books the "characters" are not *character*, but a selected idiosyncrasy or two. Often and inevitably in the case of one who is not the inexhaustible and fecund creator, like Dickens.

But there is the humour. . . .

Now we have come to it. In the first place, Mr. Lincoln shows the quick faculty evidenced from the outset by Mary Roberts Rinehart of getting the humour on every page. Mrs. Rinehart has not always practised with that intention, but Mr. Lincoln has never neglected the rapid shift of the reader's mood. To insure it, he does not hesitate to sacrifice something of his more important scenes, making them if necessary less dramatic. The common-sensicality running through his stories is a solvent to drama and a feeder to the spirit of fun; if it makes it impossible for his story ever to leave the ground, it also kills to a large extent the language, or lingo, of sentimentality so-called, that terrible jargon in which so much popular fiction is sugared and preserved. Mr. Lincoln pickles his stories in this salty common-sensibleness, rather—a breath of Cape Cod air and a dip in the ocean brine. All his "atmosphere" is as matter of fact as a dip in the ocean, and the temperature is much more unvarying and satisfactory . . . unless you may find it tepid. He is a funmaker, resorting without hesitation to such crude and cheerful devices as the spree in which Henry Ward Beecher Payson breaks his "Sunday best," or cork, leg. And yet fun warms the heart. We laugh inanely, and afterward we have the feeling of having laughed inanely, a sense of a slight immoderacy or excess, of a mild dissipation which perhaps has not really done us any good (though the harm be passing and inconsiderable); but when the moment comes we are ready to laugh again.

vii

A final note on that debateable Yankee shrewdness, then. . . .

Can we not find its fruitful exercise in Mr. Lincoln's own case? I think we can. Here was a man of around thirty whose observation was keen, whose caution was used to direct him in a proper self-committal, whose own personal sense of humour was of a sufficient dryness to keep him from the easy trails of self-deception. Just as his friend, Captain Lorenzo Baker, of Wellfleet, Massachusetts, was able to discern in the casual remarks of a West Indian the commercial possibilities of the yellow banana, so Joseph C. Lincoln could perceive from a token or two the personal possibilities of Cape Cod as he could put it on paper. And acuteness, or, as the Yankee says, 'cuteness, having done its work, that other trait of Yankee shrewdness, the caution which restrains and then goes in headlong, was brought into play. Mr. Lincoln committed himself wholeheartedly to his fictional enterprise. He put all his money, or rather, the energy which was his equivalent for money, on the bob-tailed nag—in a little sloop which was his own boat rather than in somebody else's two-masted schooner. The rest was plain sailing and persistence that could have been fatally spoiled if that inner dryness of wit and clearness of perception had ever failed him. But he never forgot that it was his own little sloop, the sailing of which must be kept within the manœuvres she could execute. He has never, for example, tried to write the great American novel which, consciously or unconsciously, has brought up into the wind, all sails shaking and way lost, the craft of more than one of his fellow sailors. A Yankee and shrewd, earning many rewards, including that of a very widespread affection.

Books by Joseph C. Lincoln

1902 *Cape Cod Ballads*
1904 *Cap'n Eri*
1905 *Partners of the Tide*
1906 *Mr. Pratt*
1907 *The "Old Home House"*
1908 *Cy Whittaker's Place*
1909 *Our Village*
1909 *Keziah Coffin*
1910 *The Depot Master*
1911 *Cap'n Warren's Wards*
1911 *The Woman-Haters*
1912 *The Postmaster*
1912 *The Rise of Roscoe Paine*
1913 *Mr. Pratt's Patients*
1914 *Cap'n Dan's Daughter*
1914 *Kent Knowles: Quahaug*
1915 *Thankful's Inheritance*
1916 *Mary-'Gusta*
1917 *Extricating Obadiah*
1918 *"Shavings"*
1919 *The Portygee*
1921 *Galusha the Magnificent*
1922 *Fair Harbor*
1923 *Doctor Nye of North Ostable*

All fiction, except *Cape Cod Ballads* (verse) and *Our Village* (sketches of life and people on the Cape).

Sources on Joseph C. Lincoln

Joseph Crosby Lincoln. Booklet published by D. APPLETON & COMPANY, 1921.

Joseph C. Lincoln's America, by Hildegarde Hawthorne. Booklet. D. APPLETON & COMPANY, 1921.

Some Samples of Yankee Shrewdness, by Joseph C. Lincoln. Article in AMERICAN MAGAZINE, July, 1919.

My Types: An Interview with Joseph C. Lincoln, by Charles Francis Reed, THE FORUM MAGAZINE, February, 1919.

Cape Cod's Genial Chronicler: An Appreciation by Hamlin Garland. PUBLISHER'S WEEKLY, 17 April, 1920.

The Men Who Make Our Novels, by George Gordon. MOFFAT, YARD & COMPANY, 1919.

Joseph Crosby Lincoln, by Adam C. Haeselbarth. BOOK NEWS MONTHLY, 1913.

20. Edith Wharton and the Time Spirit

i

AT just past sixty Edith Wharton's is still a name for the literary conjuror in search of an impressive effect. She has lived a long time—in the literary sense—and comparisons are not easy; she has outlived, as a writer, most comparisons, including the one which would probably have been fatal to anyone else, the comparison with Henry James. She has outlived, in the physical sense, Henry James himself; there are no more of his frequent letters to "Dear Edith." It is among the subtler tributes to Mrs. Wharton, the person, that the intellectual relation between her and the man who was once called her "Master" is now seen in a light which considerably enhances the dignity of the woman who was once called "Pupil." For who, after reading the correspondence of Henry James, published since his death, believes any longer that Mrs. Wharton ever owed anything to that man's patronage so nicely tinctured with snobbery? Victor Hugo permitted himself to be surrounded by those who worshipped him as a god, but Hugo posed, god-like; whereas Henry James——

Mrs. Atherton is several years older than Edith Wharton, both as person and author; Mary Johnston, born eight years later, is of almost exactly the same literary age; but the first is a superb journalist and a born storyteller and the second is a mystic and a historian. Mrs. Wharton's journalism in fiction is pretty well confined to *The House of Mirth* and *The Fruit of the Tree;* she invites comparison with Mary Johnston only in that ambitious novel of mediæval Italy, *The Valley of Decision.* In the two books on which Mrs. Wharton's fame definitely rests at the present, *Ethan Frome* and *The Age of Innocence*, she achieves a success and an individuality only the more interesting because it finds so strikingly different expressions.

In fact, on the evidence of the two stories, it would be superficially impossible to assert that the "sterile" tragedy of New England hillsides was from the same hand that wrote the minutely detailed story of New York society in the 1870s. Considered for their meaning and origin, *Ethan Frome* and *The Age of Innocence* are both seen to be tales of frustration, both tales of the America that Mrs. Wharton quitted some fifteen years ago but can't get out of her system, and both stories in which the background is responsible for the actors themselves as well as the play.

ii

Edith Newbold Jones was born in New York, 24 January, 1862, the daughter of Frederic Jones who had married Lucretia Stevens Rhinelander. One grandparent was a Stevens, another a Schermerhorn. A great deal of her childhood was spent in

EDITH WHARTON

Europe—there was one stretch of five years in which the family didn't return to America—and education proceeded wholly with the aid of tutors and governesses. The child learned French, German and Italian. Such summers as the family devoted to America were lived in a house at Newport, on the bay, halfway out towards Fort Adams. When Miss Jones was twenty-three she became the wife of Edward Wharton, of Boston. They lived in New York and Newport and later at Lenox in the summer, frequent visits to Europe continuing. Miss Jones and Mrs. Wharton were equally interested in writing and read extensively Goethe, Balzac, Thackeray, Dickens, Flaubert, George Eliot, Meredith and—Henry James? That last one had begun as author while Miss Jones was still in her teens. Twenty years were to pass before she started to overtake him. Mrs. Wharton was thirty-seven in the year when her first book was published, *The Greater Inclination*, containing, according to Katharine Fullerton Gerould, "two of the best stories she ever wrote" ("The Pelican" and "Souls Belated").

Six years later came *The House of Mirth*, "the tragedy of the woman who is a little too weak to do without money and what it buys, or to earn it for herself, and a little too good to sell herself." The story of Lily Bart had to a high degree that provocative quality which can generally be relied upon to make a novel a best-seller; and a best-seller it became. Soon afterward, with a feeling in which satisfaction, distaste, caution and physical preferences were obscurely blended, Mrs. Wharton settled in France—winter home in Provence, summer home near Paris. In 1914 she opened a workroom for skilled woman workers thrown out of employment by the miscalculations of Napoleon III. a generation earlier. She also opened restaurants where French and Belgian refugees were fed at less than cost, and lodgings where they might sleep. Mrs. Wharton took full charge of over 600 Belgian children who had been withdrawn from orphanages near Furnes and Poperinghe and established them, with the nuns who had the children's care, in four colonies, where the girls were taught fine sewing and lace-making, in anticipation of a day when fine sewing and lace-making would again be demanded. For these services the French Government, in 1915, conferred on the American novelist the cross of the Legion of Honour. During the war Mrs. Wharton wrote little. *Fighting France* records her visits to the French fronts; she contributed to *The Book of the Homeless;* in 1918 was published her long short story of an American boy in the war, under the title, *The Marne;* in 1920, *In Morocco* gave an account of a visit to that country which she made with General Lyautey, by invitation of the French Government. *French Ways and Their Meaning* appeared in 1919. The total roll of Mrs. Wharton's non-fiction is considerable and includes *Italian Villas and Their Gardens* (1904), *Italian Backgrounds* (1905), *A Motor-Flight Through France* (1908), *Artemis to Actæon and Other Verse* (1909), *The Decoration of Houses*, as well as the books just mentioned. No article on Mrs. Wharton would be complete unless mention was made of her passion for gardening and her art in developing beautiful gardens, both at her home in Hyères and at St. Brice, near Paris.

iii

We have had it all carefully explained for us by Mrs. Gerould how much more desirable it is that Mrs. Wharton should give us—as she has generally given us—studies of sophisticated people. Speaking of *Ethan Frome*, and, in fact, merely mentioning that masterpiece, for which, it would appear, she is without admiration, Mrs. Gerould says of Mrs. Wharton:

"She did not abandon her civilised and sophisticated folk, for any length of time, to deal with rustics. Let us hope that she never will abandon them. There is vital truth in the Shakesperean dictum that 'the hand of little employment hath the daintier sense.' To put it roughly"—as a rustic, no doubt, might put it—"the people who have leisure to experience their own emotions, and the education to show them how the emotions fit into the traditions of the race, are more interesting in themselves than the people whose emotions are bound to be on a more nearly animal plane. It is less interesting, morally, to the average man to know how the sub-average man conducts himself than to know how the super-average man conducts himself. It does not in the least matter to the average intelligent citizen—except as it may touch his social conscience—how the characters in certain modern novels behave, because those characters are not the real fruit of civilisation. They are, at best, its sorry by-products.

They do not help him out in his own problems; they do not stand to him for vicarious experience. Whereas it is of interest to a civilised man to know how other civilised beings, in situations his own or other, behave; even if they behave badly. Theirs are dramas that he can feel, theirs is conduct that he is competent to judge; they respond, or fail to respond, to an admitted code of moral taste. No creature was beyond the range of Shakespeare's sympathetic understanding; but when he wished to probe the human heart most deeply, he usually chose the heart of a king. The insensitive and the subnormal served him chiefly for comedy.

"So that a positive purpose is served by the competent novelist's choosing to deal with the more fortunate classes. Inhibitions have more chance; and inhibitions are as necessary to real drama as are passions. There is also—naturally—more opportunity for satire; and satiric comment is inveterate in Mrs. Wharton's work. If the person who has had every chance is not fine, then he is relatively uglier than the person who has had no chance at all. She does not spare her aristocrats who had an opportunity for moral fineness and neglected it. The baser emotions are more shocking in a world where there is less excuse for them. And since it is real life with which Mrs. Wharton is dealing, the baser emotions frequently appear."

These words were written after, not before, the publication of Mrs. Wharton's novel, *The Glimpses of the Moon* (1922).

At sixty, one either prepares to die or one faces life anew. In the latter event one knows, if one chances to be a writer, the heavenly and earthly certitudes . . . and the escape from platitudes is final. Thus, for example, it is given to understand that a reputation will at least last for the remainder of a lifetime but that markets change. And, after all, as Mrs. Wharton once remarked, cleanliness and comfort are the two most expensive things on earth—comfort implying whatever degree of luxury is essential to a state of mind in which one can do work to purchase continued comfort. At sixty, though one may now and again bounce it high in the air, the real and right concern is to keep the ball a-rolling. . . . Let people think what they like and say what they like (and the follies of attack and fence are always equal), the unerring perception is directed toward the next thing that is to be written. One may exercise a choice from the very limited amount of material one has or can acquire; at sixty, it is too late to acquire much additional. Of course, a finely cultivated imagination in early years might come to the rescue with a second blooming; but suppose one's imagination has always moved in the best society? No, it doesn't do, it most decidedly doesn't do to speculate any longer about anything; let others pretend what they like, there is a positive relief in the knowledge that one writes what one can when one has to—and be it good, bad, indifferent or astonishing the aim was an honest aim and the result achieved was, at least, intelligent.

iv

And what could place Mrs. Wharton in a clearer, finer light than just this situation of fact? What could be more in keeping with the two traditions that have bound her life?—the tradition of an older New York and the literary tradition of France, both strict and both congenial, both so severe as by their very classicism to give the greatest possible scope to personality. The New York of the Age of Innocence into which she was born, the literary Europe of the nineteenth century to which she so early attached herself—these were the ideal forcing-beds of a personality such as hers. You come upon her expressing in vigorous words her delighted enthusiasm for the first novel of William Gerhardi: "You not only make your people live, but move and grow —and that's the very devil to achieve. Do, for all our sakes, keep it up!" There is no flabbiness about her. She is past the pitfall of fanaticism and safe beyond the quagmire of adulation. She does not need to practise the conventional literary dishonesties which close like traps upon novelists whose fame is on the make and who still have much to lose. She can say frankly: "There are moments —to me at least—in the greatest of Russian novels, and just as I feel the directing pressure of the novelist most strongly on my shoulder, when somehow I stumble, the path fades to a trail, the trail to a sand-heap, and hopelessly I perceive that the clue is gone, and that I no longer know which way the master is seeking to propel me, because his people are behaving as I never knew people to behave."

What heresy! Here we all are kneeling on the ground, touching foreheads and breathing the overpowering incense burnt before the shrine of Dostoievsky, and a voice is distinctly heard to remark that the literary deity is perhaps not as luminous as he should be! How many would dare such a remark, or, if they ventured it, would command from any of us the bravery of timid, relieved assents? Not many; scarcely a one.

She has not always been so free; who, indeed, is born to freedom? Saint Paul said he was, but a price had been paid formerly; it always is. Henry James, tormented to the end of his days by the fact that his books really didn't sell, wasn't able to pay the price. Thomas Hardy paid it at the cost of silence as a novelist after the reception accorded to *Jude the Obscure*. O. Henry, confronted with the heavy total, shivered and shuddered. Every man has his price, indeed, in quite another sense from what that saying was coined to convey; it is a price he must manage if he is to have the truth for himself or tell it about others.

Mrs. Wharton's greatest good fortune has probably consisted, after all, in her realisation of this. Did she learn it in France, that country where truth lies at the bottom of a well . . . and is not drawn up but used as a mirror? You can see the perception through nearly all of Mrs. Wharton's work. In her long novel of eighteenth century Italy, *The Valley of Decision*, she is painting away with grand strokes on a magnificent canvas; she wants to find out if she really is suited to the execution of fictions like the *Romola* of that George Eliot she once read so attentively. Well, no; the result satisfies her that she isn't. So then she goes on with those short stories in the writing of which she is so proficient, and, a few years later, produces *The House of Mirth*. The result is instructive; one might almost say it was destructive. Mrs. Wharton definitely learned that here was a kind of thing she could successfully do, in terms of money and popularity. But in other terms?

This was a question less easily answered. Two years after *The House of Mirth* came *The Fruit of the Tree*, with its highly interesting "problem" as to whether it can ever be right for a physician or nurse to accelerate and ease the death of a doomed patient. This has been called, by the Folletts, Mrs. Wharton's "one lapse into artistic disintegration." But Mrs. Wharton was not thinking of art, but of life. It had sharply come over her that the pursuit of art in one or another form of preciosity would land her where she didn't wish to be landed. She might be, as was charged, the woman who of all women wrote most like a man; but she didn't desire to write like some men. If she could have been Gustave Flaubert, perhaps . . . but she saw no use in being George Moore or—Henry James? The whole contemporary French school left her unaffected; she read them, but experienced no wish to write like them; and in the midst of a freshly-running sea of Continental literature she became more than ever aware of her absolute and inescapable Americanism. In a way, it was a tragedy. To think that one could grow up in Europe, be, as it were, a part of Europe, definitely adopt Europe, and yet not to Europe belong! After steadily eyeing this situation for a while she reacted without either tears or temperament; and her reaction took the form of a short novel which is among the most perfect pieces of workmanship in English, the story of *Ethan Frome*. The "hard shapeliness" of that tale was the hard shapeliness of a full self-recognition, the so-called "sterility" was the result of an individual adjustment to the deepest personal need of her remarkable nature. What she would once have so wanted to give, she now knew she never could give to the world, and her awakened consciousness strove for the fit expression of this discovery in terms of an art of which she knew something. *Ethan Frome*, whatever else it may be (and it is many things, some strange and all beautiful) is the Magnificat of a woman in the hour of profoundest personal disappointment. Such works of fiction are especially rare, but, given the genuinely capable writer, given the one hour of a lifetime, the masterpiece is quite possible, yes, almost certain.

Ah! She had written it at last . . . and she could afford to let it stand there to her credit while, with calmness and admirable fortitude she returned to the region of *The House of Mirth* and *The Fruit of the Tree* to add a study of divorce and parasitic marriage called *The Custom of the Country*. The resumption of the general warfare which has been the custom of Europe during odd generations for several centuries didn't interfere with *Summer* (1917), wherein Mrs. Wharton tried to combine her established "material" with some of the qualities of *Ethan Frome*—an experiment only moderately a success. When she came later to write *The Age of Innocence* she was, to all appearances, in the happy position of desiring only to do a definite and modest thing, a first-rate story of very marketable quality, and then achieving something distinctly beyond that.

V

Mrs. Wharton's new novel, *A Son at the Front*, is primarily a study of character and a portrayal of the relation between a father and his son. The father is Campton, a lame painter of some distinction living in Paris. His son, George, has just finished his education and the father is counting on a trip to Italy for the chance, at last, to get acquainted with the boy. Campton's wife, Julia, after divorcing him, married a rich American named Brandt. The two also live in Paris and George has for some years been supported by the Brandts, spending part of his time with them. With this position when the novel opens, end of July, 1914, war intervenes, taking George from them because of his French birth. Campton and Brandt, drawn together by a common interest, pull what wires they can to secure a clerical appointment for George. The intensity of the war and initial reverses bring Campton to regret that George should have been willing to remain behind the lines. But word comes that the son is lying wounded in hospital; he has all the time been at the front but has concealed the fact in writing home. Brought back to Paris, an effort is made to keep him there, a shallow little married woman of George's acquaintance lending what help she can; the huge compulsion of the war is too great, however, and on his return to the front George is again wounded, this time fatally. He lives to hear that America is at last in the conflict and to know that Campton and the rest have an undivided aim while the war lasts. When George dies, the others, feeling they have lost everything except the hope of victory, bend themselves to help toward that with such courage as they have left.

The record of wartime Paris, the shift of ideals and the gradual sacrifice of all lesser purposes, the resolution of smaller loyalties in a larger, the intimacy of personal emotions—these, of course, are the true substance of Mrs. Wharton's story.

vi

You may comprehend her, in discourse with that familiar of hers, the Time Spirit, in a dialogue running somewhat as follows:

TIME SPIRIT: So, then, you've settled it with yourself? You haven't too many regrets, I hope?

MRS. WHARTON: Oh, no, thank you. You can't know what a sense of freedom, of satisfaction both outer and inner, it gives! You see, I always had, for ever so long, a few illusions—about myself and my own work, I mean.

TIME SPIRIT (*dryly*): Most writers do. But now that you are rid of them all, you aren't finding it impossible to go on?

MRS. WHARTON: I find it far more possible to go on. I go on with ease and a lightness of heart.

There isn't anything I wouldn't write now, that I mightn't wake up and find myself to have written, except the kind of thing I once was determined to write. That sounds cloudy, no doubt; but what I mean is very simple: I discovered that, contrary to the old saying, it is life that is long and art that's fleeting.

TIME SPIRIT: Yes?

MRS. WHARTON: Exactly. We live a long time, and we write for a time not so long but pretty long, too. If in those years of writing we achieve art once or twice, we are among the rare, fortunate ones.

TIME SPIRIT: And the rest of the time?

MRS. WHARTON: The rest of the time we must be industrious, but it is so much better if we are clear in our own minds about it.

TIME SPIRIT: But, you know, you are really an artist!

MRS. WHARTON: *Retro me, Sathanas!* I beg your pardon, though; you couldn't tempt me. I know what I know. There are things I have had, and have, to do without; but I don't live with them; I live with what I have. Of course, all kinds of aims, and quite possibly some forms of achievement will be conferred upon me by those who practise the craft of fiction under the guise of criticism. But I am clearly not responsible for what they say, and it may not be used against me. I am only responsible for what I myself say—and that is: Nothing.

TIME SPIRIT: So you refuse to answer? On the usual ground, of course; it might tend to incriminate or degrade you?

MRS. WHARTON: I refuse to answer on the ground that it might incriminate and degrade others who write about me like this: "*The House of Mirth, Ethan Frome*—these are orchestral in their richly subtle clashing of overtones, a sort of infra-discordance which is among the rare improbable finenesses accessible to the artist, on condition of his readiness to take infinite pains for infinitesimal effects."

TIME SPIRIT: Madame, permit me to deal lightly with you.

MRS. WHARTON: *Merci, monsieur.* But I think we have concluded our bargain, haven't we? *Au 'voir.*

Books by Edith Wharton

1899 *The Greater Inclination*
1900 *The Touchstone*
1901 *Crucial Instances*
1902 *The Valley of Decision*
1903 *Sanctuary*
1904 *The Descent of Man, and Other Stories*
1904 *Italian Villas and Their Gardens*
1905 *Italian Backgrounds*
1905 *The House of Mirth*
1907 *Madame de Treymes*
1907 *The Fruit of the Tree*
1908 *The Hermit and the Wild Woman*
1908 *A Motor-Flight Through France*
1909 *Artemis to Actæon and Other Verse*
1910 *Tales of Men and Ghosts*
1911 *Ethan Frome*

1912 *The Reef*
1913 *The Custom of the Country*
1915 *The Book of the Homeless*
1915 *Fighting France*
The Decoration of Houses
The Joy of Living
1917 *Xingu and Other Stories*
1917 *Summer*
1918 *The Marne*
1919 *French Ways and Their Meaning*
1919 *In Morocco*
1920 *The Age of Innocence*
1922 *The Glimpses of the Moon*
1923 *A Son at the Front*

Sources on Edith Wharton

Contemporary American Novelists, 1900–1920, by Carl Van Doren. THE MACMILLAN COMPANY, 1922.

Some Modern Novelists, by Helen Thomas Follett and Wilson Follett. HENRY HOLT & COMPANY, 1918. The chapter deals with Mrs. Wharton's work up to and including *Summer*. Her novel, *The Valley of Decision*, is singled out for especial emphasis.

Edith Wharton, A Critical Study, by Katharine Fullerton Gerould. Booklet published by D. APPLETON & COMPANY, 1922. A spirited exposition of what are conceived to be Mrs. Wharton's special qualities by a woman whose interest lies particularly in Mrs. Wharton's material.

21. *The Unclassified Case of Christopher Morley*

i

TO know Christopher Morley is to be interested, amused, enthusiastic, sceptical or even secretly puzzled; but to have him for a friend is to learn the meaning of friendliness in a degree that is very exceptional. And few escape being his friends, though this is less true than formerly. There was, indeed, once a time when the friendship of Morley was among the two or three serious responsibilities of an individual's life—like marriage, or filial duty or a conscience in regard to one's chosen craft. Practically every day, sometimes twice in a day, the evidence of Morley's friendliness would appear in a brief letter or hastily-penned note about this or that or the other thing under the sun.

An image arose of an ever-active, a sleepless mind; of an emotional nature more unresting than the Atlantic and quantitatively as great. This awful abstraction slowly faded out into a visual image of a "burly" man with a smiling face and a lighted pipe, and that, in turn, gave place to the fear lest so much confidence in the human race should prove fatally misplaced. . . . Somewhat, it has; but what we didn't foresee was that the change, coming about gradually, would operate as a gradual salvation of (1) his friends from Morley, (2) Morley from his friends, (3) Morley's work from Friend Morley.

Yet this beneficial and important transformation has been accomplished in the most salutary manner, with a result that may accrue with permanence and advantage to American literature.

ii

As lately as 1920 one estimating American talents could observe of Morley: "His gift is purely journalistic, isn't it?" and receive the answer from Morley's friend: "Purely"—an answer conceived in entire truthfulness. Both the asker and the answerer were pretty certain to regard the assumed fact as a great pity. But as to the fact!—why, what further evidence was needed to establish it? Morley had been writing for several years, had averaged several books a year of prose and verse, and nowhere gave the least sign of doing work of a different character. What, then, was the character of his work in those years? He began at Oxford with a book of verse; from a more actual standpoint his beginnings had been made with *Parnassus on Wheels*, published in 1917. This really capital conceit had engendered a sequel, *The Haunted Bookshop*, published two years later. There were certain books of essays—*Shandygaff*, *Mince Pie*, *Pipefuls*—pleasant, partly serious, sometimes sentimental and showing a deplorable fondness for the pun. There were books of verse—*Songs for a*

CHRISTOPHER MORLEY

Little House, *The Rocking Horse*, *Hide and Seek*. *Travels in Philadelphia*, the short story, *Kathleen*, and an unfortunate collaboration called *In the Sweet Dry and Dry* completed the roll. It is no reflection upon these volumes to say that they gave the impression of a talent strictly journalistic; the best journalism is more than ephemeral and most of the titles enumerated are still actively in demand. The quality we call "journalism" is not an affair of perishability but something very difficult to define, something in the approach, something in the treatment rather than in the choice of subjects. In the last analysis it is probable that the effort to define it would end with hands flung out hopelessly before the mystery of a personal temperament.

The facts were these: Morley had been educated at Haverford College and Oxford; he had then come to Garden City to work for the publishing house which, principally, has published his prose, and his first enterprises as an author were precociously instructed by an "inside" acquaintance with what James Branch Cabell would call the auctorial career. The influence upon his own work of this very special knowledge is not easy to estimate. He saw, as only one in a publishing house sees, the facts of authorship after the author's child is born. For example: the immense effect upon the fortunes of a writer's book, or books, of the attitude toward them of the bookseller. And that attitude is quite rightly fixed by what the bookseller (1) knows he can sell, or, less frequently (2), by what he thinks he can sell.

Morley saw that books are sold through bookstores. Looking a little further, he discerned that books which are not in bookstores are, with certain class exceptions, very rarely sold. He learned, as everyone in a publishing house learns, that three-quarters of the books that are sold to retail purchasers are bought because retail purchasers have had these books thrust directly under their noses. He suffered, no doubt, the customary amazement on discovering the vast number of people who (1) either enter the bookstore with no particular book in mind, or (2), on being unable to obtain the book in mind, readily take something else. It was brought to his keen attention that, as Frank Swinnerton reiterates in his admirable brochure on "Authors and Advertising," direct advertising, as in newspapers and magazines (the commonest mediums) does not sell books. Being a young man of alert perceptions, it cannot have been lost upon him that book reviews do not, with any reliability, sell books, either. What does sell books is talk—in some instances—but the hard rock foundation of book sales is a favourable attitude on the part of "the trade."

To know the people in the bookstore, to have and to cultivate and to deserve their good will (for, in the long run, you must deserve it), and thus to insure the sale of your book to the bookseller and to enlist his energy and enterprise in re-selling it to his customers—this is the "favourable attitude" just mentioned. Few authors succeed in establishing it; fewer succeed in maintaining it. Mr. Morley has done both, with the result that in five years from the time of his *Parnassus on Wheels* he has been able to publish a highly imaginative, refined and polished satire and see it become, in its field, a pronounced best seller.

iii

One would about as soon expect to see a fantasy by Lord Dunsany a best seller as witness the sale, in tens of thousands, of Morley's *Where the Blue Begins*—if one were making one's estimate solely on the work itself. *Where the Blue Begins* is the story of the dog Gissing's search for God—a search conducted in various places and circumstances parallel to human life of the present day by an animal discreetly analogued to the human animal. Such a piece of writing has ordinarily no hope except from unusual and very favourable (or acutely controversial) critical attention; and the hope from that quarter is relatively small. By "hope," of course, is meant a hope of a considerable sale. *Where the Blue Begins* belongs to that class of literature which is written because it has lain in the author's heart to write it, regardless of its fate after it lies on paper. In the case of Mr. Morley, the work has received merited praise; but it would be naïve to suppose that this notice and commendation sold the book; and the book trade might even justifiably be indignant at such a supposition. Did not they, the booksellers, buy *Where the Blue Begins* because it was Morley's new book? And did not they and their clerks "push" the book for the same reason? The Ayes have it, to both questions, and unanimously.

On the other hand, the sceptical soul who argues that Chris Morley wrote *Parnassus on Wheels*, in the first place, because it was a story about a bookseller calculated to "get him in right" with the trade—that man does not know Morley and shows that he does not know him. It is possible to detect in the character of Morley's work, in the circumstance of its publication and in the accessories provided for that publication evidences of a singularly intelligent literary campaign; it is possible to detect them and believe them to be such; but it is not possible to over-estimate the part played by Morley's own naïveté, affectionate nature and formerly unchecked and indiscriminate enthusiasm.

Such an attitude is always open to misconstruction. But it takes real intelligence to go beneath the surface; and among Morley's friends were many who could do that. These perceived his genuineness without being in the least able to predict the outcome of his generosity. Ours is a world thus and thus and so and so. The ultimate effect upon Morley himself of a disposition which he would unquestionably see suffer and change was the problem. It would be very easy for him to come a tremendous cropper of any one of several sorts; and then should we have a soured, an embittered young man? Prophecy was worthless.

Meanwhile, with the auspicious beginning of *Parnassus on Wheels*, the young man went gaily on. His first book of verse (barring the Oxford experiment) was published in the same year under the valuable title, *Songs for a Little House;* and at once the small beginnings of a Morley vogue were faintly perceptible. The suspicion that such a title harboured a spirit committed to the sentimental attitude toward life was confirmed within a year by the publication of a book of essays, *Shandygaff*, named after a reputed or actual beverage and got up with a deliberately quaint title page. One was left in no doubt that Morley liked Stevenson, was affectionately fond of Robert Cortes Holliday, and worshipped the genius of Don Marquis. The seeds of literary jealousy were sown, to be harvested several years later in accusations of log-rolling * that were levelled at others a-plenty besides Morley. Here, however, it should be explained that Morley had come from Oxford to go to work, at the age of twenty-three, at Garden City; that while learning the publishing business he had married Miss Helen Booth Fairchild, a New York girl whom he

* The term is borrowed from the Congress of the United States, where it has long been employed, quite unofficially, to describe an exchange of favors among Congressmen, some voting for another's bill in exchange for his favorable vote upon their pet measures. As here used, it refers to the alleged praise of one writer by another in tacit exchange for similar praise back; the public being expected to take both encomiums at face value and without any discounting for personal friendship, etc. Whether the public has ever quite done so is possibly to be doubted; but, at any rate, in the winter of 1921-22, New York and some other literary circles were so openly under suspicion of log-rolling that the suspects were not able to ignore the charges openly made. The boldest method of counter-attack adopted was that of Heywood Broun, who ridiculed the accusation, not quite successfully from every standpoint. There was, however, an immediate and noticeable diminution of enthusiasm among some of the younger writers for each other's work, publicly expressed. Morley himself, discussing the matter of log-rolling, explained that the accusers had the cart before the horse; that commonly one liked another man's work and praised it, and in consequence thereof came into a personal acquaintance. This is without doubt frequently the true situation.

had met in England. If, therefore, he modestly undertook to become the American poet of domesticity with his songs for households "of two or more," the guilt should by no means be made personal to him, but may justly be laid at the door of the race.

The year following *Shandygaff* witnessed the appearance of another book of verse, *The Rocking Horse;* the sequel to *Parnassus on Wheels*, entitled *The Haunted Bookshop;* and a book done in collaboration with Bart Haley. Called *In the Sweet Dry and Dry*, this is quite exceptional among Morley books, and not too common among any books, for its badness. An extravaganza on the subject of prohibition, the plot may be said to have resided mainly in incessant and outrageous puns, at that time a pronounced Morley weakness. But again it is necessary to point out a detail which, taken in one light, and, as I think, the proper light, reflects great personal credit on Mr. Morley; he has never disowned the bad book. He could not do so openly, of course—copies probably exist—but he has not done so tacitly, as he might have without question or comment. I have in mind a little booklet on Christopher Morley published in 1922 and concluding with a bibliography. There it stands: "*In the Sweet Dry and Dry*, Boni and Liveright, 1919. (In collaboration with Bart Haley, out of print.)" The book, no doubt. George Moore and Henry James, not to mention other men of literary genius, have had occasion to be ashamed of their work and to drop it quietly from the roll. I like Mr. Morley for not doing so.

iv

Christopher Darlington Morley was born at Haverford, Pennsylvania, 5 May, 1890, of parents both English by birth but long Americans by residence. Dr. Frank Morley, an English Quaker of Woodbridge, Suffolk—the home of Edward Fitzgerald—was graduated at Cambridge and came to Haverford in 1887 as professor of mathematics. His wife was Lilian Janet Bird, of Hayward's Heath, in Sussex, a woman of some musical and poetical gifts, the daughter of a man at one time with the London publishing house of Chapman and Hall. CDM frequently praises her cooking, which blended as an influence on his boyhood with the Haverford campus, where cricket is played. In 1900 Professor Morley went to Baltimore and Johns Hopkins. His son entered Haverford in 1906, was graduated in 1910 and, in the same year, was chosen as Rhodes Scholar representing Maryland. The three years at Oxford were spent at New College. In the title-poem of a new book of verse, *Parson's Pleasure*—the name of the old bathing pool on the Cherwell at Oxford—occur the lines:

> Two breeding-places I have known
> Where germinal my heart was sown;
> Two places from which I inherit
> The present business of my spirit:
> Haverford, Oxford, quietly
> May make a poet out of me.

The confused exigencies of his native land, however, were, more immediately, to make something else out of him. Repairing to Garden City, he interviewed Mr. F. N. Doubleday, otherwise FND ("Effendi") on the matter of a job. Mr. Doubleday has preserved the record of that interview in an amusing account which fully displays the youth, eagerness, enthusiasm and amiable audacity of the twenty-three-year-old. The noted Effendi, whose philosophy of life is not without its Oriental suggestions and whose sense of humour is at such times gently active, was feeling "a little weighted down that morning with the difficulties of the job which the President of Doubleday, Page & Company takes as a daily routine," and therefore finally told Morley "to go to work at all his manifold plans and literary philanderings, reserving the right to restrain his commitments if necessary."

It was Morley who discovered William McFee. English sheets of that long and very fine novel, *Casuals of the Sea*, had been submitted to the firm for consideration and possible purchase. Ultimately it became necessary to set up type for the novel in America. "We were accustomed," Mr. Doubleday explains, "to hold what we called a 'book-meeting,' when each member of the staff gave his suggestion about authors and books. For months when it came Christopher's turn to speak he always began, 'Now, about McFee—we don't appreciate what a comer he is' and so on for five minutes without taking a breath until finally it became the joke of the meeting that nothing could be done until Morley's McFee speech had been made. Our jibes influenced him not at all. His only reply to our efforts in humour was to bring on a look of great seriousness and the eternal phrase, 'Now, about McFee.' "

In leaving Garden City after a stay of nearly four years to become, in his own phrase, one of the "little group of wilful men who edit the Ladies' Home Journal," CDM departed from the well-established tradition under which so many men in the book publishing business have fallen. It is some kind of a tribute to Doubleday, Page & Company that the house has been the training-place of a considerable number of the heads in other publishing houses. In Philadelphia a term on the Ladies' Home Journal was followed by work as a columnist on the Evening Public Ledger, the direct preliminary to Morley's column on the editorial page of the New York Evening Post, with which he has been since 1920. The book, *Travels in Philadelphia;* the personal acquaintance of A. Edward Newton, author of *The Amenities of Book Collecting and Kindred Affections;* and a deepened interest in Walt Whitman, are some of the concomitants of the Philadelphia period. Also, I think, Morley's gradual disillusionment began then. The collection of essays called *Mince Pie* was published late in 1919 and there were still to appear, in 1920, certain overflowings of the Morley of the first period—the story of an Oxford undergraduate prank, called *Kathleen;* a book of verse, *Hide and Seek;* and more essays in *Pipefuls.* But that was to be about all. Something very definite had happened to the young man who was so friendly with everybody, who was forever talking about William McFee, who wrote forty-leven letters and notes a day, who had made a cult of quaintness and who liked to be called Kit and to have the resemblance of his name to that of Christopher Marlowe's stretched into a fanciful resemblance of personalities and writing. Some lone reviewer, speaking harshly; or some slight wound received in the house of one of his friends; or the shifts and vicissitudes of commercial enterprise—dissatisfaction with what he had already done, a thirtieth birthday, a wish to do something he had yet to do—together or singly may have been the agents of the change. Only the change itself matters. And what was that? It was not that Chris became less friendly, or autographed fewer dozens of copies of a new book of his, or loved the Elizabethans less or the work of Theodore Dreiser more. But a retractation took place, an alteration of ideas went on . . . aided, it may be, by the uniformity with which American magazine editors rejected a short story called "Referred to the Author," one of the contents of Morley's book *Tales from a Rolltop Desk*—a story which Morley himself thinks marks the definite line between his old work and new.

V

Those who care for the poet of "households of two or more" will find him most readily now in the volume called *Chimneysmoke* (1921), which is a representative selection from the earlier books of verse, *Songs for a Little House*, *The Rocking Horse*, and *Hide and Seek*. Vincent O'Sullivan has said that the Morley here represented belongs with "the

English intimists, Herrick, George Herbert, Cowper, Crabbe." Writing an introduction for the English edition of *Chimneysmoke*, E. V. Lucas remarked: "Domesticity has had many celebrants, but I cannot remember any one work in which such a number of the expressions of Everyman, in his capacity as householder, husband and father, have been touched upon, and touched upon so happily and with such deep and simple sincerity. The poet of 'The Angel in the House' was, I suppose, a predecessor; but Coventry Patmore was a mystic and a rhapsodist, whereas Mr. Morley keeps on a more normal plane and puts in verse, thoughts and feelings and excitements that most of us have known but have lacked the skill or will to epigrammatise. If we are to look in literature for a kindred spirit to Mr. Morley's we find it rather in the author of 'The Cotter's Saturday Night.' "

Morley's new book of essays, *The Powder of Sympathy*, shows the man changed and changing. It would be impossible to detect any loss of humour or cheerfulness in such papers as those on Sir Kenelm Digby or the Morley automobile, Dame Quickly (to be succeeded some day by the more impressive Dean Swift). But the satire in "The Story of Ginger Cubes" is not less complete or sharp for being throughout good-natured; and in his piece on "The Unknown Citizen" Morley seems to me to strike a single magnificent chord in which satire and humour are simply notes underlain by the deep bass of pathos and truth. The new book of poems, *Parson's Pleasure*, shows that where there was so much *Chimneysmoke* a fire burns also. This book has an inspiring and inspiriting essay for preface—one far too quotable; I must resist it. Instead, let me give the first sonnet in the "Memoranda for a Sonnet Sequence":

The herb Lunaria, old books aver,
If gathered thus and so, in moony patches,
Has property of mystic opener
When laid upon the fastest locks and latches.
In this respect, the moonplant duly matches
The magic of the poets, who bestir
Their art to loosen spirit's careful catches
And split our secret bolts like gossamer.

To sprinkle moonseed on the tight-locked soul
Bidding it open, or stand soft ajar—
To sprinkle moonseed, gathered thus and so,
This is the poet's honourable rôle.
Like some old Tudor captain bound afar
I hear him crying *Inward! Inward Ho!*

Books by Christopher Morley

1912 *The Eighth Sin.* Oxford: B. H. BLACKWELL. Out of print
1917 *Parnassus on Wheels*
1917 *Songs for a Little House*
1918 *Shandygaff*
1919 *The Rocking Horse*
1919 *The Haunted Bookshop*
1919 *In the Sweet Dry and Dry.* Written in collaboration with Bart Haley. Out of print
1919 *Mince Pie*
1920 *Travels in Philadelphia.* DAVID MCKAY COMPANY

1920 *Kathleen*
1920 *Hide and Seek*
1920 *Pipefuls*
1921 *Tales from a Rolltop Desk*
1921 *Plum Pudding*
1921 *Chimneysmoke*
1921 *Modern Essays* (an anthology, selected and with an introduction and biographical notes by Christopher Morley). HARCOURT, BRACE & COMPANY
1922 *Thursday Evening* (a one-act play). STEWART & KIDD COMPANY
1922 *Translations from the Chinese*
1922 *Where the Blue Begins*
1922 *Rehearsal* (a one-act play, included in *A Treasury of Plays for Women*, edited by Frank Shay. LITTLE, BROWN & COMPANY
1923 *The Powder of Sympathy*
1923 *Pandora Lifts the Lid* (with DON MARQUIS)
1923 *Parson's Pleasure*

Sources on Christopher Morley

Christopher Morley: A Biographical Sketch. Booklet published by DOUBLEDAY, PAGE & CO., 1922.
Private Information.

22. *The Prophecies of Lothrop Stoddard*

i

PROPHECY is a very old business. It has become our habit to think of ourselves as a people without prophets; and yet there was never a time when mankind had more seers or more interesting ones. What is H. G. Wells but a prophesier, and from whom do we receive counsel if not from Mr. Chesterton? Mr. Shaw is our Job's comforter, and George Horace Lorimer, on the editorial page of Saturday Evening Post, calls us to repentance. A few years ago I had the adventure of reading Madison Grant's *The Passing of the Great Race*, an impassioned proclamation of the merits of the blond Nordic race, and a lamentation over its decay. At that time such a book was in the nature of a revelation whether you gave faith to its assertions and proofs or scoffed at them. The thing that struck me was the impossibility (as it seemed to me) of any reader remaining unmoved; I thought him bound to be carried to a high pitch of enthusiastic affirmation or else roused to fierce resentment and furious denial. And so, in the event, I believe it mainly turned out. At that time, although he was the author of several books, I had not heard of Lothrop Stoddard, unless as a special writer and correspondent for magazines. It was not until April, 1920, that *The Rising Tide of Color Against White World-Supremacy* was published. Even so, attention is not readily attracted to a book of this type. Many who have since read it with excitement knew nothing of the volume until, in a speech at Birmingham, Alabama, on 26 October, 1921, President Harding said: "Whoever will take the time to read and ponder Mr. Lothrop Stoddard's book on *The Rising Tide of Color* . . . must realise that our race problem here in the United States is only a phase of a race issue that the whole world confronts." The late Lord Northcliffe, returning from a trip around the world, declared: "Two far-seeing books, *The New World of Islam* and *The Rising Tide of Color*, should be in the library of every one who wants to know something about the world of 1950." Several months before he died, Northcliffe spoke again to a newspaper correspondent: "Have you read *The Rising Tide of Color*? Then I want you to read it. I want every white man to read it."

ii

The New World of Islam followed *The Rising Tide of Color* from Mr. Stoddard's pen, or more probably, as authors work nowadays, from his typewriter. It brings out with detail and vividness a situation which Hilaire Belloc made vivid also in his American lectures in the spring of 1923, when he remarked that, after all, we must remember it was only two hundred years since the armies of Mohammed stood outside the walls of Vienna. But Mr. Belloc in a lecture had no time for details; he stressed the remarkable spiritual unity (something beyond merely religious unity) of Islam, tending to match the condition of Europe in those centuries when it was possible to lead Crusade after Crusade. Mr. Stoddard, however, is a master of detail. His book on the Mohammedan world is compact of facts and figures, and concludes with one of the most significant maps the world allows to be drawn today. For it is not a day of satisfactory map-making; too much is changing; but the great patches of green on the chart at the close of *The New World of Islam* do not change. The day is never past when some dark-skinned Mahdi, like that false one in Lytton Strachey's portrait of "Chinese" Gordon, may sit his horse "letting the scene grow under his eyes," watching the assembly of turbulent but vast and unanimous armies, looking down upon the thousands of upturned, fanatical faces, in a scene "dark and violent and beautiful" . . . and of enormous import to the peoples of the earth.

His study of the coloured races and their gradual predominance and his account of Islam seem to me to be but preparatory, however, to Mr. Stoddard's book on *The Revolt Against Civilization*. This has already passed through many editions, like the two preceding volumes. "The reason why *The Revolt Against Civilization* has attracted such an extraordinary amount of attention is not far to seek," comments the Saturday Evening Post. "It is, so far as we know, the first successful attempt to present a scientific explanation of the worldwide epidemic of unrest that broke out during the Great War and still rages in both hemispheres." The book is a considered and noteworthily documented argument against the Underman—to be conceived of as the opposite of Nietzsche's Superman. It was Macaulay who remarked that if civilization is again overthrown it will not be by the barbarian from without but by the barbarian within—and Mr. Stoddard's case is, quite simply, that we have in our civilisation an immense mass of inferior men, of Undermen, who will drag us down and whom we cannot lift up. Nor is he among those who advocate terrorism. He would grant and secure to those whom he regards as the foes of civilisation a wider freedom of thought and speech than would many who share his view of the actual situation. And as a prophet is not allowed any longer to prophesy unless he is prepared with a programme—must not cry, "Woe! Woe!" unless he does so constructively—Mr. Stoddard closes his book with two chapters in which he disregards with something like a surgeon's magnificence and coolness the rooted prejudices and inherited opinions of ordinary men and women. This, he says very clearly and with precision, is the path out; and he suggests that we go to no further compromise than may be absolutely inevitable in our mixed circumstances. Nothing is more admirable in this American prophet than his daring unless it is the level admixture of his common sense.

iii

Who is Lothrop Stoddard? In the first place, his name is Theodore Lothrop Stoddard. He is the son of John Lawson Stoddard, and both father and son were born in Brookline, Massachusetts, where at 1768 Beacon Street, the son now has his residence. The senior Stoddard travelled widely and was known as the promoter of the Stoddard lectures in the larger American cities for over twenty years. His travel lectures fill fifteen volumes. Mr. Stoddard retired from the platform in 1897 and lives in the Italian Tyrol. The son, born in 1883, was graduated from Harvard in 1905. He is unmarried. The interests that lie back of his volumes are reflected in his membership in the American Historical Association, the American Political Science Association, the American Sociological Society, the Academy of Political Science, the National Institute of Social Sciences, the American Genetic Association and the Galton Society. But let Mr. Stoddard speak for himself:

"I have aways been interested in world affairs. I spent a good deal of my early life in Europe and as an undergraduate at Harvard most of my work was along those lines, that is, history, politics, sociology, and so forth. The four men who stimulated me most were Professors A. C. Coolidge, T. N. Carver, Toy, and R. M. Johnston. At that time, however, I was intending to make the law my profession and I took the law course and was admitted to the Massachusetts bar at the beginning of 1908. The immediate occasion for my undertaking my present profession was a trip to Europe which I took at that time. This trip was an extensive journey through western and central Europe, occupying most of the year 1908; it was in the nature of a 'grand tour' before settling down to the practice of law. But when I was in Europe during that year (the year of the second great political crisis preceding the European War) I became convinced of what I had already suspected, that a cataclysm was inevitable in Europe within a relatively short time. I further realised that in any such cataclysmic struggle the United States would either be directly involved or would at least be drawn out of its isolation into the stream of world affairs. The idea shaped itself strongly in my mind to fit myself to become an expert on world affairs. I believe that such experts were at that time very few in number in America. However, I realised that if America should be situated as I felt she would be after a European disaster, such experts would be greatly needed. To me such a career implied extensive preparation and special training. In my opinion the expert on world affairs must have a high degree of technical knowledge such as cannot result from the knowledge gained by travel, ordinary reading or experience, however accurate that knowledge may be. Especially is a thorough historical background a prime necessity.

"Accordingly I proceeded to acquire the technical knowledge and training which I judged necessary by entering the Harvard Graduate School where I spent four and a half years, from the autumn of 1909 to January, 1914, gaining incidentally my

A.M. and Ph.D. degrees. I was ready then actively to practise my new profession. Nevertheless for the first two or three years I did much more research work on contemporary world affairs and future tendencies than actual writing. I planned out a long schedule of writing; and *The Rising Tide of Color* is the first large item in that schedule."

Books by Lothrop Stoddard

1914 *The French Revolution in San Domingo*
1917 *Present-Day Europe—Its National States of Mind*
1918 *The Stakes of the War*
1919 Harper's Pictorial Library of the World War (Volume 6, *The World at War*)
1920 *The Rising Tide of Color Against White World Supremacy*
1921 *The New World of Islam*
1923 *The Revolt Against Civilization*

Sources on Lothrop Stoddard

Who's Who in America, Volume 12, 1922-23.
Private Information.

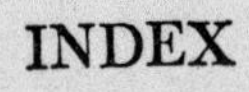
INDEX

INDEX

INDEX

INDEX

INDEX

INDEX

INDEX

INDEX

INDEX

INDEX

INDEX

INDEX

INDEX

INDEX

INDEX

INDEX

INDEX

INDEX

INDEX

INDEX

INDEX

INDEX

INDEX

INDEX

INDEX